中英双语

图说 **根** 台湾民俗文化

文／邱杰　摄影／吴景腾　翻译／Lewis James Wright

Roots
Customs and Traditions in Taiwan

外文出版社
FOREIGN LANGUAGES PRESS

图书在版编目（CIP）数据

根：图说台湾民俗文化 / 吴景腾主编. — 北京：外文出版社，2019.9
ISBN 978-7-119-12179-6

Ⅰ. ①根… Ⅱ. ①吴… Ⅲ. ①风俗习惯 – 台湾 – 图集
Ⅳ. ① K892.458-64

中国版本图书馆 CIP 数据核字（2019）第 214706 号

出版指导：徐　步
出版策划：吴景腾　张瑞琪　胡开敏
责任编辑：蔡　箐　李　湲
封面设计：闽江文化
内文排版：瑞东国际
印刷监制：秦　蒙

根——图说台湾民俗文化

撰　　文：邱　杰
摄　　影：吴景腾等
翻　　译：Lewis James Wright

© 外文出版社有限责任公司
出 版 人：徐　步
出版发行：外文出版社有限责任公司
地　　址：北京市西城区百万庄大街 24 号　　邮政编码：100037
网　　址：http://www.flp.com.cn　　电子邮箱：flp@cipg.org.cn
电　　话：008610-68320579（总编室）
　　　　　008610-68995852（发行部）
　　　　　008610-68996183（投稿电话）
印　　刷：北京盛通印刷股份有限公司
经　　销：新华书店 / 外文书店
规　　格：184mm×260mm　　印　张：18
版　　次：2019 年 9 月第 1 版　　印　次：2020 年 1 月第 1 次印刷
书　　号：ISBN 978-7-119-12179-6
定　　价：110.00 元

版权所有　侵权必究

图说
台湾民俗文化

根

Roots
Customs and Traditions
in Taiwan

目录

序 一 i
序 二 v

文化篇

传统戏剧 002
现代舞 018
郑成功与台南府城 032
台北故宫博物院 040
祭孔大典 046
中式建筑 052
张廖家庙 058
柴烧制陶 063
竹编艺术 068
传统铸剑 073
手工制墨 078
制笔艺术 085
铸字与印章 092
蔬果雕 100

民俗篇

过新年 108
欢喜元宵节 126

三月疯妈祖 146

清明节习俗 157

端午节习俗 167

客家义民节 181

舞狮和舞龙 187

神秘的王船祭 196

生活篇

台湾的茶文化 206

台湾的中药故事 212

米食和面食 218

迪化街：台北第一大街 228

下象棋 234

咬牙切齿来挽脸 240

成年礼与高考祈福 245

童玩趣味多 251

周岁抓周 260

圆仔旋风 265

Contents

Foreword iii

Preface viii

Culture

Traditional Opera 010

Modern Dance 025

Zheng Chenggong and the Prefecture of Tainan . . . 037

Palace Museum of Taipei 044

Confucian Ceremonies 049

Chinese Architecture 056

Zhang-Liao Family Shrine 061

Wood-Fired Pottery 066

Woven Bamboo Art 071

Traditional Sword-Making 076

Hand-Made Ink 082

The Art of Brush Making 089

Typefounding and Seals 096

Vegetable and Fruit Sculptures 103

Folk Customs

Chinese New Year 117

Lantern Festival 136

Mazu March Mania 152

Qingming Festival 162

Dragon Boat Festival 174

Hakka Yimin Festival 184

Dancing Lions and Dragons 192

The Mysterious Lords' Boat Ceremony 201

Lifestyle

Tea Culture in Taiwan 210

Stories of Chinese Medicine in Taiwan 215

Rice- and Wheat-Based Dishes 223

Dihua St: Taipei's First Main Street 232

Playing *Xiangqi* (Chinese Chess) 238

Pain Is Beauty: The Art of Threading 243

Coming-of-Age Ceremonies and Prayers for College

    Entrance Examination. 248

The Joy of Children's Toys 256

Zhuazhou, A First Birthday Tradition 263

Yuan-Zai Mania 269

序一

  原本是一趟寻找雪地残荷之旅，却"好运莲连"催生了《根》这本书。

  话说 2017 年 1 月 31 日的春节期间，我接到一通电话，是《淮安日报》摄影部主任程钢打来的，他跟我说："淮安下雪了。"

  下雪有什么特别的？对我来说当然特别，因为我从高中开始拍荷花以来，40 多年来拍了无数荷花照片，却独缺"雪地残荷"，而淮安正是拥有号称全球最大、品种最全、花期最长观荷园的淮安金湖荷花荡景区，淮安下雪对我可是天大的事。

  所以，次日我就搭飞机冲到南京再转到淮安，并且准备第二天好好地拍他一番。但是，老天喜欢开玩笑，我 5 点多起床后，眼前看到的是红艳艳的大太阳，雪被太阳融光了。我是来拍残荷的，看到的却是连残雪都称不上的景象，"雪地残荷"有荷无雪。

  程钢告诉我，根据气象预报，2 月 8 日会再下雪，算算要等四五天。我决定干脆先转到北京访友拜年。在北京我见到了新华社第一位派驻台湾的摄影记者，现在是外文出版社社长的徐步，以及新华社摄影部国际编辑室主任张瑞祺。他们是我 2009 年在德国采访世界大学生运动会时认识，并一直交往到现在的朋友。

  当天晚上的聚会里，徐步谈起他派驻台湾时的采访记忆。他谈到在台湾采访过程中，感受到台湾保存着许多中华传统文化，他也提到这些美好的文化在现代工商业社会中正逐渐消失。"作为摄影记者有责任把它记录并保留下来。"徐步说，"要让全世界华人了解中华文化之美。"

  就在这一晚以中华文化话题佐酒的餐聚间，徐步决定要出版《根》这本书，并要我在台湾收集照片，一些有关台湾传统风俗习惯及乡土民情的照片。

  回台湾后，我用电话与在北京的张瑞祺主任及外文出版社编辑沟通商量，规划出文化篇、民俗篇、生活篇三大主题，每个主题包含多个子题。之后，我开始收集照片，立刻获得资深摄影记者王远茂、杨锦煌、何叔娟、于志旭、陈柏亨、徐大昌等人的大力支持。他们提供了许多精美照片。

照片收集完成后，我邀请台湾知名作家邱杰（他也是一位资深的报社编辑）为我们每一篇题目写文稿、说故事。邱杰老师经历丰富，文笔之快让我惊讶，32篇文章在一个月左右就完成写作。他说出许多失传的小故事，道尽了台湾保存至今的原汁原味中华文化的精髓。

宋词《西江月·听说金公两字》有言：寻枝寻叶必知根。或许这句词就能道尽《根》这本书出版的必要。

没追到残荷（后来在哈尔滨追到了），误撞出这本《根》，老天这回玩笑开得还算不赖。坚持对美好事物的追求，必有美好的回报。

吴景腾

2017年12月20日于台北

Foreword

Appropriately, it was during a search for lotuses in the snow that the idea for *Roots* was born.

The story goes that during the Spring Festival on 31 January, 2017, I received a phone call from Cheng Gang, Head of Photography at the *Huai'an Daily*, who told me, "It's snowing in Huai'an."

What's so special about snow? Of course, snow was terribly special for me, because, in the more than 40 years since I started taking photos of lotus flowers in high school, the only photo I'd never taken on this theme was of a lotus rising out of the snow. As it happens, Huai'an boasts the Jinhu Lotus Scenic Area: the largest lotus park with the greatest variety of lotuses and the longest flowering season in the world. A bit of snow in Huai'an was an event of momentous significance for me.

Therefore, the next day I hopped on a flight to Huai'an via Nanjing with the intention of spending most of the following day taking photos. However, it would seem that the fates were playing tricks on me that day: I woke up shortly after five that morning, only to be greeted by a dazzling sun that had all but melted the snow. The lotuses were well and truly in bloom, but the scene of lotuses peeking out from underneath a blanket of snow was nowhere to be found.

Cheng Gang told me that according to the weather forecast, there would be more snow a few days later, on February 8. I decided to visit my friends in Beijing in the meantime and give them my wishes for the Chinese New Year. While in Beijing, I met Xu Bu, who was once the first resident photojournalist in Taiwan for Xinhua News Agency and who has since become Director of the Foreign Languages Press (FLP), as well as Zhang Ruiqi, Director of Xinhua Photographic News Department International Desk. I met them in 2009 while we were interviewing athletes at the World University Games in Germany. Since then, we have remained good friends.

At a gathering that evening, Xu Bu recalled his experiences interviewing people in Taiwan and said that they left him with the impression that many elements of traditional

Chinese culture still existed there. However, he felt that this culture was gradually disappearing under the influence of modern industry and commerce. "As photojournalists, we have a responsibility to document and preserve these things," he said. "We have to make all people of Chinese descent throughout the world see just how beautiful our culture is."

Within the space of this evening where the topic of Chinese culture was paired with a healthy quantity of wine, Xu Bu came up with the plan of *Roots* and assigned me the task of taking photos that captured local traditions and customs in Taiwan.

After returning to Taiwan and discussing the details over the phone with Zhang Ruiqi and FLP's project editor in Beijing, we decided to divide the book into three parts: Culture, Folk Customs and Lifestyle, each of which would have a number of subsections. Shortly after, I began to collect photos. Veteran photographers Wang Yuanmao, Yang Jinhuang, He Shujuan, Yu Zhixu, Chen Boheng and Xu Dachang were of great assistance, providing me with a number of exquisite images.

Once we had gathered all the photos we needed, I invited renowned author (and seasoned newspaper editor) Qiu Jie to write a short discursive summary of each topic. Qiu Jie has lived a full and interesting life, and writes at a startling pace. In only a month or so, he completed all 32 short essays, in which he shares a number of previously forgotten stories and evokes the true essence of Chinese culture as preserved in Taiwan.

There is a line in the Song Dynasty poem *Moon over the West River*: "If you seek the branches and the leaves, you must know the root." Perhaps this line alone can summarize the necessity of this book.

Who'd have thought that my failed attempts to find a lotus in the snow (I later succeeded in Harbin) would lead to the genesis of *Roots*? The fates sure do know how to pull a good prank. We are always rewarded for pursuing the things we desire — even if it's not the reward we expect.

Wu Jingteng
20 December, 2017 in Taipei

　　写这一本书，我非常快意，也非常自在，一路走笔如策马奔腾于原野。因为所写皆身边事物，所有的题材从小一直陪伴在我的身边，如同空气之存在于大地，虽不曾时时检视有无，却明明白白地存在着。我跟着阿公从台湾北部到中部拜妈祖；我上学开始学书法课；我过年忙着贴春联，痴痴坐在大灶边享受妈妈蒸年糕的香甜气味……我到海水浴场去采访龙舟比赛；我看着大年大节舞龙队伍穿行于小街。直到现在我和老妻当了阿公阿婆，在儿孙辈盛情簇拥之下来到饭店享受除夕围炉大餐，进了大饭店两头五彩醒狮咚咚咚呛呛呛迎上来，只见大大的迎客敞厅倒贴着一个喜感十足的福字，而后，两包压岁钱被晚辈恭恭敬敬塞到了我和老妻的手中……

　　这一切都是那么自然，无人注意其存在，而确确实实就是我们的生活写真。而今提笔书写，一面写一面豁然而感，啊！原来就是这样呀！万物皆有律，所有生活上的一切，原来也是其生皆有律而非偶然间蹦出来。这让我得以一一回眸探看其本其源。

回眸

回眸1

云山重重万载树
枝繁叶茂淘天覆
海峡难断情牵系
回首悠悠来时路

回眸 2

我忽然问我我何人
我忽然再问我我何来？何往？
我何所事何所为
千古悠悠而我无以回复
我只一脸茫茫然
这不是一向自信饱满勇往直前之我
我追寻而不愿给自己真相
我挣扎切不断那牢牢锁链
我惊醒始见那只是轻如风柔如粉之脐带
竟然无锁链也无捆绑
而真相就在眼前
明朗如我亲手所画
我书写因为我要书写
我行笔如云因为我无隐瞒无避忌
我一路驰骋畅快奔行
我只不否认我谁能拦阻我
我的彩笔每一笔皆是我亲历的累积
我回眸，望见来时路

2017年5月23日，我在计算机中按了个"新建文档"键，建立一个新文档，然后开始书写。这一本新的书稿于是正式开工。

二十多天来，我尽量维持着正常生活作息，赴该赴的约、聚该聚的会。我去了一趟文化局，去了一趟户政事务所，去了八德市民大学的公共论坛谈了一场搭乘时光机的轻旅行，去了一个文化馆讲了一场桃园文化浅说，去了五趟闽南文化节计划的小区操作进度访视和一趟远距离的社造参访，去了一个美美的山野露营了两天，为了检查还跑了四趟医院……呵，还真忙哪！最重要的是我依然维持平时的写作习惯，平均每两天写一个小品文寄出去。如此忙碌而又如此轻松，二十几天竟然就把这一本书稿完成了。比我预定的书写时间还提前了十几天。

这并不是我所书写中最快交卷的一本，却是我九十多种出版品中写来最是轻盈愉快的一本。因为我只要轻松自在地、直言无隐地书写便成，所有的题材都是我身边出现、我所经历，比写自传还更简单。我还没想到为自己写传，看到别人的自传总是避这隐那地写得好不痛苦，何苦。

这本书让我有机会复习身边一切视为平常之景与物，更让我有机会进一步思索我在今日应当有的作为，重新检视我的眼界与格局。七十之我，真乃大收获。

写完了也松了一口气。感谢徐步社长不但策划如此精彩壮阔之题材并付梓，还如此信赖我而付与我此项光荣的任务，感谢摄影名家吴景腾先生偕同朋友提供精美丰富又详实的照片大大充实这本著作的价值。在撰稿期间景腾时时扮演着桥梁的角色，善尽沟通之职，且亦师亦友多所指点匡正，让我少去许多无谓的摸索而得以顺利挥洒。谢谢一切善美因缘促成了这本意义非凡的大书之出版。

邱 杰
2017 年 6 月 17 日
于中国台湾白石庄

Preface

Writing this book was a thoroughly enjoyable experience, because the subject matter has formed an integral part of my world since a young age. As a young boy, I would accompany my grandfather to pay respects to Mazu: the Maternal Ancestor of the Minnan people, who keeps watch over the seas. I studied calligraphy, and every Spring Festival, I would help make *chun lian* — the banners of auspicious characters that families hang above their doors on Chinese New Year — before sitting down to enjoy my mother's *nian gao*, or "New Year's pudding", with the rest of the family. I recall with a similar fondness the dragon boat races held at the local seaside baths, and the "dancing dragon" processions that would weave their way through the lanes of my town on holidays.

These days, my wife and I have grandchildren of our own. Last New Year's Eve, we went to celebrate at a restaurant, accompanied by our children and their children. Upon entering the restaurant, two dancing lions rushed up to greet us as they moved to the rumbling thunder of drums and gongs. Amid this excitement, our kin humbly handed my wife and I two red envelopes filled with money...

This scene, as outlandish as it may seem to Western readers, was perfectly natural for us — after all, we have been practicing these customs for as long as we can remember. As I wrote this book, there were times when I couldn't help but exclaim to myself, "So that's how it came to be!" As I untangled the origins of different cultural phenomena, I realized that nothing truly emerges "out of the blue" — everything in this world is the result of a certain context or set of circumstances. In this book, I hope to trace the ancient traditions and customs of Taiwan back to their roots.

On 23 May 2017, I made a new document on my computer and began to type. Throughout the writing process, I tried to the best of my ability to maintain a regular work schedule as well as respecting my numerous meetings and planned visits. I visited the Office of Cultural Affairs and the Household Registration Office, as well as attending an open university conference. I went to the Cultural Centre to give a talk on the culture of Taoyuan County, and I took part five times in the Minnan Culture Festival. I also went on a spectacular mountainside camping expedition and went to the hospital on four occasions for tests... It truly was a hectic time. Most importantly, I regularly sat down at my desk to write. On average, it took me about two days to write each small essay. Despite this packed schedule, writing this book was a relaxed process. To my great surprise, I was able to finish this book in a little more than three weeks — around two weeks sooner than I had originally predicted.

While I have been able to complete other books within a shorter period of time, this book was, out of the more than 90 books that I have published, the most pleasant to write. This is because writing this book merely required me to explain with levity and succinctness the phenomena that have defined my world since I was a child. In this sense, writing this book was even simpler than writing an autobiography — an endeavor that I have not yet considered undertaking. Reading other authors' memoirs, I have often been struck by how uncomfortable it would be to highlight certain moments of one's life and conceal others.

This book gave me an opportunity to reappreciate all of the sights and objects that I have come to take for granted. It also encouraged me to further consider my role in conserving traditional culture within a global context. Even though I am already 70 years old, writing this book taught me much about myself and my place of origin, and I had a great sense of achievement upon finishing it.

I would like to thank President Xu of the Foreign Languages Press for choosing such a vast and exciting topic, as well as the outstanding photographer Wu Jingteng and his friends for producing such a beautiful and elaborate selection of photos. During the writing process, Jingteng would act as an intermediary who would convey my feelings to the publishers, and vice versa. He also often gave me constructive advice from the perspective of a professional and a friend that saved me much unnecessary searching. Thank you to all the serendipitous connections that sped up the production of this most meaningful work.

Qiu Jie
17 June, 2017

文化篇 Culture

传统戏剧

传唱不辍的京剧

京剧在台湾地区曾长时期被称作"国剧"或平剧。称作"国剧"的原因是蒋介石部队东渡来台后，为了强调其"正统"地位而希望台湾民众接受此一具有强烈政治意味之名称。而北京市曾一度被国民党政府改名为北平，京剧源自北平，就被称作平剧了。

中国戏曲种类繁多，各具特色。京剧以北京为发源中心，在徽剧的基础上汲取汉剧、秦腔、昆曲、梆子、弋阳腔等多种表演艺术精华而逐步形成。乾隆五十五年，来自南方的四个徽剧班三庆班、四喜班、和春班、春台班（称为四大徽班）陆续来到北京。1828年前后的道光年间，大量的湖广演员进京表演，带来了汉调，造成剧团的大融合。受北京语音与腔调的影响，他们的唱腔有了"京音"的特色。后来他们到上海演出，上海人就把这种带有北京特点的皮黄戏叫作"京戏"，也叫"京剧"。这便是京剧的由来。

由于台湾的京剧观众绝大多数都是外省人，无法与本地文化相互融合，等到老一辈的外省人逐渐凋零，京剧便失去了忠实观众而没落。幸好台湾出现重要的戏剧院和戏曲学院，有计划地保存、传承、推广京剧，迄今仍有四大京剧团：国光剧团、复兴剧团（现已改名为台湾戏曲学院

文化篇 Culture

台湾戏曲学院京剧戏学生演出《文昭关》。摄影：吴景腾
Peking opera students at the Taiwan College of Performing Arts perform *The Wenzhao Pass*. Photography: Wu Jingteng

京剧团）、台北新剧团（李宝春主持）、当代传奇剧场（吴兴国主持）。经常演出京剧的场地有四个：（木栅）国光剧场、（内湖）复兴剧场、（内湖）碧湖剧场、（台泥大楼）台北戏棚。每年还有不定期在重要演艺场所进行的大型公演。

2010年京剧通过了联合国教科文组织的审议，入选为非物质文化遗产。台湾地区也对振兴京剧不遗余力，甚至有人指出：将京剧推上世界三大艺术节舞台，带领传统走入当代的是吴兴国。吴兴国曾是台湾"云门舞集"的舞者，创立当代传奇剧场全力复兴京剧。保守派指责他大逆不道，是京剧逆子，而丹麦的欧丁剧场大师EugenioBarba则认为：他不仅撼动了自己的传统，也撼动了欧洲莎士比亚的传统。在80年代有人悲叹"国剧"气数已尽时，吴兴国带领一群年轻人在京剧中加入新元素。"我要让更多人来看戏。"

虽然步履坎坷，当代传奇剧场一度宣告闭团，但纵使环境再差，吴兴国仍不愿放

北京京剧院武生名家"李(万春)派"传人韩增祥教授(左)指导国光剧团演员。
Famous actor of *wusheng* (male protagonists well-versed in martial arts) from the Jingju Theatre Company of Beijing, Professor Han Zengxiang, visits Taiwan to give actors guidance.

台湾京剧名家吴兴国带领上海戏曲学院年轻演员演出《水浒108——忠义堂》。
Famous actor and director of Peking opera, Wu Xingguo, leads young actors in a performance of *Outlaws of the Marsh*.

摄影:吴景腾
Photography: Wu Jingteng

弃，复团后的首部创作《李尔在此》，以独角戏打通生旦净末丑，一人饰演十二个角色，采用"一角色一章节"的诠释方法，重新解构莎士比亚的《李尔王》。复团以来的作品，从希腊悲剧、莎士比亚、西方当代文学再到中国传奇故事等，取材多元，成绩惊人，锲而不舍地打造台湾京剧新美学，也写出京剧在台湾地区的闪亮诗篇。

布袋戏里的民族英雄

在台湾地区，中年一辈只要提起"云州大儒侠"这个名号，没有人不立时眼睛一亮；小学生考试答题，列举出几位民族英雄，史艳文往往高居排行榜之首。史艳文的名号大大压倒了史可法和戚继光，而事实上史艳文只是布袋戏《云州大儒侠》中一个虚拟出来的人物。

当年全台湾只有三个电视台，每当播映《云州大儒侠》节目时，电视机前总是挤满聚精会神的老少观众。里头许多角色如今依然深植人心，几首主题曲也仍传唱至今，写下了台湾布袋戏传奇之页。时至今日，布袋戏不但不被扬弃，竟还以更惊人的气势登场，在电视节目中占有不可撼动的一席之地。布袋戏所衍生的外围文化创意产业与商品丰富多元而且广受欢迎。

布袋戏起源于17世纪福建泉州，也在当时流传至台湾。布袋戏之名称有说是因为戏偶都缝成一个个小布袋，再伸进手掌去操作而称布袋戏；另一说法则是无分主角配角、王孙贵族，演完统统朝布袋里一扔便提走，因此有了布袋戏之通称。

人们早期聘布袋戏班演出是因其价格较廉。民间酬神谢愿要演戏，但演一场歌仔戏价格不低，所以改用布袋戏代替。当然在排场和规格上相去甚远，只能说是聊胜于无。后来有了电视传播，创作者发挥创意巧思，推出精彩戏码，竟是一炮而红轰动全岛。其中李天禄、黄海岱等大师的贡献更是居功甚伟，为了方便传艺，他们亲笔写下剧本纲要传授给徒弟。黄海岱著名的布袋戏剧本有《五虎战青龙》《大唐五虎将》《三门街》《昆岛逸史》《秘道遗书》等。其子黄俊雄的著名布袋戏作品《云州大儒侠》就来自黄海岱的《忠孝义勇传》。

至1995年，霹雳布袋戏成立首家以布袋戏播放为核心的独立电视台霹雳卫星电视台，无论演出水平之精进与科技运用之炫奇以及相关产值无不连创佳绩，为台湾布

台湾庙宇节庆时总会邀请布袋戏班来演戏。
Glove puppet opera troupes are always invited to perform at temples throughout Taiwan on important celebrations.

布袋戏班在小货车上搭出舞台,机动十足,四处演出。
A glove puppet opera troupe sets up a makeshift stage on the back of a truck.

摄影:吴景腾
Photography: Wu Jingteng

袋戏发展写下新页。

布袋戏偶基本结构包括身架、服饰、盔帽。身架包括了头，布身，手（文手或武手，木制），实心的布腿，鞋（靴子，木制）。传统戏偶高度约30厘米。霹雳布袋戏在摄影棚中拍摄的新戏偶动辄一米身高，制作精美、身价非凡。

云林县有台湾第一座布袋戏馆。布袋戏馆原为云林县虎尾镇的旧警察分局馆舍，建立于1922年间，是一栋古色古香的老建筑物，2013年由虎尾厝文化创意馆进驻经营布袋戏馆，并以"向掌中大师致敬"作为开幕首展。这个馆专门介绍了台湾布袋戏南北四大门派的名师，如亦宛然的陈锡煌大师、小西园的许王大师、西螺新兴阁的钟任壁大师、虎尾五洲园的黄俊雄大师等，展示了四大名师的家族发展、经典角色和老照片文物。馆内还有交互式游戏，让展示更有趣味也更活泼，布袋戏偶不再是冷冰冰的展品，而成了活泼可亲的新的生命。馆内还有定期演出，动态、静态、展演俱足，有如一座小型博物馆。台湾布袋戏总算有了自己的家。

台湾歌仔戏

歌仔戏一般被认为发源于宜兰，是台湾地区唯一土生土长的戏曲剧种，至今约有一百多年的历史。但是歌仔戏的演出内容，像"山伯英台""陈三五娘"等历史故事或民间传说，则毫无疑问几乎完全取材于中华文化。

据1963年宜兰县文献委员会编的《宜兰县志》，以及1971年出版的《台湾省通志》记载，歌仔戏为宜兰地区的一种民谣曲调，传唱者乃是员山乡结头份一个名叫阿助的人。时人不知其名姓，乃称之为"歌仔助"。学者曾永义先生则在《台湾歌仔戏的发展与变迁》一书中介绍称，这位歌仔助先生名叫欧来助，从小就随着父母迁居宜兰市，先住在午崁街（现西后街）。他父亲叫欧接成，在那里摆菜摊子，后来搬到西城门外（今旧城北路）经营金德发商号。欧来助以善歌名闻乡里，他在大约40岁时（1910年），应乡中父老邀请，每天晚饭后偕同好友、家里开金纸店的翁南一同搭渡船过西门溪，沿着田间走半个小时的羊肠小道，再穿过一条竹巷，到达一处槟榔园。在那里有一座由乡民用桂竹和稻草搭盖的棚寮，两人就在里头教乡中子弟演唱"本地歌仔"。这个棚寮因此被称作"歌仔寮"。他们演唱的故事是梁山伯与祝英台。后来，歌仔助的名气越来越大，曾先后到过台北县的卯澳和宜兰员山乡的十八磱（今湖北村）开班授徒，并且在迎神赛会的场合登台演唱，所谓的歌仔戏就从此诞生了，欧来助也成了台湾歌仔戏的鼻祖。

民俗专家陈建铭也有考证称，欧来助所传唱的歌，原是流传于大陆闽南地区，后来随着移民传入台湾地区而传唱起来的"歌仔"。歌仔的内容大多描述日常生活，后来才发展成说唱故事，最初并没有演员，也没有布景、道具，称为"念歌仔"。后来结合了车鼓戏的表演身段、角色及装扮，从第三人称的说唱故事，变成由第一人称来铺演故事。但这时仅有简单的故事情节，角色亦仅有小生、旦和小丑三种，是为三小戏的表演形式，多于农闲之际在大树下、草垛旁演唱，为自娱娱人的性质。

粗具戏剧雏形的歌仔戏，后来渐渐参与庙会活动，成为迎神赛会的阵头之一，称为"歌仔阵"；当阵头在空地或庙埕停下来，以竹竿定出四个角落，由演员"踏四门"，划出表演区来演出，则称为"落地扫"。后来再转到舞台上表演，戏出也由段子戏扩充为全本戏，即为"老歌仔戏"或称为"本地歌仔"。目前宜兰地区仍可见这种表演形式的歌仔戏。

"本地歌仔"经不断吸收、融合其他剧种的菁华，渐渐形成大戏形态的歌仔戏。再融入北管戏、南管戏、四平戏、外江戏曲等表演艺术的音乐曲调、锣鼓点、武打、服饰、装扮、彩绘布景，和其他剧种的戏码、身段、道具、乐器等，发展成一种兼容并蓄、内容丰富的新剧种，歌仔戏终于完备。

歌仔戏迅速风行全台，并且产生了职业戏班，还渡海去厦门传授、公演，一度使得歌仔戏风行于福建地区。现今闽南地区的芗剧，就是从台湾的歌仔戏发展而成的。

歌仔戏在台湾地区的发展并非一帆风顺。外来殖民政府总有去之而后快之念而设法禁止，但歌仔戏总是能在低谷时峰回路转重获生机。其中不可不提的廖琼枝老师，从艺逾六十载，终身岁月全部投注于歌仔戏的薪尽火传上，培育了数不清的学生，是台湾当代歌仔戏发展最重要的推手。廖老师的唱腔、身段优美而且演技精湛，被誉为"台湾第一苦旦"，也先后获得许多重要大奖，被指定为"重要传统艺术歌仔戏保存者"，堪称实至名归。

文化篇 Culture

台湾春美歌剧团演出武侠大戏《义薄云天》。
The Chunmei Opera Troupe perform the great martial arts opera *Highest Integrity*.

歌仔戏《穆桂英》一幕。
An act from the gezai opera *Mu Guiying*.

摄影：吴景腾
Photography: Wu Jingteng

Traditional Opera

Peking Opera

For a long period of time, Peking opera was referred to in Taiwan as *guo ju* ("national opera") or *ping ju* ("peace opera"). The term "national opera" originates from the period following the retreat of Chiang Kai-shek's army and government to Taiwan. In order to emphasize the "legitimacy" of their rule, the Kuomintang imposed this highly politicized term on the local people. Similarly, as the city of Beijing had at one point been renamed Beiping ("Northern Peace") by the Kuomintang, Peking opera was called "peace opera" in reference to their place of origin.

There are many types of Chinese opera, each with their own characteristics. As suggested by its name, Peking opera originated in Beijing (formerly transcribed into English as "Peking"). The genre is largely based on Hui opera, although, throughout its development, it absorbed the essence of a variety of Chinese performing arts, such as Han opera, *qin qiang* (tunes of Qin), *Hui Opera*, *bang zi* (woodblock tunes) and *yiyang qiang* (tunes of Yiyang County). In the 55th year of Emperor Qianlong's reign during the Qing Dynasty, four Hui opera troupes came up from the south of China to Beijing. Around 1828, during the reign of Emperor Daoguang of Qing, a large number of actors from Huguang (modern-day Hunan and Hubei) went to perform in Beijing, thus introducing the cadences of Han opera to the Northern Capital

文化篇 Culture

台湾戏曲学院附设京剧团老师与青年演员们，在开学第一天依古礼举行开台仪式。
Students at the Taiwan College of Performing Arts perform a traditional "opening the stage" ritual on the first day of the academic year.

演员化妆准备登台表演。
Actors apply make-up in preparation for an on-stage performance.

一群票友在公园里吊嗓子。
A group of amateur Peking opera performers train their voices in a park.

摄影：吴景腾
Photography: Wu Jingteng

and contributing to the fusion of styles that would come to define Peking opera.

Because the majority of Peking opera spectators in Taiwan were originally from the mainland, Peking opera was unable to successfully take root in local culture. As this generation of mainland spectators grew old and passed away, Peking opera would, having lost its loyal fan base, gradually fade into obscurity. Fortunately, some of Taiwan's most prestigious theatres and conservatories intervened and carefully planned the conservation, impartation and promotion of Peking opera. To this day, four major Peking opera troupes are still active in Taiwan: Guoguang Opera Troupe, Fuxing Opera Troupe, Taipei Li-yuan Peking Opera Theatre and the Contemporary Legends Theatre. Every year, these troupes stage public performances at major venues throughout Taiwan.

In 2010, UNESCO included Peking opera on its Representative List of the Intangible Cultural Heritage of Humanity. Indefatigable efforts have been made to revive and conserve Peking opera. The man responsible for leading the introduction of this traditional genre to contemporary audiences is Wu Xingguo. In the 1980s, as people lamented that the days of Peking opera were numbered, Wu Xingguo led a troupe of fellow young actors in order to lend new life to this genre, saying, "I want more people to see Peking opera." In one of his productions, *Lear is Here*, Wu Xingguo plays all 12 parts of *King Lear* in a deconstructed version of Shakespeare's play. His Peking operas are based on a number of stories, including Ancient Greek tragedies, Shakespearean plays, works of contemporary Western literature, as well as Chinese legends. These productions have continued to dazzle audiences, irrevocably changing the face of Peking opera in Taiwan.

Glove-Puppet Opera

In Taiwan, middle-aged people are invariably familiar with the name "The Scholar Swordsman", and, when elementary students are asked to name popular local heroes, "Shi Yanwen" is often high on the list of most common answers. In reality, however, Shi Yanwen is just a fictional character from the glove-puppet opera *The Scholar Swordsman*.

At a time when Taiwan only had three TV stations, whenever a new episode of *The Scholar Swordsman* was broadcast, families would huddle around their TV sets, their eyes glued to the screen. Some of the theme songs used for the series are still known and sung to

传统布袋戏后场管弦乐器以唢呐、笛、二胡、三弦、椰胡为主，称之为"文场"。摄影：吴景腾

The traditional string and woodwind instruments used in the background music to glove puppet operas are the *suona* (a double-reed woodwind instrument), di (transverse flute), *erhu* (two-stringed fiddle), *sanxian* (three-stringed lute) and *yehu* (fiddle with a coconut shell resonator). Photography: Wu Jingteng

孩子们玩起布偶很开心。摄影：吴景腾
Children having fun playing with glove puppet dolls. Photography: Wu Jingteng

this day, and television broadcasts of glove-puppet dramas continue to receive high ratings. The cultural industry and range of products derived from glove-puppet opera broadly appeal to Taiwan's consumers.

Glove-puppet opera originated during the 17th century in Quanzhou, Fujian Province, and was soon after introduced to and popularized throughout Taiwan. The Chinese name for this genre literally translates to "fabric-bag opera". It is commonly believed that this name is due to the puppets' material and shape: they are essentially "bags" made of two pieces of fabric sewn together, into which the puppeteer inserts their hand and manipulates using their fingers. Another theory concerning the origin of this name is that all of the puppets used in each opera — whether they be lead characters or extras, noblemen or peasants — are carried away in the one fabric bag at the end of each performance.

Initially, when organizing performances in order to express gratitude to local deities, local people would often choose glove-puppet operas because of their relatively low cost. Following the invention of the television, producers worked with puppeteers in order to develop exciting repertoires of televised glove-puppet shows, causing the genre to become famous throughout the island. Of these master puppeteers, Li Tianlu and Huang Haidai are particularly celebrated for their contributions to the popularization of glove-puppet opera. Huang Haidai is known for creating scripts such as *The Five Tigers Battle the Azure Dragon*, *The Five Tiger Generals of the Tang Dynasty* and *Three-Gate Street*. His son, Huang Junxiong, is the creator of *The Scholar* Swordsman.

In 1995, PiliTV, a channel that primarily broadcasts glove-puppet dramas, was founded. Whether it be in terms of the quality of performances, the application of new technologies,

传统布袋戏加上声光、爆破,发展成令人称奇的霹雳布袋戏。摄影:吴景腾

Televised glove puppet operas add stunning visual and sound effects, such as explosions, to traditional performances. Photography: Wu Jingteng

or the creation of stunning visual effects, the foundation of this station marked a new phase in the development of glove-puppet opera in Taiwan.

Glove puppets are essentially composed of a frame, clothing, and a hat or helmet. Traditional glove puppets are approximately 30 cm tall. The glove puppets filmed in studios are generally a meter tall and are made with painstaking attention to detail.

In Yunlin County, there is a glove puppet museum. This museum is dedicated to explaining, through the use of artefacts such as old photos, the typical character types and intra-familial impartation of the four great schools of glove puppet opera. Inside the museum, one can find interactive games that make the exhibition more interesting and lively. The museum also organizes regular performances.

Gezai Opera

Gezai opera is also known simply as "local opera" as it is the only known type of opera to have originated in Taiwan. It is thought to come from Yilan County and has over one hundred years of history. However, the content of gezai opera is almost entirely based on historical events and folklore from traditional Chinese culture, such as *The Butterfly Lovers*.

According to historical records, gezai opera was originally a type of folk tune from the region of Yilan. One of its most important practitioners and conveyors is a native of Yilan named Ah Zhu. Ah Zhu was well known throughout his village because of his talent for singing. When he was around 40 (in 1910), he and his close friends began to give daily singing lessons to children of the village in the local betel palm orchard. The story that they would sing to the children was *The Butterfly Lovers*, also named *Liang Shanbo and Zhu Yingtai* after its two protagonists. Later, as his reputation began to grow, Ah Zhu was invited to perform at festivals in honor of local deities, thus spawning gezai opera.

Research by the ethnologist Chen Jianming offers evidence that the songs transmitted by Ah Zhu originated from southern Fujian Province. Initially, the majority of these gezai operas were simple vocal performances with no actors, backdrops or props. Eventually, these vocal performances would develop simple plotlines featuring three roles: a male and female lead, as well as a jester. They were mostly performed in the shade of a big tree or a haystack during breaks from farm work. Over time, these performances were increasingly included in temple ceremonies and celebrations. As their popularity rose, they were eventually introduced to the stage, where they gradually developed into major productions.

Subsequently, instruments, tunes, martial arts, make-up and backdrops from other types of opera were integrated into these performances in order to create a new genre with diverse content. As gezai opera took Taiwan by storm, a number of professional gezai opera troupes emerged. These troupes would regularly cross the Taiwan Straits and perform in Xiamen, thus beginning the popularization of gezai opera throughout Fujian. The genre of *xiangju* in southern Fujian is an offshoot of gezai opera.

It is important to note that the development of gezai opera in Taiwan was not totally unencumbered. Colonial governments attempted to ban gezai opera, but the genre has always found a way to survive these attempts and return with renewed vigor. The contemporary dancer Liao Qiongzhi played an indispensable role in promoting the development of Taiwan's contemporary gezai opera. Her singing voice and elegant figure, as well as her consummate acting skills, earned her the reputation of Taiwan's best *kudan* ("sorrowful female lead"). She has been designated an "important conservationist of the traditional artform of gezai opera."

在"台北市歌仔戏观摩汇演"上，一心戏剧团带来"群仙献瑞，财神临福"的开场表演，吸引许多民众观赏。
摄影：吴景腾
Opening performance of the Taipei Gezai Opera Gala and Exchange, entitled *The Fairies Bring Good Tidings and the God of Wealth Brings Good Fortune*. Photography: Wu Jingteng

现代舞

龙飞凤舞董阳孜

舞蹈也可以舞出书法之美吗？书法之美也可以借舞蹈来做出完美的诠释吗？

台湾的书法家董阳孜以最传统来表现最现代，淋漓尽致的将书法与舞蹈完整结合，这样的展示，真乃直击人心！

"我们总不能落到有一天要到日本去学书法嘛！我们自己不努力，难道巴望由别人来帮我们传承？"这是董阳孜常常挂在嘴边的一句话。她耗费大半生致力于研究书法、推广书法，目的无他，咬定了这是中华文化之精髓，一分一秒也舍不得放下。

董阳孜生于1942年，原籍浙江，出生于上海，在台湾师范大学艺术系毕业后赴美国深造，取得麻州大学艺术硕士后回台湾，她在书法创作中大量融入西洋构图的理论，兼具现代平面设计与传统书法的美学，而形塑出个人独特的风格。

她最擅长也最教人震惊者乃巨幅草书创作，个子不高大的她持比身体还长的巨笔，在一整面大墙、一整个敞厅的地面上以雄浑笔力奔放挥洒，开创了书法艺术的新风貌。

文化篇 Culture

台湾知名书法家董阳孜为了让大家深刻感受中国文字的美感及丰富层次，邀请编舞家布拉瑞扬·帕格勒法、罗文瑾、多媒体创作者陈彦任，及爵士演奏家魏广皓、张坤德、山田洋平等人，糅合书法线条、人体线条、音乐线条，共同创造出跨界作品《骚》。摄影：吴景腾

Renowned calligrapher, Dong Yangzi, fuses modern dance, multimedia and jazz music into her interdisciplinary work *Sao* as a means of expressing the aesthetics and richness of Chinese text. Photography: Wu Jingteng

　　2016年间，她的《骚2016》跨界剧场，结合书法线条、多媒体影像、爵士乐、现代舞各种元素跨界共同演出。她所创作的一百幅书法作品，经过多媒体科技转化后，从平面变立体，再搭配现场爵士乐与现代舞在舞台上即兴挥洒，再一次震惊社会。大众惊异于书法艺术竟然可以如此自在活泼呈现，董阳孜则潇洒表示："书法是线条，乐句是线条、舞者的身体也是线条。希望观众从看演出开始酝酿骚动，结束时在台下蠢蠢欲动，恨不得到台上跟舞者乐手一起飙舞飙乐！"显然，她已在这一次演出中得到了肯定和心中的预期。

　　以龙飞凤舞来形容董阳孜的书法堪称匀当合宜，近年来她一直努力将书法美学融入当代生活与视觉艺术创作中，如云门舞集、新舞台、金石堂文化广场，到公共电视节目《孽子》、青春版昆剧《牡丹亭》题字、方文山的MV《兰亭序》，乃至国家音乐厅引自诗经"瑟兮僩兮，赫兮咺兮"的逸品、高雄捷运大型灯箱装置，以及诚品书店农历新年赠送读者的"福"字春联等，都出自她之手，一直佳评如潮。

创作四十年,董阳孜三字几乎已成为书法之代名词。她先后在德国、美国、加拿大、英国、日本、韩国、香港及台湾等国家和地区,举办超过六十场书法展览,最近多年来更以跨界艺术创作展演为重心,透过和绘画、影像、音乐、雕塑等不同艺术形式创新者的合作,彰显书法艺术的当代性。重要展演包括:《沉墨似金》《心弦,无声之音》《对话》《无中生有:书法—符号—空间》《墨韵无边》《无声的乐章》《一字箴言——诚》《独乐》等。她大胆创新的跨界创作,希望在网络时代里活化书写的艺术,并且让书法不断探索介入当代艺术的创作当中,以延续这项东方传统艺术的当代生命光彩。

林怀民和云门舞集

中国古书《吕氏春秋》中有这样一句话:"黄帝时,大容作云门,大卷……",这句话解释了炎黄子孙之始祖黄帝的时代,舞蹈的名称就是云门。这便是台湾享誉四海的"云门舞集"命名之由来。

云门舞集是台湾一个现代舞蹈表演团体,创办于1973年。创办者林怀民先生是曾任嘉义县长的林金生先生之子,据说林金生对爱子不肯继承衣钵,竟然想去跳舞,一度恼火得不得了。但林怀民却是意志坚定的勇往直前,一路诸苦备尝,终于闯出了傲人的一片天。多年来云门先后推出许多舞蹈作品,包括《薪传》《家族合唱》《流浪者之歌》《水月》《竹梦》《行草》《九歌》(舞剧)等等。1999年另创"云门舞集2",舞台上呈现舞作从古典文学、民间故事、台湾历史到社会现象的衍化发挥,乃至前卫观念的尝试均无所不包。展演场地从台北戏剧院,到各县市文化中心、体育馆、乡镇学校礼堂,另还包括平均每场观众高达六万人的户外演出。此外云门也经常应邀赴海外公演,堪称是国际重要艺术节的常客。舞团在台湾地区及欧、美、亚、澳各洲两百多个舞台上,演出已将近两千场,以独特的创意、精湛的舞技,获得各地观众与舞评家的热烈赞赏。

2008年,一场无名大火将云门位于淡水河畔的八里练舞场烧成灰烬。万幸的是云门并没有被击倒,在各界的关怀、勉励和支持下,云门历经7年之后重生于淡水河北岸的淡水小镇上。新的馆区坐落于沪尾炮台后方,隐匿在层层树林之间,美如现代桃花源。云门人辛勤于此,脑力激荡、流淌汗水,游客也得以在安排下局部性参观与

文化篇 Culture

云门舞集以中国书法、太极及拳术入舞的"行草三部曲"。摄影：吴景腾
The Cloud Gate Dance Theatre performs *Cursive in Three Parts*, a production that blends Chinese calligraphy, tai chi and martial arts.
Photography: Wu Jingteng

参与，这里俨然成为淡水无声却有力的闪亮文化新焦点。

回首三十年，林怀民以中国最古老的舞名——云门——作为现代舞团的名称。这是台湾地区第一个职业舞团。中国传统文化加上这块芬芳土地的滋润，是云门舞集艺术的母体；文学经典、历史、传说和民间故事，都是林怀民创作的源泉。站在这个巨人的肩膀上，林怀民展现了他努力开创终于开花结果的高度。

刘凤学的新古典

1925年，刘凤学出生于黑龙江齐齐哈尔市，是什么因缘让这个东北女子跨越海峡，在台湾发出璀璨的光，以70年的努力不懈写下难有人能与之并驾的新古典美学现代舞风格？

"我是东北人，特别喜欢苍凉和悲壮的感觉"，刘凤学对于家乡始终有着不能忘却的眷恋。她在创作舞蹈作品《北大荒》与《大漠孤烟直》中，展现的辽远风情，被认为正是对家乡的怀念。

70年来，刘凤学致力于中国现代舞的创作，不同于其他舞者往西方去学习，她朝着中国古乐舞的方向去寻根。她从史籍文献中考古，发现中国近代颠沛的历史造成许多珍贵的乐舞资料失传佚散。她前往日本宫内厅、韩国及法国国家图书馆等地埋首寻找，手抄携回珍贵的乐谱及舞谱，再细加翻译。唐代的乐谱每一种乐器的乐谱符号都和现代不同，她只好化身为今人古人之间的桥，一一苦心翻译，试着让原音重现。舞谱也是一样，古代的舞谱有文无图，以一句一句的文字来描绘繁复的舞蹈动作，刘凤学以计算机协助翻译这些文字成图画舞谱，工程浩大而艰巨，她却甘之如饴。

刘凤学的老家是个多民族混居的城市，满族、朝鲜族、蒙古族、回族、达斡尔族、锡伯族、赫哲族、鄂伦春族、鄂温克族和柯尔克族等不同族群和睦共处。刘凤学有满族血统，从小与白俄小朋友一起学芭蕾舞。刘凤学在国立长白师范学院主修舞蹈、辅修音乐，于1949年毕业，随即来台，开启了她毕生对美学的追求之旅。

原本刘凤学一心在现代舞创作的世界里悠游探索，1957年，她的系主任江良规博士问她："你想创造中国现代舞，但是你对中国古典舞有什么了解？"这个问题给了她莫大的震撼，从此一头栽入中国古典舞的殿堂。她从经史子集中去探索，也从《乐

文化篇 Culture

台湾编舞家刘凤学博士费尽六十年心血，重建唐宫廷乐舞《倾杯乐》。摄影：吴景腾

The choreographer Dr. Liu Fengxue devoted 60 years of her life to recreating the musical performance from the Tang imperial court, *Emptying the Cup*. Photography: Wu Jingteng

律全书》《北堂书抄》《古今图书集成》等文献中寻找。最后因为得知日本还保存许多唐代传过去的乐舞，1965年直接闯进日本筑波大学研究，进到宫内厅书绫部，花了7个月时间，手抄2050页的乐谱及舞谱。唐代的乐谱每一种乐器的乐谱符号都和现代不同，她苦心翻译，试着让原音重现。古代的舞谱有文无图，刘凤学以电脑协助将文字转化为图画舞谱。经多方钻研请教，终于陆续重建失传的盛唐乐舞《拔头》、北齐武舞《兰陵王》、唐高宗时代的《春莺啭》，以及在公元8世纪传入日本的《皇帝破阵乐》。

1972年和1974年，她两度前往韩国研究宋代传至韩国的儒家舞蹈，以及韩国在15世纪模仿儒家舞蹈所创作的宗庙舞蹈，整理出儒家文舞"化成天下之舞"以及武舞"威加四海"。接下来更是远赴德国法国的漫长学习之旅，所谓礼失而求诸野，向外国人学中国，没想到竟是一条艰苦的快捷之径！

长期以来，刘凤学在台湾深入少数民族部落及乡村偏郊，整理她的创作灵感，汲取地方养分，而后以十百倍的作品回馈这块土地。她的作品《沉默的杵音》及《云豹之乡》便是长期深入部落创作出来的重要代表作。

刘凤学和一群献身舞蹈文化的学生创办的"新古典舞团"于1976年成立，以深度的人文内涵，融会西方艺术，将历史春秋之情化成天下之舞，透过研究、创作和演出，呈现多元化的风貌。新古典不但足迹遍及台湾地区，更受邀至美国、德国、法国、奥地利、新加坡等地演出，其中应法国政府之邀，参加比利牛斯民俗舞蹈节，共演出22场，观众累计达10万人次。在纽约文化中心台北剧场、俄罗斯新西伯利亚、法国国家舞蹈中心及返回大陆，在深圳、广州、中山巡回演出，无不受尽观众、舞蹈界、学界及媒体新闻界一致赞誉，写下了台湾舞艺辉煌新页。

文化篇 Culture

Modern Dance

Dance and Calligraphy

Is dance capable of conveying the beauty of Chinese calligraphy? The calligrapher Dong Yangzi has fused traditional calligraphy and modern dance into a profoundly moving art form. She firmly believes that calligraphy is the essence of Chinese culture, and has devoted most of her life to researching and promoting it.

Dong Yangzi was born in Shanghai, in 1942. Her ancestral home is in Zhejiang Province. After graduating from Taiwan Normal University, she moved to the United States to pursue her studies at a higher level. Upon obtaining her master's degree in Art, she returned to Taiwan, where she started her career as an artist. In her works, she blends Western principles of composition and graphic design with the aesthetic criteria of traditional Chinese calligraphy. Dong Yangzi's most startling and successful works are large-scale pieces where she wields a brush that towers above her petite frame and writes in flowing cursive text along the entire face of a wall, or across the floor of a spacious hall.

In 2016, her work *Sao 2016* was presented in theatres. In this groundbreaking performance, she used a variety of media and technologies to combine 100 of her past works into a moving three-dimensional display. She then invited jazz musicians and contemporary dancers to improvise a

现代舞者运用肢体表现书法线条、人体线条、音乐线条之美。摄影：吴景腾
Contemporary dancers use movement to convey the parallel beauty of calligraphy, the human form and musical notation, all defined by their flowing lines. Photography: Wu Jingteng

performance, using this display for inspiration. While audiences are startled by how organic and spontaneous Yangzi's creative process is, she humbly explains: "Calligraphy, musical sentences and the dancers' bodies are all composed of lines. I hope that, as the performance commences, the audience will start to reflect on the nature of spontaneous movement — and that, by the end, they will be itching to get up on stage and get carried away by the music!"

Over the course of 40-year career, Dong Yangzi's name has become synonymous with calligraphy. She has organized over 60 calligraphy exhibitions in many countries and regions, including Germany, the US, Canada, the UK, Japan, South Korea, Hong Kong and Taiwan. In recent years, she has largely focused on exhibitions that blend different disciplines and media. By mixing calligraphy with disciplines such as painting, video, music and sculptures, Yangzi reaffirms calligraphy's relevance in the art world and introduces its glory to modern audiences.

Cloud Gate Dance Theatre

The Cloud Gate Dance Theatre is a contemporary dance troupe founded in 1973 by Lin Huaimin, the son of Lin Jinsheng — the former Governor of Chiayi County. Apparently, when Huaimin announced to his father that he wished to become a dancer rather than following in his footsteps, Jinsheng flew into a fit of rage. However, thanks to his determination and courage, Huaimin was able to carve out a path for himself in the field of his dreams.

Yunmen (literally "cloud gate") is China's oldest dance. The name Cloud Gate was inspired by descriptions of this dance in the *Spring and Autumn Annals of Master Lü*, a book from approximately 300 BC. Over the last few decades, this troupe has staged a number of productions, including *Passing the Flame*, *Nine Songs*, *Familial Harmony*, *Song of the Wanderer*, *Water Moon*, *Bamboo Dream* and *Walking in the Grasses*. The subject matter of new productions of 1999 — Clound Gate II — is largely taken from classical literature, folk stories, Taiwan's history, and current societal phenomena — although some of the productions are more abstract and avant-garde in nature. The Cloud Gate Dance Theatre is also regularly invited to give performances overseas and is a popular addition to prominent arts festivals around the globe. The troupe has performed over 2,000 times on more than 200 stages, both in Taiwan and across the globe, in North America, Europe, Asia and Australia. Their performances have won fervent praise from both critics and the public.

In 2008, a fire tragically reduced Cloud Gate's dance studio to ashes. Fortunately, this tragedy did not mark the end for the theatre troupe — in 2015, a new facility was constructed in the small town of Danshui, located on the north shore of the river of the same name. Discreetly tucked away in a resplendent grove of trees, the new facility is like a modern-day "peach blossom spring" (a utopia commonly represented in Chinese art). It has become the cultural hub of Danshui.

云门舞者与水墨流影共舞,挥洒出奇幻壮丽的泼墨山水。摄影:吴景腾

Members of the Cloud Gate Dance Theatre engage in a dance with the flowing ink on the screen, conjuring up magnificent landscapes. Photography: Wu Jingteng

文化篇 Culture

Neo-Classical Dance

In 1925, Liu Fengxue was born in Qiqihar, Heilongjiang Province. This woman from the northeastern extremities of the mainland would later move to Taiwan and devote 70 years of her life to creating a form of modern dance with a neo-classical twist.

"I'm from the Northeast, and I very much like the majestic sadness and austere scenery of that part of the world." Throughout her life, Liu Fengxue has felt an unbreakable bond with her hometown. The distant lands evoked in her dance performances *The Great Northern Wilderness* and *In the Desert, A Lone Tower of Smoke Rises* are thought to reflect Fengxue's longing for her hometown.

Liu's hometown is a melting pot of different ethnicities. She herself is of Manchurian descent, and she has studied ballet with the Russian children since she was a little girl. Liu Fengxue studied dance and music at Changbai Normal Academy, and, after graduating in 1949, moved to Taiwan, where she would begin her lifelong pursuit of dance aesthetics.

In 1957, her department head, Dr. Jiang Lianggui, asked her: "You want to create a modern Chinese dance, but what do you know about China's classical dance?" This question left Liu speechless. From that very moment, she decided to plunge headfirst into the world of classical Chinese dance. She learned through her research that Japan had preserved many dances from China's Tang Dynasty, and in 1965, she went to study at Tsukuba University. In the seven months that she spent in Japan, she copied 2,050 pages of dance choreography and sheet music by hand. The forms of musical notation for every instrument during the Tang Dynasty significantly differ from the system used today, meaning that Liu Fengxue had to painstakingly "translate" these ancient scores in an attempt to reproduce their original sound. Meanwhile, the ancient dance instructions were pure text, with no illustrations. With the assistance of a computer, Liu was able to create visual representations of the ancient dances based on these textual descriptions. Thanks to her tireless research, she finally succeeded in reviving the music and dances from the Tang Empire's most prosperous era.

In 1972 and 1974, she visited South Korea in order to research the Confucian dances that were introduced to Korea during the Song Dynasty, as well as the religious dances that Koreans created during the 15th century in imitation of China's Confucian dances. Thanks to this research, she was able to distinguish and define Confucian dances belonging to two

文化篇 Culture

categories: "cultural dances" and "military dances". Subsequently, Liu Fengxue spent much time immersing herself in, and seeking inspiration from, the culture of Taiwan's indigenous communities and rural villages.

In 1976, she founded the Neo-Classical Dance Troupe, which has since performed all throughout Taiwan, as well as performing upon invitation in the United States, Germany, France, Austria and Singapore. Their performances have garnered the unanimous praise of spectators, dance critics and academics.

刘凤学致力于中国现代舞的创作，朝着古乐舞的方向寻根。摄影：吴景腾

Liu Fengxue traces ancient songs and dances to their roots as part of her lifelong objective to create a uniquely Chinese modern dance.
Photography: Wu Jingteng

郑成功与台南府城

郑惠仁撰述 / 邱杰整理

台南是两岸历史浓得化不开的古城，三百多年前郑成功打着反清复明旗帜，登陆北汕尾鹿耳门，打败荷兰军队，随着这场中国历史上第一次打败西方强权的战役，也在这儿让文化开枝散叶。昔称"一府二鹿三艋舺"，台南是台湾的府城，更是文化的散播地，至今依然在各个层面中传承不辍。

早期许多福建先民就渡海来到台湾拓垦，明末清初两大海上强权西班牙、荷兰分别占据台湾北部与台湾南部。郑成功为反清复明，规划以台湾为基地，公元1661年4月25日统率四百多艘战舰、两万五千多名官兵，从金门料罗湾出发东进台湾。途中遭遇台风，避风澎湖，但因粮食不足，4月29日不得不下令冒着不适航的风浪，强攻台南。

当时荷兰军队驻守热兰遮城（今台南安平古堡），若要攻打热兰遮城，必须进入台南二仁溪出海口到八掌溪出海口间，长20公里、宽80公里的台江内海。当时台江内海有两大咽喉，南是大员港，北是鹿耳门港。若从北进入，因有暗礁，若非涨潮，连小船都不易进入，更别说是大型战舰。因此，荷兰驻军认定郑成功必将从大员港进入，把重兵摆在大员

文化篇 Culture

严阵以待。

郑成功看准这点，选择从"府城天险"鹿耳门港进入，除了认为因台风影响，出海口溪水暴涨，又值海水大潮，有机会登陆鹿耳门；且若能扼住鹿耳门港，就能阻止敌方求援之路，也可切断东印度公司南下的援军。另一个考虑更因在北汕尾岛的"热律菲堡"炮台已在1655年毁于台风仍未修复，郑成功认为取道鹿耳门进军不啻是"天助我也"好时机，而做此决定。

1661年4月30日上午，郑军先派小型舰艇驶抵鹿耳门港西南方的北汕尾岛，截断荷兰驻军向东印度求援路线。接着郑成功亲在北汕尾岛摆香案祝祷天地，祈求潮水高涨，助他顺利登陆。两个钟头后的午时，潮水大涨至水深5米以上，已可供大小战舰从鹿耳门港进入台江内海。

郑军先直攻目前是台南市北区的鸭母寮市场"禾寮港"，因港小无法容纳太多船只，大小战船分散停靠到台江内海其他小港，然后再集结，也和荷军展开数次大小战役，并在大员港击沉荷兰多艘战船，5月3日终于攻下行政商业中心普罗民遮城（赤崁楼）。

荷军仍认为郑成功缺少粮食，若坚守一定能突围。未料到郑成功采取"寓兵于农"

台南安平古堡即为当年荷兰军队侵占的热兰遮城。摄影：刘军喜

The fort held by the Dutch troops during their occupation of Taiwan. Photography: Liu Junxi

措施，就地屯垦、种田，半年后粮食已足，一举发动大围攻。1662年1月强攻，2月间荷兰总督揆一见大势已去，只能缴械投降。

物换星移，300多年后的今天"鹿耳门港"已非港，而成为鹿耳门溪出海口，不复昔日样貌；出海口竖立起"府城天险"石碑，旁边盖了一座镇门宫，供奉着郑成功的母亲。今日游客，有多少人知道这里曾是早期台江内海的首要军事、经贸大港。许多居民的祖先跟随郑成功来台首到此处，这里更是近代史中打败西方强权的重要战役处，也改写了台湾历史。

郑成功长得什么样呢？荷兰人菲利普·梅（Philippus Daniel Meij van Meijensteen）所写的一段文字，可能是全世界唯一亲见郑成功并且用文字书写下来的描述。菲利普是17世纪荷兰联合东印度公司派到台湾工作的土地测量师，在台湾居住长达19年。公元1661年5月4日，菲利普奉命带着求和信到中国军队大营见郑成功。他惶恐地跪在郑成功面前，近距离看着这位令人敬畏的中国将军，事后，他在日记里记录下了他对郑成功的印象："他身穿一件未漂白的麻纱长袍，头戴顶褐色尖角帽，式样像便帽，帽檐约有一个拇指宽，上头饰有一个小金片，在那小金片上挂着一根白色羽毛……年约四十岁，皮肤略白，面貌端正，眼睛又大又黑，那对眼睛很少有静止的时候，不断到处闪视。嘴巴常常张开，嘴里有四五颗很长，磨得圆圆、间隔大大的牙齿。胡子不多，长及胸部……说话的声音非常严厉，咆哮又激昂，说话时动作古怪，好像要用双手和双脚飞起来。"关于郑成功的身材，菲利普形容说他是中等身材，有一条腿较为笨重，右手拇指戴着一个大的骨制指环用以拉弓。

1993年，在担任鹿耳门天后宫文教公益基金会活动组长时，台南市鹿耳小区项目经理蔡登进配合台湾文艺季举办"发现鹿耳门"活动，举办文化营，广邀各地奉祀郑成功的庙宇之执事人员，会聚参加郑成功秋祭大典。还以胶筏改装成古战船，让居民、学生穿着盔甲、战袍，扮演士兵，拿着旌旗、军旗、三连旗、反清复明等旗帜，模仿郑成功登陆，一时海上战舰如云，仿若重回三百年前。

2011年蔡登进发起再办"重回北汕尾鹿耳门——模仿郑成功登陆活动"，希望借鹿耳门的沧桑变迁，以及郑成功的复台故事，串起历史故事、地理演变、史迹遗存、宗教信仰的延续各亮点，以趣味化、生活化的活动，召唤更多人关注与寻访郑成功登陆的足迹。

2011年首办时仅有居民、学生共63人参加，第二年增到150余人。第三年纳入台南市郑成功文化季活动，许多大学、高中、小区都加入，并且把登陆鹿耳门港的场

文化篇 Culture

"重回北汕尾鹿耳门——模仿郑成功登陆"活动,一群群众演员扮演国姓爷大军,分乘10艘战舰上溯鹿耳门溪。
During the reenactments of Zheng Chenggong arriving on the shore, a crowd of volunteers play the role of Chenggong's troops, riding makeshift war vessels in groups of 10.

"国姓爷大军"上岸后,浩浩荡荡涌向鹿耳门天后宫,以鞭炮代表炮声,锣鼓喧天、旌旗飞扬。
During the event, actors beat their drums and wave their flags as firecrackers imitate the sound of gunfire.

摄影:刘军喜

Photography: Liu Junxi

景延伸到攻打鹿耳门，还有艺阵大会串，人数随之倍增。2017年是郑成功登陆鹿耳门356年，共有500多人参加，主办单位特别再添购两艘战船，共有10艘参与登陆。蔡登进说，明式战船以胶筏改装，从悬吊上岸、装潢装饰、粉刷底漆、彩绘船身、下水、首航都按传统的民俗信仰完成。虽然没有枪林弹雨，但使用炮竹代替火炮、火枪，参与者手持旗帜，战鼓齐鸣中登陆鹿耳门，别具历史意义。而在大军围攻赤崁楼时，许多游客临时获知讯息，都自动为参与的学生、居民鼓掌致意，更让参与者振奋不已。

在最近一次活动中也吸引来德国人Jockenhofer、英国人辛蓓卡参加，他们穿着明式军装，坐着战船登陆，感受着从未有过的体验。

模仿郑成功登陆活动已成鹿耳小区每年最重要的大事，家家户户几乎都是总动员，连旅外乡亲也回来帮忙。学生帮忙彩绘战船，小区居民协助聘雇吊车、租借胶筏、整修及装潢战船、烹煮餐食、运输、茶水供应、医护等，成为小区的大团结，也是令人感动的活动！

从模仿郑成功登陆活动，通过居民与学者的介绍，也让学生及游客进一步了解到台南市许多特色小吃和郑成功有关。例如郑成功在澎湖躲避台风时，因粮食不足，征用岛上居民的食物为粮，但仍不足一餐，只好将番薯粉等淀粉类的东西加水干煎来果腹。后来加上蚵，就是现在的蚵仔煎。若将蚵裹起来炸，就是蚵嗲，目前这两道料理已成安平最知名的特色小吃之一，也是风靡全台各地的美食。

另如虱目鱼也称国姓鱼，相传郑成功来台后，有人献上虱目鱼，郑成功问是什么鱼，民众误以为国姓爷说的是这种鱼的名称就叫什么鱼（虱目鱼），此后便称此鱼为虱目鱼。台南沿海养殖最多的就是虱目鱼，产量居台湾之冠，虱目鱼丸、虱目鱼粥、虱目鱼干等相关料理都是这里最有名的特色小吃，也是观光客来台南必吃的佳肴。

如果时间抓得准，说不定在下一届的"模仿郑成功登陆活动"中，你将有机会身披战甲，和高举反清复明旗帜的战士同登战舰，在战鼓中鼓浪前行，然后抢滩上岸，当一位大战"红毛番"的大英雄！

Zheng Chenggong and the Prefecture of Tainan

Written by Zheng Huiren and adapted by Qiu Jie

Tainan was once the prefectural seat of Taiwan. It was in Tainan that the great admiral of the Ming Dynasty, Zheng Chenggong, defeated the Dutch army and restored Taiwan, over 300 years ago. After this battle, which constitutes China's first military victory over a Western power, Chinese culture spread from this city throughout the whole of Taiwan.

While, initially, many Fujian ancestors settled along the coast of Taiwan, it was occupied at the end of the Ming Dynasty and the beginning of the Qing Dynasty by the two great maritime powers of the time: Spain and the Netherlands, who respectively colonized the north and the south of Taiwan. Zheng Chenggong led a battalion of over 400 navy vessels carrying more than 25,000 soldiers from the east coast of the mainland towards the main island of Taiwan. On the way, they encountered a typhoon and took shelter in the Penghu Islands. As his troops were running out of reserves, Zheng Chenggong decided on 29 April that they had no choice but to brave the storm and take Tainan by force. They engaged in a number of battles with the Dutch army, sinking many of their opponent's ships. On 3 May, Zheng Chenggong's troops stormed the commercial and administrative center of Tainan. The Dutch soldiers believed that Zheng Chenggong's army would soon run out of rations, and that, if they persevered long enough, they could surely make a sortie. Little did they know, however, that Zheng Chenggong had ordered his troops to gradually open up wasteland and plant crops. After half a year, they were able to reap a significant harvest. In January 1662, Chenggong launched a large-scale offensive against the Dutch. By February, the Dutch troops had no choice but to surrender.

More than 300 years later, at the estuary of Lu'ermen Brook, one can find a stone inscription and a small palace that serve to remind people of its history as a strategic military point and trade port. The ancestors of many of Tainan's residents came to Tainan not long after Zheng Chenggong's conquest, arriving at this very port.

What did Zheng Chenggong look like? Philippus Daniel Meij van Meijenstee is perhaps the only person in the world to have described Chenggong's appearance in writing. On 4 May 1666, Philippus Daniel Meijvan Meijenstee visited the base of the Chinese army to deliver a letter requesting peace to Zheng Chenggong. Afterwards, he wrote some of his impressions of the admiral in his diary: "He was approximately 40 years of age, had regular features, and a somewhat pale complexion. He had an extremely strict speaking manner, and would bellow each phrase in an imposing, impassioned way. ... On his right thumb, he wore a ring made of bone designed for pulling the string on his bow."

Every year, the locals organize events where they recreate the arrival of Zheng Chenggong at the port. During these events, people redecorate traditional rafts into ancient war vessels. The decorations of the ship body, its placement in the water and its maiden voyage are all carried out according to popular beliefs and traditional customs. Residents and students put on helmets, carry flags and beat war drums, as well as setting off fire crackers to mimic the sound of gunfire. For a moment, the port is a flurry of excitement as an immense fleet of ships approaches the shore, just as it would have done, over 300 years ago. These reenactments have, over time, become the most momentous occasion of the year for locals, with families all throughout the vicinity actively taking part. Students help to paint the war boats in traditional colors, while adults help out with transportation and repairs, as well as providing food and first aid.

Many of Tainan's small delicacies are in some way related to Zheng Chenggong. For instance, when Zheng Chenggong and his troops began to run low on rations as they took shelter from the typhoon, the admiral learned from the local of Penghu Islands that one can make a filling snack by cooking dough made with sweet potato flour and water into flat cakes. Later, people would add eggs and oysters to the recipe in order to create a dish known in Minnan dialect as *ô-á-chian*, or oyster omelette. Alternatively, the oysters may be wrapped up in the omelette and deep-fried: a dish known as ô-te. These two dishes have since become delicacies that sell like hotcakes throughout the entire island.

文化篇 Culture

竹筏改装成古战船，模拟郑成功舰队登台攻打荷兰侵占军。
Traditional bamboo rafts are converted into ancient war vessels.

"洋将"插花！来自英国、德国及蒙古等国家的朋友粉墨登场，扮演郑成功部队的将军、士兵。
Tourists from countries such as England, Germany and Mongolia also join "Zheng Chenggong's battalion".

摄影：刘军喜
Photography: Liu Junxi

台北故宫博物院

一眼览尽八千年

走进一个建筑物，可以一眼看尽 8000 年！这是一个魔术空间吗？这里是台北故宫博物院。

台北故宫博物院可以说是中华文化精品最重要的收藏、展示中心，馆藏中华文物之丰富难有可与之匹敌之所在。这座台湾地区规模最大，也号称世界顶尖博物馆之一的博物馆，坐落于台北市士林区外双溪，占地总面积约 16 公顷，依山傍水，气势宏伟；外观碧瓦黄墙，充满了中国传统的宫殿色彩；1965 年落成，1966 年启用，藏有近 70 万件 / 册文物。

馆藏主要源自原北平故宫博物院、中央博物院筹备处和北平图书馆等机构所藏来自紫禁城、盛京行宫、清帝避暑山庄、颐和园、静宜园和国子监等处皇家旧藏的精华，内容对象年代始于 10 世纪中期当朝统治者的珍藏，时间跨度则涵盖新石器时代至今长达 8000 年。

博物院的主体建筑分为四层，正院呈梅花形，在第三层后面建有一座 26 米长的隧道，直通凿在山腹里头的山洞库房，山洞离地面 50 米高，内有拱形洞库三座，每座长 180 米，高、宽均为 3.6 米，再分隔成许多小库房，分类收藏各种文物。

文化篇 Culture

海峡两岸故宫博物院文物首次合璧展出"雍正——清世宗文物大展",北京故宫博物院郑欣淼院长(右)与台北故宫博物院周功鑫院长(左)互赠礼物。

At the first joint exhibition of the Palace Museums of Beijing and Taipei, the "Grand Exhibition of Emperor Yongzheng's Artefacts", the museums' respective directors, Zheng Xinmiao (right) and Zhou Gongxin (left), exchange gifts.

游客聚精会神观赏"翠玉白菜"。

Tourists at the Palace Museum of Taipei intently admire the "Jadeite Cabbage".

摄影:吴景腾
Photography: Wu Jingteng

抗日战争中，文物南迁汉口、重庆以躲避战火。1948年，蒋介石领导的国民党军一路节节败逃，在眼见人民解放军即将获得全面胜利之下紧急将这批贵重文物以军舰转运台湾。1950年4月先行暂藏于台中郊外雾峰乡吉峰村仓库。1957年在库房之外新建一座小型陈列室，将少量文物轮批公开展览供民众参观。1965年才在外双溪现址建成新馆。新馆为纪念孙中山先生百岁诞辰而命名为中山博物院，后来才正名台北故宫博物院。

台北的历史博物馆和郑州的河南博物院都记载着这样一段历史：1937年"七七事变"爆发，日本侵略者长驱直入，为避免苦心收藏的文物受损，河南博物院精心挑选文物珍品5678件，拓片1162张，图书1472套（册），分装68箱运往汉口，1938年又运至重庆。

1948年底，国民政府令故宫博物院挑选贵重文物以军舰转运台湾。从1948年12月21日到次年2月22日的64天里，南京下关到基隆港这条水道上，总共有6个机构的5522箱顶级国宝被运到了台湾。

海峡两岸开放以来，各省市民众与学术单位、学者专家、艺术家纷纷走进这座台北市郊的中华文物殿堂，沐浴在中华文物的氛围中，感受着炎黄子孙的共同骄傲，故宫博物院也成了必访景点名单之首。而由于博物馆本身也兼负教育责任，多年来也相继举办了轰动世界的多个重大活动。例如《富春山居图》的合体便称得上惊人之举。

黄公望的传世国宝数十年来分居两岸，2011年6月，由海峡两岸携手合办的合璧特展中，还出现运用新媒体的"山水觉——神会黄公望、山水新演绎"，将浙江省博物馆的重要收藏《剩山图》（横51.4米，占原画十四分之一）运来台北，与台北故宫博物院珍藏的《富春山居图·无用师卷》（横636.9米，占原画十四分之十二）完成世纪性的合璧，写下中华文物传奇美谈之新页。

随后相继推出国人耳熟能详的《清明上河图》之原图动画设计，运用3D技术和摄影效果，让观众得以在数字视觉效果中神游画境，与古人遥望互动、鱼鸟徜徉，或呼应山水、风起絮飞，用动画形式呈现出画作的历史与传奇故事，让游客有如身历其境。

近年来台北故宫博物院另行筹建南院，目的在带动台湾中南部地区的文化、教育、社会、经济发展，自2004年12月15日核定动工，2015年12月28日开馆。新馆设在嘉义县太保市，主体建筑内部共分四层及一阁楼层，展厅面积约8800平方米，其中有五座常设展厅、一座多媒体展厅、一座专题展厅、一座借展厅，还有一座儿童

文化篇 Culture

浙江省博物馆收藏的《剩山图》和台北故宫博物院的《富春山居图·无用师卷》首度合体在台北展出。
摄影：吴景腾
The two sections of Huang Gongwang's iconic work *Dwelling in the Fuchun Mountains* — one of which, *The Remaining Mountain*, is kept at the Zhejiang Provincial Museum, while the other, *Master Wuyong's Scroll*, is kept at the Palace Museum of Taipei — were reunited for the first time and displayed in Taipei in 2011. Photography: Wu Jingteng

创意中心。常设展包括"奔流不息——嘉义发展史""佛陀形影——院藏亚洲佛教艺术之美""芳茗远播——亚洲茶文化展""锦绣缤纷——院藏亚洲织品展""认识亚洲——新媒体艺术展"五大主题。院方还和台南吉美博物馆、东京国立博物馆、九州岛国立博物馆及大阪市立东洋陶瓷美术馆等馆签约，陆续举办特展，也达到了预期设馆目标。

Palace Museum of Taipei

There is a building in Taiwan where one can witness over 8,000 years of history within the span of one visit. This building is none other than the Palace Museum of Taipei. It is the largest museum in Taiwan and boasts what could be considered the world's most important collection of Chinese cultural artefacts.

The Palace Museum of Taipei is a majestic structure that occupies a plot of approximately 16 ha offering views of adjacent mountains and creeks. With its turquoise roof tiles and yellow walls, it has the typical style of a traditional Chinese palace. The main building has four stories. Before it lies an immense courtyard arranged into five points, much like the "5" on a dice. The museum was completed in 1965 and opened to the public in 1966. It has close to 700,000 artefacts and artworks in its collection. These artefacts are all heirlooms of the Qing imperial court. The oldest item of this collection dates from 8,000 years ago, during the Neolithic era.

Over many years, the museum has also hosted a number of major events. The painting *Dwelling in the Fuchun Mountains* by the Yuan Dynasty artist Huang Gongwang is a national treasure that has been passed down from one dynasty to the next. Currently, the Zhejiang Provincial Museum has one piece, accounting for 1/14 of the entire original painting, while the Palace Museum of Taipei has the larger piece, accounting for 12/14. In June 2011, the Zhejiang Provincial Museum and the Palace Museum of Taipei organized an exhibition where the two segments were reunited — a momentous occasion in the history of Chinese culture!

The Palace Museum of Taipei has also produced a 3D animated version of the work *Along the River during the Qingming Festival*, which allows visitors to plunge headfirst into this famous artwork from the Northern Song Dynasty, come face to face with their ancestors, and immerse themselves in the sights and sounds of that era.

民众参观定窑"婴儿枕"。
Members of the public appreciate the Northern Song "Ding-ware" sculpture entitled *Reclining Infant*.

游客观赏"清19世纪广东镂雕象牙云龙纹套球",直径约12厘米,表面以高浮雕刻成九龙穿梭于祥云间,内部雕刻各种镂空精致的锦地几何纹样,共24层,每层皆可灵活转动。层层相套,玲珑剔透且制作繁复的象牙球,可说是清代晚期牙雕工艺之代表。

Tourists marvel at the *Ivory Ball*, an ingenious work from the 19th century (late Qing Dynasty) with a diameter of approximately 12 cm, composed of multiple concentric spheres. The outer layer has a profoundly three-dimensional relief of nine dragons weaving through the clouds, while on the inside, there are 24 concentric spheres featuring intricate geometric engravings. Each of these spheres can move independently of the others. With its painstaking craftsmanship and ingenious, multi-layered design, the ivory ball is perhaps the most iconic ivory sculpture of the late Qing Dynasty.

摄影:吴景腾
Photography: Wu Jingteng

祭孔大典

9月28日是至圣先师孔子诞辰日,这个日子在台湾还被定为教师节,而早期台湾各级学校大多立有孔子铜像供学子早晚瞻仰,孔诞日当天,设有孔庙的地方都要由地方首长率领各主管及地方硕彦隆重举办祭孔典礼。笔者曾多次应邀参与祭孔,担任分献官,引为荣耀。而台湾祭孔要员中以孔子第七十九代嫡孙孔垂长在祭孔大典亲任奉祀官最受瞩目,至圣先生之后人亲自参加祭孔,实属难得之佳话。

台湾孔庙最重要的是台南市和台北市这两地所设者,规模宏大,且具历史典故。台南孔庙是全台湾建成的第一座孔庙,大成殿上方悬有清康熙"万世师表"、雍正"生民未有"、乾隆"与天地参"、同治"圣神天纵"、光绪"斯文在兹"匾额。在其他各孔庙中,坐落于虎头山麓的桃园孔庙建造最晚,环境优雅,也是学子们考季参拜的热门地点。桃园本无孔庙,在一座市区公园内建有文昌庙,祀奉文昌君,孔子神位和塑像栖身文昌庙中,地方逢孔子诞辰日便在庙内中庭举办祭典,直到80年代才另建孔庙,祭典也移到新孔庙举办。但因孔庙依例不设孔子像而只立牌位,移来的孔子塑像便供奉在内部侧殿。

传统孔庙不但不立塑像,另外有别于一般寺庙的是整座孔庙里里外外无一副对联,传说中人们知晓孔夫子学问大,因此无人胆敢在他的庙里写对联了。此说带着几分幽默,究竟是真是假无从查考,孔庙没有对

文化篇 Culture

台南孔庙大成殿上方悬有清代康熙"万世师表"、雍正"生民未有"、乾隆"与天地参"、同治"圣神天纵"、光绪"斯文在兹"牌匾。
At the Confucius Temple of Tainan, one can find honorary plaques from five Qing Dynasty emperors: Kangxi, Yongzheng, Qianlong, Tongzhi and Guangxu.

孔子第七十九代嫡孙孔垂长在祭孔大典亲任奉祀官。
Confucius' 79th generation descendant, Kong Chuichang, acts as a ceremonial official during a large-scale Confucian ceremony.

摄影：吴景腾
Photography: Wu Jingteng

联倒是事实。

　　祭祀大成至圣先师孔子的典礼，称为"释奠礼"。释、奠都有陈设、呈献的意思，指的是在祭典中，陈设音乐、舞蹈，并且呈献牲、酒等祭品，对孔子表示崇敬之意。而这个典礼古来传承已久，《礼记·文王世子》记载，周朝时学校便要按四季释奠先师，表示尊师重道之意。不过当时所谓的先师，并不是指特定的某一个人或某些人；凡是过去对教育有贡献的，已过世的都是祭祀的对象。后来释奠的对象才逐渐改为孔子为主。隋朝时孔子被尊称为"先师"，释奠才成为祭孔典礼的专属名称。

　　孔子生于周灵王二十一年（公元前551年），卒于公元前479年，享年73岁。死后来年鲁哀公下令在曲阜阙里孔子的旧宅立庙，将孔子生前使用的衣、冠、车、琴、书册等保存起来，并且按岁时祭祀。这是诸侯祭孔的开始。至汉高祖十二年，汉高祖以太牢祭祀孔子，成为帝王祭孔之始。台湾的祭孔典礼于1970年综合古礼制定释奠礼仪节，年年依礼举办至今。

根 图说台湾民俗文化
Roots: Customs and Traditions in Taiwan

"祭孔释奠礼"依古礼在庄严肃穆的典礼中进行,除了向"至圣先师"孔子致敬,也通过仪式重新展现儒学的精神。
摄影:吴景腾

The veneration of Confucius takes place in the form of ancient rituals and solemn ceremonies. In addition to expressing the people's reverence for Confucius, these rituals also seek to revive the scholarly spirit of his disciples. Photography: Wu Jingteng

Confucian Ceremonies

Rather than celebrating Teacher's Day on October 5, as is the case elsewhere, Taiwan celebrates its teachers on 28 September, which is believed to be Confucius' birthday. A number of bronze statues of Confucius were erected at many of Taiwan's primary and secondary schools, as well as universities, to serve as inspiration to students. On Confucius' birthday, local governments invite locally renowned figures to partake in grandiose ceremonies in his honor. To my great honor, I have, on multiple occasions, been invited to take part in these commemorative events as a ceremonial official. In Taiwan, we are also lucky enough to sometimes receive the 79th generation descendant of Confucius, Kong Chuichang, at these ceremonies.

The Confucius Temple in Tainan is the first temple to be built in Confucius' honor in Taiwan. Inside, one can find honorific plaques from five different Qing Dynasty emperors: Kangxi, Yongzheng, Qianlong, Tongzhi, and Guangxu.

The Confucius Temple at Taoyuan is the most recently constructed Confucius temple in Taiwan, and a popular place for students to come and pray for good results in the lead-up to major exams. Unlike other temples, the Confucius Temple in Taoyuan is not decorated with matching couplets. This is supposedly in recognition of Confucius' learnedness and wisdom — who would dare to presume that their couplet, however witty, was worthy of his name?

台北市大龙小学的佾舞教练以师徒传受的方式传承八佾舞。佾生所穿的服装是明代的书生服。摄影：吴景腾
A trainer teaches the steps of the ceremonial dances. Dancers wear the traditional garb of Ming Dynasty scholars. Photography: Wu Jingteng

During these ceremonies, people express their reverence for Confucius by performing songs and dances in his honor, as well as humbly presenting offerings such as meat and wine. This tradition has been imparted over thousands of years — according to the *King Wen's Descendants* chapter in the *Book of Rites*, schools during the Zhou Dynasty would hold ceremonies in honor of Confucius at different times throughout the year as a means of instilling students with respect for their teachers, as well as a sense of moral integrity. At the time, the ceremonies didn't serve to honor any teacher in particular — rather, they commemorated anyone deceased who had made a contribution to education in their lifetime. It was only later on that ceremonies began to focus exclusively on Confucius.

Confucius was born in 551 BC, in the State of Lu during the Zhou Dynasty, and died in 479 BC. The year after he died, the Duke of Lu ordered that a temple be erected in

Confucius' honor at his former residence in his hometown, Qufu, and that his things — such as his clothes, cap, carriage, zither and books — be conserved there. The Duke also stipulated that, from that year onward, ceremonies be held annually in his honor. This marked the beginning of the collective reverence of Confucius. Later, during the Han Dynasty, Emperor Gaozu became the first emperor to host a Confucian ceremony within the imperial court. In 1970, Taiwan defined an official protocol for Confucian ceremonies, based on the way these ceremonies were held in ancient times. Since then, Confucius temples in Taiwan have adhered to this protocol year after year.

台南孔庙是台湾第一座孔庙，建于明永历年间。清初也是全台童生唯一入学之所，因此称"全台首学"。康熙年间在大门外立一块下马碑，以满汉文并刻"文武官员军民人等至此下马"，威仪十足。摄影：吴景腾

The Confucius Temple in Tainan is the first temple to be built in Confucius' honor in Taiwan. It was built during the Ming Dynasty. At the beginning of the Qing Dynasty, it was also the only school in Taiwan to accept young children. During the reign of Emperor Kangxi of Qing, a hitching post was erected out of the main entrance, on which one can read in both Manchurian and Chinese: "Cultural and military officials, soldiers and civilians may tie up their horses here."
Photography: Wu Jingteng

中式建筑

台湾有很多地方建过城,只要有城,几乎都有北门口这样的地名。许许多多的北门中,最精彩的莫过于台北城的北门,无论格局、造型、坐落地点乃至历史价值,全岛无出其右者。

台北市北门正式名称为承恩门,坐落在现今台北市忠孝西路、延平南路与博爱路交叉口,落成于清光绪十年(1884年),为当时台北府城五大城门中唯一保持建城原貌的一座。承恩门也是台北市区目前所剩无几的清代建筑之一,称得上是台北市重要地标。

北门建筑重视防御功能,设计风格独特。20世纪60年代为了拓宽马路曾濒临拆除,在学者极力争取下才幸免于难。2016年除夕当天,台北市政府将城门旁一座高架桥拆了,老城门终于重现风华。

台北的中正纪念堂园区内,有两座知名度与地位都很高的建筑物,颇有故宫的样式,这便是"两厅院"中的音乐厅和戏剧院。

戏剧院造型采中国传统明清殿堂式建筑,屋顶是尊位最高的庑殿顶,近似故宫的太和殿;音乐厅屋顶设计为歇山顶,类似故宫的保和殿。

两厅院皆为20世纪80年代的同期作品,音乐厅设2064个观众席,其中安装的管风琴由享有盛名的Flentrop管风琴公司制作,长14米,高9米,深3米,共有4172根管子,号称亚洲最大。

戏剧院接待大厅的水晶灯高达四楼,展示着傲人的气势。观众席分

文化篇 Culture

台北市北门是目前所剩无几的清代建筑之一，也是台北市重要地标。
The North Gate is one of Taipei's few remaining structures from the Qing Dynasty, as well as one of its most important landmarks.

台北戏剧院造型采中国传统明清殿堂式建筑，屋顶为尊位最高的庑殿顶，类似北京故宫的太和殿。
The Theatre of Taipei adopts the same architectural style as the palaces and halls of the Qing and Ming Dynasties. It has a hip roof similar to that of the Hall of Supreme Harmony at the Forbidden City in Beijing — a style of roof reserved for only the most prestigious buildings.

摄影：吴景腾
Photography: Wu Jingteng

四层，共1498席。演出节目包罗万象，连台湾歌仔戏也多次登场献演。

另一座重要的地标建筑是台北圆山大饭店。

圆山大饭店主建筑楼高其实仅十四层，却因造型颇具特色，又坐落在一座小山丘上，旁边少有高大建筑，因而显得倍加壮观醒目。除了歇山式飞檐屋顶及雕梁画栋的传统宫殿风格，建筑上还采用相当多的龙形雕刻，以浮雕、圆雕等手法安排在天花板、地板、栏杆等不同位置，故有人称此饭店为"龙宫"；除了龙，还有石狮、梅花等中国建筑常用的图案。而在主建筑的八个客房楼层里，也分别以商周、秦汉、魏晋南北朝、唐、宋、明、清等不同朝代为主题，打造出不同年代的风格。客房内的红木家具与床单、沙发布、窗帘皆依据历史考证，以现代纺织技术重现。

谈及圆山大饭店不能遗漏一个更见特色的题材，那便是神秘的圆山秘道。

由于这座饭店常用以接待重要宾客，也是当年蒋介石经常到访之处，饭店内部设有秘密通道，让蒋介石在紧急时可以从秘道遁走。密道有两条，入口都位于地下二楼，其中一条朝东走，全长78米，沿途设有45盏照明灯，可通到北安公园。另一条反方向朝西走，可以抵达80米外的圆山联谊会剑潭公园。出口设在公园的用意是公园有宽阔草坪，紧急时可以停驻直升机。但因出口设有巨石屏档，外人不易见到。两条密道高度都是2.3米，宽2.1米，可容纳二至三人同时并行。密道内部蜿蜒曲折，一路向下盘旋，而最特殊的是西侧的密道旁还设计了一座约一人宽、以磨石子为底，类似滑梯的滑行道。据说这个设计也是专为蒋先生紧急逃生时使用，让他可以不必在慌乱中跌跌撞撞奔走，只要学小朋友玩滑梯便可安全又迅速滑行而去。

文化篇 Culture

圆山大饭店建筑大量采用龙的图案，因而常有人称此饭店为"龙宫"。摄影：吴景腾
The Grand Hotel of Taipei is often referred to as the Dragon Palace due to the liberal use of dragon motifs in the hotel's interior design. Photography: Wu Jingteng

Chinese Architecture

The North City Gate of Taipei's official name is "Cheng'en Gate". The gate, which was completed in 1884 (the 10th year of Emperor Guangxu's reign), is one of the few structures of the Qing Dynasty to remain standing in Taipei and can be considered one of the city's most important landmarks. In the 1960s, the gate was almost demolished in order to widen an adjacent road, but was saved from this unjust fate thanks to the efforts of scholars. On the eve of the Lunar New Year, in 2016, the Taipei Municipal Government demolished a high bridge next to the city gate, thus allowing the gate to return to its former glory.

Within the grounds of Taipei's Chiang Kai-shek Memorial Hall, there are two renowned and prestigious buildings: the Theatre and the Concert Hall. These structures were both built in the 1980s. The architectural design of the theatre is inspired by palaces and other similarly important structures from the Qing and Ming dynasties. It has a hipped roof similar to that of the Hall of Supreme Harmony. In the theatre's expansive lobby, there is a crystal lamp that reaches four stories high. The seating is also spread over four stories and can accommodate a total of 1,498 spectators. Meanwhile, the Concert Hall has an East Asian hip-and-gable roof similar to that of the Hall of Preserving Harmony and has a total of 2,064 seats. Its organ was built by the renowned organ manufacturer Flentrop and is said to be the largest in Asia.

Another important work of traditional architecture is the Grand Hotel of Taipei. In addition to having the typical style of a traditional Chinese palace — with its hip-and-gable roof, upturned eaves, engraved beams, and painted rafters — the hotel also features a number of dragon sculptures and reliefs on ceilings, floors and banisters. It is for this reason that the hotel is sometimes referred to as the "Dragon Palace". However, besides dragons, the hotel is also decorated with other traditional imagery, such as stone lions and plum blossoms. Each of the eight guest floors of the hotel reflects, in its decor and motifs, a certain era; as one ascends the building, one is propelled through China's history. The themes of the floors are, in order: the Shang and Zhou dynasties; the Qin and Han dynasties; "the Period of Division" (from the foundation of the Wei Kingdom to the end of the Northern and Southern Dynasties); the Tang Dynasty; the Song Dynasty; the Ming Dynasty; and the Qing Dynasty.

No description of the hotel would be complete without mentioning its two secret passageways, located two floors underground. One of these passageways leads east and has a total length of 78 m, while the other leads west and is 80 m long. Both of the passageways open out onto parks on either side of the hotel.

台北音乐厅屋顶设计为歇山顶，类似北京故宫的保和殿。摄影：吴景腾
The Concert Hall of Taipei has a quintessentially East Asian hip-and-gable roof, similar to that of the Hall of Preserving Harmony at the Forbidden City in Beijing. Photography: Wu Jingteng

张廖家庙

早期台中地方原为一片大荒野。清收复台湾之后，闽粤移民大举入垦，在中部地区争相以"割地换水"方式与当地少数民族订立垦约，大举开拓，未几荒野快速变成了聚居地。

台中盆地北端之大甲溪冲积扇延伸地带，为第四纪冲积层，由于引进水源较为便利，成为早期移民垦殖之重要据点。当时有廖朝孔，初居云林县二仑，1734年间接受台中岸里五社总通张达京的邀请，与秦登舰、姚德心、江又金、陈周文等垦首，合组"六馆业户"，以割地换水方式共同开发台湾中部平原，并集资开垦葫芦墩圳。当时以廖朝孔为垦首的持有地分布在永兴庄一带（即今西屯港尾里），廖朝孔遂成为开发西屯区的重要人物，其子孙繁衍也多分布在这一地区。廖朝孔后来还获张达京等人聘请协助开辟水圳，在完工之后，田园益见茂美，子孙繁衍也越来越多。

廖朝孔乃"张廖家族"重要一员。张廖家族源自明初的张元子，原属于同宗，堂号清武，是从张氏的郡号清河与廖氏的郡号武威，各取堂号前一字构成。此张廖家庙即是张公廖妈之后代子孙所建，俗称张廖公厅。光绪十三年（公元1887年）开始兴建，1911年落成，并继续增建左、右护龙（即围屋），1916年完成所有建筑。

在建筑格局上，张廖家庙整座庙堂坐西朝东，是一座两进两廊四护

文化篇 Culture

张廖家庙是由三川殿、左右护龙及两座山门相互连接，形成一个格局完整的传统式建筑。摄影：翁清雅
The Zhang-Liao Family Shrine is composed of a main hall, known as Sanchuandian ("Three Rivers Hall"); the left and right wings; and two main entrances. All these structures are interconnected according to the layout of a traditional courtyard house. Photography: Weng Qingya

龙的四合院祠宇建筑。前有宽广的前埕及半月形的门口塘，建筑格局与中部地区的传统民居近似，但建筑本体以中轴线分左右，做法各有不同却也成为一大特色。

三开间的前厅与正厅，均用柱廊形式，柱廊内，左右次间为红砖斗仔砌墙体，前厅红砖墙上开八卦三棂竹节窗，窗外框以砖雕构成，两边图案及雕法各有明显差异。正厅红砖墙上开直棂木窗，形式较前厅简单。厅堂室内大木结构多用硬山桷檩，只有两厅的前檐廊及左右墙廊有雕刻及彩绘的抬梁结构。屋顶全为硬山形式，两厅及内外护龙的院门屋顶都有弯曲起翘的燕尾脊。

整体建筑由正殿、三川殿、过水廊、左右护龙及两个山门连接，形成一个格局壮阔的长形立面。从空中鸟瞰可发现三川殿透过两条过水廊连上拜殿、正殿，形成一个宽敞的封闭空间，这个空间于祭祀仪典时可以充分显现其不受外界尘嚣干扰的神圣性。精致的木结构以及彩绘、屋梁上用以镇邪和稳定大梁的造型奇特的狮座，以及蓝漆圆窗配以灰色条纹的万字图案，充分表现出协调而朴拙的建筑艺术风格。

这座家庙的格局与传统客家建筑特色颇为相似，主体建筑以传统三堂二过水加一围屋之客家常见环形土楼特性来营建。其斗栱形式之多样尤为少见，斗栱有方形、八角、碗形、菱形、花瓶形等，非常的精彩多变，称得上是民族建筑风格技法传承之经典作品。

传统家庙有俗称"红庙、黑祖厝"的特色，张廖家庙将此特色展露无余，从正殿、过水及围屋外墙粉饰成黑色便可窥见。

1985年张廖家庙获指定为三级古迹，目前仍保持传统家庙的功能，而张廖家族仍然以此作为家族的精神象征与宗族的聚会场所，所以也可以称得上是一座活古迹。

砖瓦及大木构，组成张廖家庙这座祠堂建筑的设计精髓。摄影：翁清雅

The architectural design of the Zhang-Liao Family Shrine is essentially composed of bricks, tiles and wooden structures. Photography: Weng Qingya

文化篇 Culture

Zhang-Liao Family Shrine

For most of Taiwan's history, the region of Taichung in central Taiwan was a vast plain of wilderness. During the Qing Dynasty, a large number of migrants from the provinces of Fujian and Guangdong arrived and rapidly constructed settlements throughout the island. In 1734, a settler named Liao Chaokong formed an alliance with six other men and settled in the central plain of Taiwan. Many of his descendants are spread throughout this region.

Liao Chaokong himself was a notable descendant of the Zhang-Liao clan. The Zhang-Liao Family Shrine's construction began in 1887 (the 13th year of Emperor Guangxu of Qing's reign). It was inaugurated in 1911 and totally completed in 1916.

In terms of its architectural outlay, the Zhang-Liao Family Shrine is an east-facing *siheyuan* ("four-walled courtyard house") with two main entrances and two decorative corridors that link the main hall with its adjoining wings. The structure can be split down the middle into two symmetrical sides. The outlay of this family shrine bears a certain resemblance to that of traditional Hakka structures, and is a classic example of the way that Hakka architectural styles and techniques were preserved and passed down in Taiwan.

In 1985, the local government designated the Zhang-Liao Family Shrine a third-level historic site. To this day, the structure still serves its traditional functions as a family shrine, acting as a symbol of the Zhang-Liao Clan's spirit as well as a venue for clan descendant reunions. In this sense, the family shrine can be considered a living piece of history.

左右厢房的拱形小门、圆形小窗，及水形马背"栋头"，简洁中带着藏不住的华丽风采。
摄影：翁清雅
The exquisitely designed side-wings feature small arched doorways, circular windows and "water-shaped horseback ridges" (a defining quality of Hakka architecture). Photography: Weng Qingya

文化篇 Culture

柴烧制陶

马玉洁撰述 / 邱杰改写

柴烧是指利用薪柴为燃料烧成的陶瓷制品。传统的柴窑烧陶曾因费时费力被视为落伍的技法，但柴火直接作用于坯体上留下的火痕和木柴燃烧后产生的自然落灰，让作品产生出变幻无穷、耐人寻味的阴阳变化，与现在流行的电窑模式化的单一美感完全不同，让许多追求返朴归真的现代人着迷不已。

台湾在荷兰殖民统治时期便出现了宋磁，但直到清朝末期，才开始自己建窑烧器，并渐渐发展出包括莺歌陶、公馆陶、苗栗陶、沙鹿陶、大甲东陶、集集陶、南投陶、八卦山陶、凤山陶等独具地方特色的技艺。

二战后，台湾的陶瓷曾因塑料制品的兴盛而没落，但随着经济起飞，人们开始回头寻找更为精致的生活方式，尤其对古老的柴烧更是着迷，陶瓷之风因而再次兴起。

众多钻研柴烧的艺术家中，54岁的陈金旺是其中之一。2010年他举家迁往台中大肚山，开始研究大肚山红土。红土往昔常被用来烧制红砖块，却在70年代因窑业式微而无人问津。陈金旺发现大肚山红土富含铁等金属元素，特性与福建南平的水吉红土尤为相似，水吉红土以含铁量高而闻名。用水吉红土为胎底，以同样高铁质的釉料为着色剂，经高

陶艺家陈金旺利用台湾大肚山红土烧制陶器。
摄影：吴景腾
The ceramic artist Chen Jinwang produces pottery using red earth from Taiwan's Dadu Plateau.
Photography: Wu Jingteng

温烧制的茶碗釉色黝黑，俗称建盏。建盏是宋朝皇室的御用茶具，宋代八大名瓷之一，以油滴、兔毫、鹧鸪斑等不同的釉面风格为人所知。

"水吉红土的含铁量为8%至9%，而我们大肚山的红土含铁量也高达6%，用它烧制的茶器甚至可以吸住磁铁。"陈金旺说，这正是他从此定居大肚山，在大肚山建窑的原因。经过无数次尝试，陈金旺成为台湾目前唯一一位不混土、用大肚山全红土烧制茶器的陶艺家。陈金旺用大肚山红土柴烧的茶器带着粗粝而质朴的特质，使用纯矿物釉烧出来的釉彩效果丰富多变，尤其是他在过去建盏油滴效果的基础上，烧出仿佛蓝色星空那么璀璨的釉质壶身，被冠以"蓝星天目"之美称，更受到藏家的欢迎。

在桃园的新屋，来自平镇的年轻艺术家范纲荣老师本着对柴烧的热爱，在大坡初级中学校园内建起柴烧基地"大坡窑"，除了学生长期前来学柴烧，连当地小区父老也竞相投入学习之行列，教室里常是男女老少济济一堂。每当柴烧日期一到，民众参与排班，24 小时不间断值班 3 到 7 天，日夜驻守窑前投柴，盯紧温度计的变化，甚至还在窑边搭帐篷轮流守夜。开窑时刻，更是人人兴奋。他们捏塑出来的麒麟、达摩、貔貅和各种花器用品，呈现出来的古朴苍劲风韵，在展出中令人惊艳。

1959 年出生于台北市，曾担任过传教士及监狱教诲师的何志隆，2009 年间前往台东山区泰原幽谷自行盖窑，名之为"志窑"，钻研柴烧技艺，自行烧窑筑梦。他历经千辛万苦，几乎散尽家财，作品终于被认定为是失传 1500 年的灰釉青瓷，其中夹带古老青瓷血脉，经命名"翡翠青瓷"而名扬两岸。

何志隆专以海岸漂流木为燃料，动辄囤柴数百吨以确保熊熊大火之质量与落灰之美，最近一连失败 6 次，终在第 7 次开窑时获得成功。作品件件都是精品，被台北知名的典藏杂志社社长简秀枝小姐誉为国宝。多位北京知名学者和艺术家亲往参与开窑大典，作品也随即获安排于 2017 年夏在北京盛大展出。

陶瓷与茶叶一样，自古以来就带有浓郁的东方色彩。陶器制作在中国已有超过一万年的历史。中国各个朝代在陶瓷工艺上都有精雕细刻、推陈出新的表现。而除了传自大陆的深厚底蕴，更出现许多像陈金旺、范纲荣这样的新锐陶瓷艺术家，在岛上各个角落大放异彩。

陈金旺以大肚山红土烧出"蓝雨夜天目"及"柿红天目"。摄影：吴景腾
Chen Jinwang is able to produce spectacular glazes thanks to the Dadu Plateau's red earth. These particular works are entitled *Celestial Eyes on a Rainy Night* and *Persimmon-Red Celestial Eyes*. Photography: Wu Jingteng

Wood-Fired Pottery

Written by Ma Yujie and adapted by Qiu Jie

Wood-fired pottery refers to pottery hardened in a wood-fired kiln. The scorch marks and ashes left on the surface of the clay by the open flames lends wood-fired pottery an infinite variety of textures, making pottery produced in an electric kiln seem sterile and dull by comparison.

At the end of the Qing Dynasty, Taiwan began to construct kilns for producing pottery, and gradually developed a technical process with local characteristics. After the Second World War, Taiwan-made pottery fell out of vogue due to the sudden popularity of plastic products. However, as the economy took off, the people of Taiwan looked to their past in search of a more refined lifestyle. This caused a resurgence in the popularity of ceramic ware. In particular, consumers fell under the spell of the ancient craft of wood-fired pottery.

Chen Jinwang is one of many artists to have delved into wood-fired pottery. He discovered that the red clay on the Dadu Plateau of Taichung is rich in iron and other metallic elements. He and his family moved to the Dadu Plateau, and, after much trial and error, he became the first person in Taiwan to produce porcelain ware using red earth sourced exclusively from the plateau. Pottery produced using pure red earth acquires a particularly rich and varied glaze. One type of work produced by Chen Jinwang has a glaze that resembles stars in the deep-blue night sky. For this reason, it has been conferred the poetic title of *Lanxing Tianmu* (*Blue Stars, Celestial Eyes*) and is coveted by collectors.

Fan Gangrong, a young artist from Taoyuan, built a pottery workshop called the Dapo Kiln and recruited local students and elders to take part in the production process. Every time the kilns are ready to be fired up, a number of Taoyuan locals volunteer in shifts for 24 hours a day over the course of three to seven days. They take turns stoking the flames, closely monitoring the changes in the kiln temperature, and even setting up camp at nighttime to guard the kilns. The opening of the kilns causes an even greater stir in the community as locals inspect the fruits of their labor. The different types of ceramic goods are primitive, yet sturdy.

He Zhilong, a former missionary and prison chaplain, built a kiln in the mountain ranges of Taitung County (along the eastern shore of Taiwan) in 2009. He stokes the kiln using debris found along the shore, which, in addition to helping maintain the right flame temperature, also produces an aesthetically pleasing coat of ash on the pottery's surface. Having overcome a seemingly endless succession of trials and tribulations which nearly left him and his family destitute, He Zhilong finally earned the recognition he deserved. Experts consider his works to be an authentic revival of "ash-glazed green ceramics", a craft that had been lost for 1,500 years. These works are now referred to "Jadeite Ceramics" due to their deep green hue.

柴烧形成的天然美色是陶艺家毕生追逐的梦。
Potters spend their entire lives pursuing the kind of natural beauty that results from firing ceramic objects in a wood-stoked kiln.

陈金旺制壶时的专注神情。
Chen Jinwang's intense concentration as he produces a kettle.

摄影：吴景腾
Photography: Wu Jingteng

竹编艺术

谈起台湾竹编艺术，首先就会想到台湾地区以竹为名的竹之重镇：南投县的竹山镇。南投位于台湾地理中心，被比拟为有如台湾的肚脐眼，也是唯一不临海的县市。而竹山，古来为进入山区的门户，竹山以竹为名，不难想见此地盛产竹材以及竹产业在这个小镇的重要性。

笔者在30年前偕同家人同游竹山，只见漫山遍野都是翠绿竹林，清雅秀丽有如仙境。小镇街肆，似乎一半以上卖的商品都与竹有关。而最有趣也最难忘的是中午随兴找了一家小餐厅，享受到的竟是全竹大餐，竹筒饭、竹笋汤、闷竹笋、爌肉竹笋、凉拌竹笋……每一道都非常有特色，也料理得极其可口，最精彩的是餐厅桌椅皆以竹编而成，餐具也都是竹雕制品，一餐饭吃得30年都忘不了。

可惜10年后再去，乃至执笔本文之数周前再去，只见竹林景观连同竹艺竹餐几乎已完全从小镇消失，残存几家竹艺品店，所售商品一如其他地方随处可见之物而无特色可言，餐厅再无全竹大餐，令人为之扼腕。

从竹山小镇的变化，可以看到台湾竹产业的兴与衰。虽是可惜可叹，却也是社会转变之下的残酷事实。如今台湾竹产业只剩若干山区成为竹材供应来源区而种植大片竹林、若干地区成为竹笋产区，提供可口的鲜笋供应零售市场及餐饮业及制造各种笋加工食材的专业人家，而竹编艺术则成为少数艺术家及技术人员认真发扬、努力传承的技艺。幸好的是

文化篇 Culture

巧手编织各种生活用品。摄影：吴景腾
A skilled craftsman weaves a variety of everyday products. Photography: Wu Jingteng

人数比例上或许仅占少数，工艺技巧却日益精进，在台湾手工艺各项竞赛或展出中大放异彩。

中国人利用竹子已有数千年，应用在生活上的器物非常多样，如：竹筷、竹碗、竹椅、竹榻、竹席、竹火笼、灯笼、针线盒、竹扫帚等，甚至还用来当作建材以建筑房舍、亭台、桥梁，乃至打造古式车辆、古式船筏、古式木船之船篷等。而各种精致的竹雕、竹编艺术，则被大量采用在提升生活美学之上，中国人崇尚的岁寒三友松竹梅、四君子梅兰竹菊，无不说明了竹与中国人密不可分的情谊。

竹编工艺最早出现在春秋战国时候的南方楚国，发现的竹编器是在小屯殷墓中发掘出土的铜戈上，细致的编竹刻纹，间接证实了当时已经有竹编器物。甚至更早年的具有7000年历史的河姆渡文化遗址出土物，已发现有竹编，证明简单竹编早在人类定居生活时期便已出现。而战国时期竹编形式变得更为丰富，在有竹乡之称的安吉出土的战国时期竹编文物有竹碗、竹盒等物。秦汉时期的竹编已被运用到了其他领域，出现了竹席、竹帘等物,西安还曾出土过底部印有竹席网格图案的"秦陵铜马车"。唐宋时期,竹编艺术融入了民间,还出现了以竹材制作的玩具,著名的竹马戏《昭君出塞》中使用的马就是竹子所编成的竹马。台湾地区的少数民族早已在生活中发展出极其精致而又实用之竹制品,历史悠远,还曾成为多伦多皇家博物馆典藏精品;随着早期移民带来的竹工艺技术,使得台湾竹材运用更加多元,而发展出台湾独特的竹制品器物与竹艺美学。光绪年间台南有竹仔街、嘉义有敢石路、竹街,还有鹿港的竹篾街都是竹工艺行业聚集地。

1929年间从日本请来编织师父教授花笼、杂物箱等的编制方法,及染色和涂装技术,所生产的竹制品返销日本;1931年间再从福州请来师父教授各种竹艺技术,所生产的竹制品也返销回大陆。当时的"竹山郡竹材工艺传习所"及后来1954年间创设的"南投县工艺研究班"对台湾传统工艺的保存及推广发挥了不可磨灭的功劳。此时期除了引进竹编技巧与涂装技术外,同时也改变了竹制品的生产方法与销售模式,从少量或订制的内销方式逐渐演变成量产外销的产业形态。

台湾竹艺大师颜水龙先生对台湾竹工艺之发展及推广功不可没,他在1949年受聘为"台湾省工艺品生产推行委员会"委员并兼任设计组长,教导台湾各地学员编织、竹细工、藤工、蓪草纸、人造花等工艺技术。另一位台湾竹编大师李荣烈师承颜水龙,从事竹艺创作逾60年.一对师徒,为台湾竹艺奉献的精神令人钦佩。

台湾竹编工艺师李荣烈(右)在竹艺工坊指导学生。
A master of woven bamboo handicrafts, Li Ronglie, instructs students in his workshop.

出自竹编工艺师巧手的小虾,栩栩如生。
In this master craftsman's dexterous hands, bamboo is transformed into a highly realistic shrimp.

摄影:吴景腾
Photography: Wu Jingteng

Woven Bamboo Art

The town of Zhushan (literally "Bamboo Mountain") in Nantou County is famous for its bamboo. Nantou is located in the center of Taiwan and is the only county that doesn't border with the sea. The region abounds in bamboo and has developed an industry out of bamboo handicrafts.

Thirty years ago, when I visited Zhushan with my family, we were enchanted by the lush grove of bamboo shoots that spread over hill and dale. Over half of the products sold in the town are related to bamboo. At noon, we enjoyed a sumptuous feast of bamboo at a local restaurant, including sticky rice cooked in bamboo tubes, soup made from bamboo shoots, as well as bamboo shoots that had been stewed — either on their own, or with meat. Everything in the restaurant — from the furniture to the tableware — was either woven or carved out of bamboo. Thirty years later, the memory is still fresh in my mind. Unfortunately, however, when I returned 10 years later, the bamboo restaurant had disappeared. All that remained were a few stores selling bamboo handicrafts.

From Zhushan's transformation, we can see the rise and decline of Taiwan's bamboo industry. These days, in Taiwan, there are only a few mountainous zones that still produce and supply bamboo — whether it be rods for use in handicrafts, or fresh shoots for use in restaurants. Although the number of bamboo artisans has decreased, the skills of those who have remained loyal to their profession continue to improve.

For thousands of years, Chinese people have been using bamboo to make a number of items, such as chopsticks, bowls, chairs, beds, mats and lanterns. Chinese people have even used bamboo as a material in the construction of houses, carriages, as well as boats and rafts. Meanwhile, exquisitely carved bamboo handicrafts have been used throughout China's history as a means of beautifying living spaces. In Chinese, the pine, bamboo and plum are collectively referred to as the "Three Friends of Winter" and are revered as symbols of endurance. The bamboo is also thought of as one of four "lords" (the other three being plums, orchids and chrysanthemums), proving that the Chinese people have an inseparable affiliation with this plant.

Bamboo handicrafts are thought to have emerged in the southern Kingdom of Chu during the Spring and Autumn period (from 771 to 476 BC), although there is evidence to suggest that it originated even earlier, about 7,000 years ago. So far, archaeologists have excavated bamboo handicrafts from the Warring States period, as well as the Qin, Han, Tang and Song dynasties. Local people have also been producing bamboo products. As migrants from the mainland introduced new techniques to Taiwan, the applications of bamboo became more diverse. Eventually, local bamboo artisans would develop their own unique product types and aesthetic criteria.

竹编工艺师编织出来的鸡年装饰品。摄影：吴景腾

Decorations for the Year of the Rooster woven by a professional bamboo artisan. Photography: Wu Jingteng

文化篇 Culture

传统铸剑

刀剑好儿郎

到佛具店购买佛菩萨各种神明之塑像不能说"买"这个字，而要毕恭毕敬说"请"神佛。同样的，前往铸剑师处，看中了某一把剑，也不能说想买这把剑回家，要说"请剑"，这是一种规矩，代表着无比的尊敬心。

中国是尊崇剑的民族，或许没有哪一种兵器能像剑一样，一直得到上至帝王、下至庶民的敬与爱。有关剑的故事多得不胜枚举，剑与侠士、剑与悲壮、剑与正气、剑与凄美似乎也画着等号。

在古中国，最早期的剑是用玉或石制造的，即使曾发现有青铜剑遗物，判断是作为长兵器之下的辅助武器，在吴、越等河川较多的地区才被作为主要武器，春秋时代的名剑也因此大多出于这些地区，其中最有名的出土古剑当属"越王勾践剑"。

而剑的历史故事中最悲壮的莫过于众所周知的干将莫邪剑了。春秋末期，吴越连年争战，吴王阖闾苦无适用兵器，遂命干将铸剑。干将偕妻莫邪从五山采来铁精，从六合收集金英，等待日月同辉，阴阳和畅之时开炉铸剑。但因气温骤降，金铁不熔，他们乃效法其师剪断头发、截断指甲，投于炉中。又命三百童男童女鼓橐装炭，加大火力，终于金铁熔融，铸成宝剑二柄。一柄剑身遍布龟甲纹，称为雄剑，取名干将。另一柄剑身隐起漫纹，称为雌剑，取名莫邪。干将藏匿雄剑，只献雌剑给吴王阖闾，吴王视若天下之珍爱不释手。

但这故事另有一本，说是令铸剑者并非吴王阖闾而是楚王。且说宝剑铸成之时，莫邪已足月即将临盆，干将对妻子说，我决意只献上雌剑，大王必定迁怒于我，我之性命难保。我死后一定要让儿子为我报仇，并告莫邪雄剑藏匿之处。干将走后，妻子

铸剑家陈重智遵循古法铸剑，开炉起火之前要先祭拜天地。
The master swordsmith Chen Chongzhi forges a blade in strict adherence to ancient customs; before firing up the stove, he first pays respects to the natural world.

手工铸剑过程，须要重复多次进行锻造、淬火。
Throughout the process of making a sword by hand, one must repeatedly forge the metal and quench it in water.

手工铸造好的剑进入最后工序：打磨。
The newly forged sword undergoes the final step: grinding.

陈重智为即将完成的剑雕刻配件、完成最后组装作业。
Chen Chongzhi carves the other components of the sword and assembles them with the completed blade.

摄影：吴景腾
Photography: Wu Jingteng

莫邪果然生了个男孩，取名赤比。赤比长大后日夜思念为父报仇，又苦无良策。一天，他一边走一边悲愤高歌，途遇一外乡人，问他何以心事重重。赤比坦言相告。外乡人说，要报仇不难，只要把剑和你的头颅交给我，我替你报仇。赤比毫不迟疑，拔剑自刎，但其尸身不倒，双手捧着头颅和干将剑交给了外乡人。楚王自从杀了干将后日夜不安，老是梦见干将的儿子前来报仇，多次派人严加搜捕。外乡人带着赤比的人头拜见楚王，楚王大喜，立即把赤比的头颅放到汤鼎熬煮，历时三天三夜仍然完整。楚王走到鼎边低头探看，外乡人立即一剑将楚王的头颅砍落鼎中，两颗人头在沸腾的鼎中捉对撕咬，胜负难分。外乡人再度挥剑，将自己的头颅也砍落鼎中。七天之后，三个头颅才溶成汤汁。

还有一说是《越绝书外记·宝剑》所记载，楚王命风胡子携重金赴吴越请欧冶子、干将铸造良剑。二人凿茨山，泄其溪，掘得铁英，铸成宝剑三柄。楚王见到宝剑十分高兴，问及剑名、物象。风胡子说三柄剑一名龙渊，一名泰阿，一名工布。又说："欲知龙渊，观其状，如登高山，临深渊；欲知泰阿，观其钚，巍巍翼翼，如流水之波；欲知工布，钚从文起，至脊而止，如珠不可衽，文若流水不绝。"这故事完美而无剑光血影，而这一段话也成为相剑者对名剑的最经典评论。

台湾近代铸剑巨匠陈重智，出身台中市沙鹿镇，乃家族第三代铸剑传人。从15岁开始学习手工铸剑技艺，22岁时铸造出自己的第一把剑。手工铸剑需要选钢、锻造、淬火、打磨、雕刻配件、组装等多个环节。工艺复杂，成品有限，他说他铸剑不单是为了销售，更是为了把手工铸剑工艺传承下去，让更多人了解这门老手艺。他的客人来自世界各地，远至德国、瑞士和法国。这些人或是武术爱好者、或是藏家，往往一见倾心。相对于高效率的机械制剑，陈重智宁可坚持传统手工艺。理由是"用机械就没了温度，没了感情"，机械和手工并没有孰好孰劣，单纯就是一种执着吧。

台湾出了如此可敬的手工铸剑师，在大陆也有同样的传统坚持者。中国远自战国时期就有精湛的折叠锻打百炼钢技艺。但有世界第一名刀之称的手工折叠锻打大马士革刀却是舶来品。一位张勇好汉为此事如鲠在喉。从16岁便发奋学习做刀技艺，苦心钻研14年，经历了无数次失败，终于完成用古法折叠锻打工艺制作的刀具，硬度与特殊纹路都不逊于千年大马士革名刀。现在，连德国人都远来选刀，世界一流名刀终于奠定！两岸争辉无负先贤先师，真乃采撷中华之光辉。

Traditional Sword-Making

When purchasing a sword from a master swordsmith in China, one must use the verb for "request" rather than "buy". This is a convention that expresses respect for the swordsmith and his craft.

Swords are revered in Chinese culture. In China's history, no other weapon has been universally cherished and respected — from the emperor to the common people — like the sword has. The sword represents noble tragedy, solemn beauty and righteousness.

And the most tragic story in the history of the Chinese sword is none other than the tale of Gan Jiang and Mo Ye. At the end of the Spring and Autumn period, when the kingdoms of Wu and Yue engaged in a war, King Helü of Wu ordered a man named Gan Jiang to cast swords for him. Gan Jiang and his wife Mo Ye travelled all throughout the land in the search of iron and gold. Upon their return, they waited for the sun and moon to appear simultaneously in the sky (symbolizing the harmony of *yin* and *yang*) before heating the stove with which they hoped to cast the sword. However, due to a sudden drop in temperature, the iron and gold would not melt. In keeping with an ancient practice, Gan Jiang and Mo Ye cut off their hair and fingernails and tossed them into the fire. They also ordered three hundred young boys and girls to stoke the flames by pressing bellows and adding coal. Finally, the gold and iron melted together, and the couple were able to cast two precious swords. One of these swords was engraved with oracle bone script, declared to be the "male" sword, and named after Gan Jiang. The other sword was engraved with decorative patterns, declared the "female" sword, and named after Mo Ye. Gan Jiang hid his sword away and only gave Mo Ye's sword to King Helü of Wu, who treasured it as though it were a divine creation.

The contemporary swordsmith, Chen Chongzhi, was born in Shalu, a town within the municipality of Taichung. He is a third-generation practitioner of ancient sword-making techniques. Chongzhi began to learn how to make swords by hand at the age 15, and successfully forged his first sword by the age of 22. The manual production of a sword comprises a number of steps, including selecting the steel, forging it over a flame, quenching it, grinding it, engraving other components such as the hilt, and fusing them together. Swordmaking is a complicated process with a relatively low output. Chongzhi says that he doesn't just forge swords in order to sell them — more importantly, he does so as a means of introducing and imparting this ancient craft to the people of today. He has customers on both sides of the Taiwan Straits, and even as far as Germany, Switzerland and France. When these customers (generally martial arts enthusiasts or collectors) see their new acquisition, it's often love at first sight. Although some would be swayed by the relative efficiency and simplicity of producing swords with the assistance of machines, Chen Chongzhi persists in making swords using traditional methods. His reasoning is that "when you use machines, there's no warmth — no emotion." There is no point in arguing that one is better than the other — it's all a question of one's personal passions.

陈重智坚持传统手工铸剑，为武术爱好者打造出梦中神品。
摄影：吴景腾

Chen Chongzhi upholds the traditional craft of forging swords by hand in order to produce stunning masterpieces for martial arts enthusiasts.
Photography: Wu Jingteng

手工制墨

巷弄中的古老文化传承人

笔者担任一家报社主编时，有位画家向我投稿，文字之外还配以水墨插图，虽然水平不错，画作却恶臭难掩，我忍不住去信要他别再用宿墨画画了，宿墨就是倒出来使用过，甚至还掺了水的隔夜墨汁，因腐败常易变质而生臭。这位作者几个月后才回我信，原来他因犯案被关押在监狱中，物质条件不好，墨汁难买，画画只好因陋就简，出狱之后再也不用宿墨啦。

笔者也爱画画，有一次一位挚友看了我的作品，诚恳提出建议：画国画不要用墨汁了，一定要乖乖研墨，以墨条研出来的墨液作画。

我非常好奇，你看得出我是用墨汁画的呀？普天之下当今又有几人看得出墨画或墨汁画？何必扬弃方便好用的现代化产品而苦苦守旧？原来她是个中专家，专门研究文物保存的学问。她说，现代墨汁作画容易毁败，保存不易。主要原因是墨汁多为合成原料制作，伤纸，画作本身也易变质，以此作画习作无妨，却不能用于艺术创作之上，收藏家内行，一见就立刻走避。

墨和墨汁怎么做出来的？果真其中学问多。

文化篇 Culture

陈嘉德先生好炉火，放置在工作台下方，以便利用热度保持墨团软化状态，再将墨团放置工作台上用手搓揉。

Chen Jiade first fires up the stove under his working surface so that he can keep the ink paste soft as he kneads it.

将墨团称好重量后，随即以手搓揉，搓揉成无缝隙接痕的圆柱形状才能进入下一步工序。

A suitable quantity of ink paste is weighed on a balance and then kneaded into a seamless column before preceding to the next step.

摄影：王远茂
Photography: Wang Yuanmao

将木模盒置于压轧椅前方,利用杠杆原理加压,使墨成型。压制过程中,陈嘉德喜欢坐在压轧椅后方,以增强压力。
摄影:王远茂
The inkstick is placed in a wooden mold on a "pressing chair", which presses it into shape using lever principles. When pressing the inksticks, Chen Jiade likes to sit on the back of the pressing chair so as to add extra pressure. Photography: Wang Yuanmao

  墨在我国已有4700年的历史,相传西周时期便已有制墨师出现,但据进一步考据,秦以前的墨大多采自天然石墨,一直到秦以后才出现近似近代人使用的制墨技术,而发展出逐渐成熟的人工造墨技术。盛唐时代,墨不仅遍及全国,其中的极品徽墨,甚至已经闻名于世界。制墨的主要原料为炭墨烟和胶,炭墨烟就是植物在不完全燃烧下产生的烟,经收集而成。最适当的植物首推松树枝条,但也可以采集菜油、豆油、猪油、皂青油、麻油、桐来燃烧,以产出的油烟造墨。另还有采自漆或矿物油为制墨材料者,各有优点,表现于墨色各不相同,质量自有高下。

  将采集的烟加入胶剂,可使墨成型,这便是墨的基础制作过程。而胶的原料取自动物骨或皮,当然为了使墨保存长久不变质又不受虫蛀,也得添加适当的防腐添加剂。好的防腐剂还可增加墨香、增添墨色及延长墨条及书画作品保存期限,原料包括极其昂贵的龙脑、麝香、丁香、檀香、熊胆、犀角粉,以及藤黄、丹参、黄连、乌头、甘松、藿香、零陵香、朱砂、雌黄、珍珠粉、金箔、银箔、硫酸铜、银朱、秦皮、地榆、紫草、茜草、黄芦、黑豆、五倍子、胡桃、牡丹皮、熏草豆、石榴皮等。不同的制墨人各有不同的配方，有些配方列为独门祖传而不外流。传统制墨程序繁杂，至少分浸油、烧烟、筛烟、和胶、用药、搜烟、杵捣锤炼、样制、修墨、阴干等工序。书画家从不嫌墨条价昂，因为深知好墨难制、好墨难求。相比之下墨汁制作显得简便太多。墨汁的主要原料为炭烟、胶料、添加剂和溶液等，一般都是机械制作。当然墨汁也分上品及劣品，视原料及制作过程而定其身价。上品者炭烟之选料、胶的来源、溶剂的种类皆经逐项考究，下品者全程化学合成物为之，习于书画者每每一用便知。由于墨条使用者日少，传统制墨行业快速没落，目前在台湾可能只剩一个人在坚持着手工制墨的传统，那便是在新北市三重区经营大有制墨厂的陈嘉德先生。他的厂房占地不大，却像一座古老的灯塔，默默散发着亘古之光。

　　陈嘉德在小学毕业后，独自从故乡嘉义北上，13岁的他就到三重台北桥下的墨庄当学徒，29岁那年自己办厂创业，初期以制作学生墨为主。由于当时原料缺乏，也缺少稳定客源，时常得自己到外推销，与文具批发店联系。经过长时间的累积以及不断的努力，好不容易才做出一番成绩。

　　20世纪90年代，台湾整个制墨市场受到外来低价倾销产品冲击严重，陈嘉德的生意也受到重大打击，工厂内十几个员工都遣散掉，工厂也暂时关闭。但是，为了一分理念与坚持，他后来大胆的采取逆向操作的手法，改以制作高级松烟墨来应对，不惜成本的加入梅片、麝香和牛皮胶等高级材料制墨，成功再创生机，几十年的制墨技术更让他成为台湾最顶尖的制墨大师。

　　转眼间入行到现在早已超过半个世纪，他还记得，几十年前台湾手工制墨业一片繁荣。无奈随着时代改变，现代人事事追求效率，生活步调绷紧，墨汁几乎完全取代传统的砚台研墨，文房四宝笔墨纸砚只剩纸笔和墨汁，写书法不研墨已大大降低书法之趣，后来一度连写书法的人都大量流失，墨香几乎已被人们所遗忘，更别提要求年轻人以此为业了。当年他四处寻找肯加入这一行的接班人，几乎无人愿意学习这种浑身乌黑看来脏兮兮的技艺，即使今天他被誉为台湾第一制墨大师，仍然苦无传承衣钵之人。他也只得继续顶着台湾唯一手工制墨师的名衔，苦苦承续着这即将失传的制墨文化薪传。

Hand-Made Ink

Back when I worked as the editor of a newspaper, a painter once submitted an article, complete with ink-wash illustrations. Although he painted quite well, the stench of the ink was overpowering. I couldn't suppress the urge to tell him in a letter that he should stop using ink left out overnight. Ink that has been repeatedly used and diluted with water over the course of an evening goes bad and releases a foul smell. This aspiring writer only responded a few months later. As it turned out, he was in prison and had difficulty acquiring fresh ink. The only way he could paint was using stale ink.

I also have a passion for ink-wash painting. Once, after a friend saw my work, she suggested that, instead of painting with ready-made ink, I should grind natural inksticks against an inkstone. I was extremely curious — who would be able to tell what kind of ink I used to paint my works? Why should I abandon the convenience of modern ink products and adhere to an outdated tradition? It just so happened that this friend was an expert who specialized in the preservation of cultural artefacts. She told me that modern inks are largely composed of synthetic ingredients that damage the paper, making it difficult to conserve. Any collector, she said, would be able to tell in a heartbeat.

How are inksticks and ink solutions made? As I expected, it's an elaborate process. The Chinese people have been making ink for 4,700 years. By the Western Zhou period, there were already a number of professional ink-makers. In pre-imperial China, ink was mostly made using natural graphite — it was only during the Qin Dynasty that the Chinese people developed techniques for producing inksticks. During the Tang Dynasty's main period of prosperity, inksticks were not only ubiquitous throughout all of China — one particularly exquisite product, named "Hui inksticks", had even garnered fame across the globe.

The main ingredients used in the production of ink are soot and animal glue. The soot itself is made by collecting the smoke produced by certain plants when they are grilled over a flame. For this step, it is recommended to use pine branches, although one can also produce soot by burning oils made from plants, animals or minerals. Different types of oil produce different colored inks.

The inkstick is then formed by adding glue to the soot and pressing it into a shape. This glue either comes from the bones or hide of animal — of course, in order to extend the ink's shelf-life and prevent it from spoiling, certain preservatives are also added. High-quality preservatives can enhance the fragrance and color of the ink and at the same time keep it fresh. Some of the then-costly ingredients used in these preservatives include Borneo camphor, musk, cloves and sandalwood. Different ink-makers use their own formulas. Some of these formulas are family secrets that have been passed on from one generation to another.

The traditional process of making ink comprises a number of steps. The basic procedure includes soaking spices in the oil, filtering the soot from the smoke as the oil burns, melting the glue, stirring in the soot and preservatives, pounding the mixture in a pestle, hammering it into shape, printing it, adding final details, and drying in a shady environment.

As the number of people who use inksticks continually decreases, traditional ink-makers have fallen on hard times. In Taiwan, the only person to have carried on the tradition of making ink by hand is perhaps Chen Jiade, from New Taipei City. At the age of 13, he went to study at Mozhuang, an ink manufacturer in Sanchong Area. The year he turned 29, he founded his own factory and began to produce inksticks for students. In the 1990s, Taiwan's ink manufacturers were hit hard as the market was inundated with cheap inks. This, however, didn't faze Chen Jiade. Sparing no expense, he began to produce his inks using high-quality pine soot, as well as other costly materials, such as a Borneo camphor known as *mei pian*, musk, and glue made from cow hide. In this way, he was able to revive his business. Several decades of experience in making ink have earned Chen Jiade the reputation of Taiwan's most skilled ink manufacturer.

放置在木模盒的墨条，经过一天定型后取出，放在室内阴干 25 天，期间还需反复翻面，以求均匀阴干。

After a day in the pressing chair, the inksticks are removed from the wooden mold and stored away from sunlight for 25 days. During this period, the inksticks must be continually flipped over to ensure that they are consistently dry.

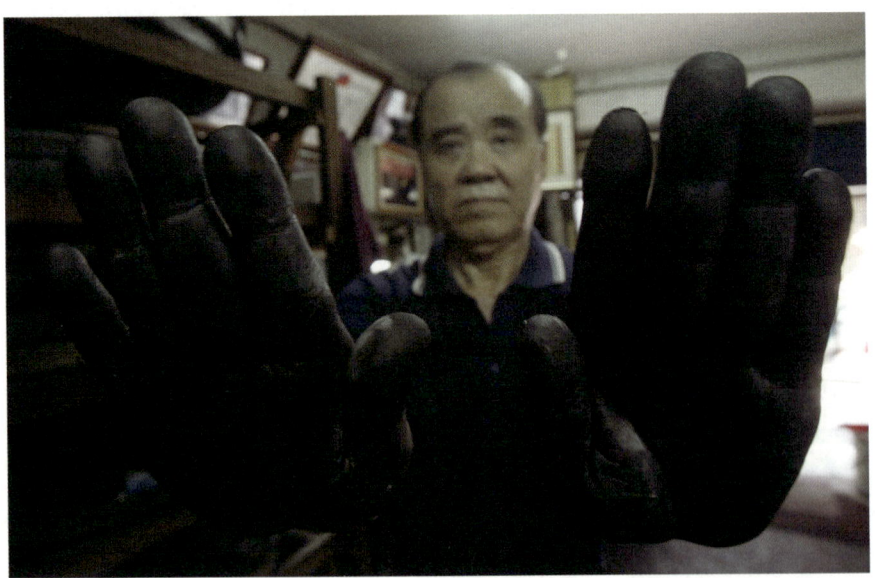

在闷热的工作环境中，整日与乌黑的墨灰为伍，在工作告一段落时，陈嘉德展示漆黑的双手，真是位默默耕耘、坚守工作岗位的老先生。

After handling soot all day in his stiflingly hot workshop, Chen Jiade's hands are as black as crows — a testament to his perseverance and devotion to his profession.

摄影：王远茂

Photography: Wang Yuanmao

制笔艺术

在文房四宝笔墨纸砚中,笔是由谁发明的呢?台湾的小学课本有着标准答案:蒙恬。

蒙恬在什么背景之下发明了毛笔呢?传说却是出于一个意外。蒙恬是战国末期秦国的一位将军,奉派镇守北疆,偶见匈奴以兽毛沾颜料绘图而大感兴趣,因为当时中国人书写不用纸笔,而用刀刻字于竹简之上,刻好竹简一卷便成为一册书卷,如此书写耗工耗力又耗时,后来有一天前方军情告急,蒙恬完全来不及一刀刀刻写战报,情急之下仿匈奴人取来兽毛,捆扎成束,直接沾了颜料在丝卷上书写,写成快马加鞭传送后方,这个紧急应变之策,不但实时传达重要战情而未误戎机,也开创下书写革命,史官将此事择要记之。蒙恬因而成为制笔之创始者而名垂青史。

其实,毛笔出现得似乎比蒙恬时代还要更早,1954 年在长沙左公山 15 号战国中期楚墓中已有出土保存依然完好的毛笔。这支笔以木作杆,用竹管将毛套在木杆上,这是今人得以亲眼目睹的原始的毛笔。而更早期,甚至还有证据显示毛笔早在商朝就出现了。

蒙恬回朝后继续研制毛笔,以柘木为管,鹿毛为柱,羊毛为被制成更便于书写之笔。蒙恬笔对于小篆的形成具有很大的意义,小篆线条婉转曲折,非硬物所能为,分析应当是用毛笔书写的。经过后世续加改进,毛笔更加完美,除了书写,更成了中国书画艺术之最重要工具。

制笔达人陈耀文，喜欢研究创新毛笔，制作215厘米的大毛笔，笔杆用竹竿制成，笔头则用了100匹内蒙古马的尾毛制成，重达50公斤，他自己都要用抱的方式才拿得动。摄影：王远茂
Even Chen Yaowen himself has to use both arms to lift his 215-cm-long brush. Photography: Wang Yuanmao

  笔按用途不同而有各种制造材料和制作方法，一般分为紫毫、兼毫、水笔、狼毫、羊毫、大笔和画笔等数种。羊毫用山羊毛制作，属大众化用品。其中又分宿羊毫、陈羊毫、净羊毫三类。紫毫用山兔背部的黑尖毫制成，毛性较为刚硬，适合写行书、草书。狼毫用黄鼠狼尾毛制成，其刚性略差于兔毛。鼠须笔用家鼠鬓须制成，笔行纯净顺遂、尖锋，写出的字体以柔带刚。鸡毫笔用鸡的胸毛制成，相当柔软，非有相当功力者难于掌握，因而不宜交初学书法者使用。猪鬃笔用猪鬃加工蒸制而成，用于书写大匾；兼毫则是将不同兽毛以不同比例掺和而成，书写可刚柔相济。如紫毫与羊毫配合，其中紫毫越多越硬，反之较柔。

  笔传来台湾始自明末时期，为数不多而未广传。台湾制笔故事最早是百余年前有

文化篇 Culture

福建安溪制笔家族成员的张扬师父来台贩卖毛笔，有一晚因行旅匆促，误了投宿时间，乃借宿一家杂货店，杂货店由一位郭老得所经营，体恤出外人离乡背井之辛劳而勤加接待，双方结成莫逆。数年交情而时相往返，有一天张扬听闻郭老得长子郭海水欲前往外地习艺，张扬为报答借宿之情，乃将一身制笔功夫倾囊传授给郭海水，郭家家族从此与毛笔结下不解之缘，亦开启台湾地区制笔的首页。

郭海水辛勤历经多年学艺成功，便自创家业，于台南府创立太阳堂，并继续学习吸收来自日本的制笔技术，开创了郭家毛笔家族至今达一世纪的制笔事业。

另外，有台湾制笔达人美誉的陈耀文，是台湾另一支制笔家族"文山社"传人。他从小与兄长帮忙家里从事的制笔工作，从最简单的挑毛开始，整毛、裁切、卷笔柱、包笔被、扎笔头、装笔杆、定型等每个步骤都要按部就班，费一番苦功学习，也因此拥有一身扎实的好功夫，一路走来、乐在其中，制笔已成为他个人最大兴趣。

谈起他的成绩与收藏，真教人不称奇也难。他曾以两年的时间仿台北故宫博物院

陈耀文这支不轻易展示的收藏笔，仿故宫康熙皇帝御用毛笔，真品笔杆收藏在台北故宫博物院，描绘康熙皇帝写毛笔的图画则收藏在北京故宫。他花了两年多时间才完成。摄影：王远茂

Chen Yaowen's replica of the brush used by Emperor Kangxi of Qing which is on display at the Palace Museum of Taipei. The brush took him over two years to complete. Photography: Wang Yuanmao

收藏的一枝康熙御用毛笔,大小比例、色泽花纹完全一致,笔杆上的镶贝一片片依样磨成有弧度的单片再逐一拼镶,失败的次数难以计数,最后总算完成。他曾制作连杆带笔仅约7厘米的"小"毛笔,也曾受托制作215厘米的"大"毛笔,这枝大笔的笔杆以竹竿为材料,笔头则用了100匹内蒙古的马尾毛才集成,重量达50公斤,必须用抱的才拿得动。古书提到的笔如:"王羲之写兰亭序的鼠须笔""明朝书法家陈宪章惯用的草笔"等,他都一一找到材料并仿造试用,制作出的笔颇得行家之赞誉。

最有趣的是他还花了12年时间完成一组十二生肖笔,每年不同的生肖来临时,便制作一枝当年之笔,材料则力求吻合生肖,唯一无法依生肖选材料的只剩龙与蛇,因为龙无法采集其毛,而蛇根本无毛可采,最后只好以绘有龙的青花瓷制成龙笔杆,以蛇皮制成蛇笔杆才集成。在陈耀文身上,我们看到了执着、对工作的热忱及无怨无悔完全投入的精神,堪称是令人骄傲的台湾之光。

陈耀文制作的十二生肖笔,巧思与创意让见者无不惊呼大开眼界。摄影:王远茂

The set of 12 zodiac brushes made by Chen Yaowen. Photography: Wang Yuanmao

The Art of Brush Making

The brush — along with ink, paper and inkstones — constitutes one of the four "treasures of the study" in Chinese culture, but who was responsible for its invention? The answer can be found in Taiwan's elementary students' textbooks: Meng Tian. Meng Tian was a general for Qin army at the end of the Warring States period who was sent to protect the Kingdom of Qin's northern border. There, he was fascinated to discover that the Xiongnu people would paint by dipping animal hairs into primitive pigments. At the time, Chinese people didn't write using a brush on paper — rather, they used a knife to carve characters into bamboo slats that would then be bound together into scrolls. This was a significantly time- and energy-consuming process. One day, when Meng Tian noticed enemies on the horizon, he didn't have enough time to carve a battlefield communiqué into bamboo slats. In this crucial moment, he decided to imitate the Xiongnu people by tying animal hairs into a bunch, dipping the bunch in paint, and writing on a silk scroll. This strike of inspiration was, without a doubt, a revolution for Chinese literature. Court historians would later record this event in official records, confirming that Meng Tian was the creator of the writing brush.

A number of techniques and materials can be used to produce brushes. Brushes made from goat hairs are well-suited to a number of purposes, while rabbit hairs are rather stiff by comparison, making them ideal for writing in cursive script. Siberian weasel hairs are slightly less stiff than rabbit hairs. As

制笔工序包括扎笔头等步骤，极为繁复。
The painstaking brushmaking process comprises a number of steps, including tying the brush hairs in a bunch.

制笔过程在完成上海菜胶、定型等步骤后，利用绳子挤压方式，将笔头多余的海菜胶挤掉。
After the brush hairs have been attached with glue and styled into the desired shape, the brushmaker uses a rope to squeeze out excess glue from the brush head.

摄影：王远茂
Photography: Wang Yuanmao

a result, brushes made from Siberian weasel hairs produce calligraphy that is equally delicate and forceful. Brushes made from chicken down are much softer. Pig-hair brushes are used to write inscriptions on horizontal boards known as *bian*, given as honorary plaques to national heroes. There were also other brushes that were made from hairs of a number of different animals.

The oldest story about brushmaking in Taiwan dates from a little over a century ago, when Zhang Yang, a professional brushmaker from Fujian Province, came to Taiwan to sell his wares. His travelling schedule was so hectic that, one evening, he was unable to find accommodation and was forced to put up at a convenience store. He quickly became good friends with the manager of the convenience store, Guo Laode. Later, Zhang Yang wholeheartedly imparted a lifetime of brushmaking experience to Guo Laode's son, Haishui. Guo Haishui went on to found a workshop called Taiyang Tang, or "Hall of the Sun", thus launching the Guo family brushmaking business.

Another person who has carried on their family's brushmaking business is Chen Yaowen, the heir of the "Wenshan Society". He once devoted two years of his life to producing a replica of a writing brush used by Emperor Kangxi of Qing (displayed at the Palace Museum of Taipei). This replica is indistinguishable from the real brush in terms of its size and proportions, as well as the decorative engravings and shells on the handle. He has made a "micro-brush" that was only 7 cm long, as well as an oversized brush that was 215 cm long. The handle of this enormous brush is composed of bamboo rods, while the head is made from tail hair of 100 Inner Mongolian horses. In total, the brush weighs 50 kg and can only be manipulated using both arms.

Another notable achievement of Chen Yaowen is a set of 12 brushes representing each of the Chinese zodiacs, which he completed in order over the course of 12 years. The materials of each brush are derived from the zodiac they represent. As there is no way to obtain the hairs of a dragon, and as snakes don't have any hairs to pluck, Chen Yaowen chose to decorate these two brushes' handles using dragon imagery for the former and snakeskin for the latter.

铸字与印章

铸字

从全盛走到唯一

印刷术是中国古代四大发明之一,是中华儿女引以为傲的一项科学技术,但活字印刷到底由哪一国最早发明呢?笔者年前赴南欧旅行,来到斯洛文尼亚布莱德湖,看到了湖畔一个小小的手工印刷店,展示满屋子的古老印刷机器及印刷品,现场还有游客学习捡字排版、手工印刷,游客们玩得开心,小店也收入滚滚、荷包满满。笔者一旁欣赏,有愧对老祖宗之叹。印刷术是我们的发明,我们的国粹,哪轮得到人家炫耀呢?

韩国一直声称他们是发明活字印刷术最早的国家,但根据台湾师范大学印刷技术研究团队依据北宋时期科学家沈括在《梦溪笔谈》中记载的一段文字逆向实验,推演文字中所载毕昇泥版活字印刷术,利用松脂、泥土烧制而成的活字泥板。证明毕昇在公元约1041年左右发明的泥版活字印刷术的确可行。并且将研究结果发表在《印刷科技》第141期刊上。

《梦溪笔谈》是一部讲述古代中国自然科学、工艺技术及社会历史现象的综合性笔记体著作。里面记载的科学研究,在国际具有公信,英国科学史家李约瑟评价为中国科学史上的里程碑,韩国的片面主张不攻

文化篇 Culture

毕昇泥活字版印刷术是中国最早的活字版印刷术，台湾师范大学印刷技术研究团队，依据沈括在《梦溪笔谈》中所记载的300多字的文字叙述，按图索骥，利用松脂、泥土烧制而成泥活字版，再进行活字版印刷，并结合3D打印雕字和牙科齿模技术，重现毕昇的泥活字版印刷术。

A research team from Taiwan Normal University specializing in printing technology recreates Bi Sheng's ceramic movable type system based on a 300-character description in Shen Kuo's *Dream Pool Essays*.

日星铸字行是台湾仅存的铸字行，老板张介冠以保存铸字技术及推广铸字工艺等中华文化为职责。

The Rixing Type Foundry is the last type foundry in Taiwan. Its manager, Zhang Jieguan, considers his professional duty to be the conservation and promotion of elements of Chinese culture, such as typefounding.

摄影：陈柏亨
Photography: Chen Boheng

自破。

　　笔者在新闻媒体服务早期,报社仍然采用活字拼版印刷,有时遇着时间紧急,记者必须跟着主编进到排字房协助改字,只见满满一间房子都是字架,排字师傅拿着记者手写的稿纸,端着拼字盒,出手如飞的从字架上取下铅字,排进盒中,组成篇章。当时发现排字房中有一个严格规定:打翻字架,记过处分,在分秒必争的排字房把字架打翻会造成什么后果不言而喻,重罚当然难免了。

　　当年台湾大街小巷各印刷厂总有大小规模不一的铅字架,密密麻麻都是铅字。曾几何时印刷业计算机化,瞬间字架上的铅字统统被扫进了历史的洪涛。全台湾唯一还保留着满墙字架,并且坚守活字印刷的铸字工程者,似乎已只剩下位于台北市太原路的日星铸字行了。

　　创办于1969年的日星,曾经号称是台北市规模最小的铸字行,却见证过台湾的经济起飞,各行各业兴盛,印刷需求量极大的环境而撑到最久。全盛时期工厂24小时轮班工作,日铸铅字达10万字之量!目前仍拥有的楷书、宋体、黑体等三种字体,不同大小各有4500字到11000字的字量。老板张介冠先生坚持着继续维持这家可能已是全球唯一繁体字活字铸字厂的事业,当作是一种无可推诿的使命。

印章

　　中国篆刻史基本上就是一部印章的历史。印章起源于夏商周时期,出土于商朝晚期都城殷墟所在地河南安阳的三枚殷铜玺可说便是证据。虽然此说犹有存疑之处,印章在战国时期已是普遍之物则无疑义。

　　古时印章的材质多为铜质,也有采用银质或玉质、动物犄角者。古时候在还没有印章的年代,人民和官府往来,或是人民与人民间的重要契约文件,印的是整只手掌的掌模。目前在博物馆或民间收藏中依然能看得到这样盖着一个完整黑手印的文契。这种掌模为契的习俗,在印章引进之后才终止。

　　随后刻印社有了社会需求,刻印师傅一技在手,生意源源上门。刻印赚的是工钱,较大宗的利润来自印材,各种石质、玉质、木质、角质印材陈列于刻印社供客人挑选,这是刻印业的美好时光。但很快就在这几年来受到了计算机科技的冲击,刻印不再是

文化篇 Culture

一件本领，计算机叫出字体或图案，和激光雕刻机一连上线，三分钟便能"烧"好一枚印章。甚至随着社会变迁，信息化时代用印机会日减，连简便的激光刻印都已快要派不上用场，或许未来将只剩下书画家会在作品上盖上印章了。

作为一位书画家，或是书画的收藏者、鉴赏者，印章（金石学）因而变成了一门必要的功课和学问。传统书画家往往必须精心研习治印之学，并为自己雕刻专用的题名章、闲章、藏书章，而收藏家和鉴赏者往往在欣赏书画本身时也会将眼光聚焦到书画作品上的印章上，外行的赝品有时连阳文阴文上下都倒置，闲章及题名章都分不清，或是盖章盖在忌讳位置、错误位置，不但贻笑大方，还直接露出膺仿之破绽。

拜网络世界所赐，透过网络学习金石之学已非难事，大致上抓紧字法、篆法、章法、刀法，边款等方向去搜索钻研，久而久之也可有所成就。

篆刻有广义与狭义两种解释，中国早期凡属于雕玉、刻石、镂竹、铭铜的范围，都叫作"篆刻"，玺印的制作只是其中的一小部分而已。到秦始皇时，将全国书体作综合整理，书分八体，印面上的文字就叫"摹印篆"。新莽定六书时称之"缪篆"，从此便明定篆书为印章印文的使用字体。唐宋之际，由于文人墨客的喜好，虽然改变了印章的体制，但仍以篆书作印。直到明清两代，印人辈出，篆刻便成为以篆书为基础，利用雕刻方法，在方寸间表现疏密、离合的艺术形态，篆刻遂由广义的雕镂铭刻，转为狭义的治印之举。而金属印章因材质特殊，一般先刻印模，再依模浇铸。因为制作有所难度，也常成为国玺、官署用印之物，就不是寻常人家随身所用的东西了。

篆刻艺术是以"文字"为载体，结合章法、笔法、刀法的"文字造型艺术"。
摄影：吴景腾

Engraving seals combines sculptural and textural art into the one medium, and comprises three fundamental techniques: *zhang fa* ("seal-making techniques"), *bi fa* ("calligraphic techniques") and *dao fa* ("knife-handling techniques").
Photography: Wu Jingteng

Typefounding and Seals

Typefounding

Printing is one of the four great inventions of ancient China and is therefore a source of much pride for the Chinese people. During my travels in Southern Europe, I came across a small printshop that abounded with antique printing presses and screens, as well as finished prints. Inside, a number of tourists were learning how to arrange typesets and operate manual printers. They were clearly having a good time, and the little shop seemed to be making a decent amount of money. I stood to one side and sighed to myself as I felt ashamed for my ancestors. Printing is our invention — how could other people flaunt it as their own?

During the Northern Song Dynasty, Bi Sheng (approximately 970-1051 AD) invented China's first movable type system using a ceramic type set. A printing research team from Taiwan Normal University created, based on a 300-character description in the Song Dynasty scientist Shen Kuo's *Dream Pool Essays*, a movable typeset out of a mixture of pine resin and clay baked in a kiln. They also incorporated 3D printing and dental modelling technology in order to recreate Bi Sheng's ceramic movable type system as authentically as possible. Their findings confirmed that Bi Sheng's invention truly did work.

When I worked for a newspaper, back in my youth, newspapers were

文化篇 Culture

still printed using movable type presses. Sometimes, when the newspaper was in a hurry to release a story, the reporter would have to assist technicians in the typesetting room. Inside, they would be overwhelmed by shelves upon shelves of typesets. The typesetter would hold the reporter's handwritten article in one hand and a case for arranging the type in the other, and whiz around the room retrieving the required metal type. They would then arrange the type in the case until they had assembled the entire text. The typesetting room had a strict rule: disciplinary action would be taken against anyone who tipped over a type shelf. In the typesetting room, where time is of the essence, one can imagine the consequences of such a mistake — natural, then, that it should be severely punished.

Later, the printing press was revolutionized by the advent of computers — in an instant, these rooms filled with lead typesets became a thing of the past. Perhaps the only place left in Taiwan that has preserved these walls of movable text and carried on the craft of manual printing is the Rixing Type Foundry, located on Taiyuan Rd in Taipei. Rixing was founded

日星铸字行的铸字机以摄氏 400 度高温熔成铅液来进行铸字，铸字行也传承了活版印刷文化。

Rixing's foundry creates type sets by melting graphite at 400 degrees Celsius and casting it in a mold.

日星铸字行库藏三十余万字的中文铅体字模，联合报将一套完整的铜铸字模转让给日星铸字行，日星铸字行成功把铅字字体数字化，提供给民众下载，让铅字文化以另一种形式流传。

In their database, Rixing has collected over 300,000 graphite type molds. They have digitalized all of these fonts and made them available for download as a means of preserving the cultural of movable type in another form.

摄影：陈柏亨
Photography: Chen Boheng

in 1969 and was once known as the smallest type foundry in Taipei. Although it belongs to a dwindling industry, the foundry has endured hard times and witnessed Taiwan's rise to prosperity. Back in its heyday, the foundry would operate day and night as workers took shifts, producing up to 100,000 lead types (individual characters) a day. They currently have three fonts — model script, Song typeface, and boldface type. Each font size has 4,500 - 11,000 types. The owner of the foundry, Zhang Jieguan, persists in operating what is perhaps the last remaining manufacturer of movable traditional Chinese type in the world. As far as he is concerned, keeping this business alive is his undeniable responsibility.

Seals

Seals originated during the Shang Dynasty, as proved by three royal seals made of copper dating from the late Shang Dynasty that were excavated from the Ruins of Yin in Anyang, Henan Province. In ancient times, before seals were in common use, people would sign written agreements using a print of their entire hand. To this day, one can still find ancient documents signed by handprint in museums and private collections.

Seal-engraving was once a lucrative industry and competent engravers had a never-ending supply of customers. Engravers mostly made their profits by offering a selection of materials — such as stones, jade, wood and animal horns — for customers to choose from. In recent years, owing to the advent of computers, seal-engraving has lost its foothold in the market. Now, one can simply upload a motif to a computer-assisted laser, which can burn a relief into a seal within three minutes. But these days, even these computer-generated seals have fallen out of use. The only people who still use seals are painters and calligraphers, who use them to sign their works.

In addition to mastering their chosen medium, traditional calligraphers and painters also learn the skills of engraving in order to produce their own unique seals. These seals include an "autographic seal", a "leisure seal", and a "book collectors' seal". Collectors and appraisers both pay great attention to the stamps on calligraphic works and paintings. The unintentional inversion of a seal's relief, the use of a leisure seal in place of an autographic seal, or the placement of a stamp in the wrong position can immediately tip off an expert that they are dealing with a counterfeit work.

The techniques involved in engraving seals are traditionally sorted into three categories:

zhang fa, or "seal-making techniques"; *bi fa*, or "calligraphic techniques"; and *dao fa*, or "knife-handling techniques". As the material is too difficult to engrave, metal seals are instead cast in a mold. Due to the relative difficulty involved in their production, metal seals were initially reserved for emperors and officials. What kind of calligraphy style is used when engraving seals? After China was unified under Qin Shihuang (the First Emperor of Qin), eight calligraphic styles from past kingdoms were identified, and it was stipulated that a specific style must be used for engraving seals. By the Ming and Qing dynasties, however, as the number of professional engravers continued to grow exponentially, seal-engraving became a diverse art form that predominantly used the most common calligraphic style.

摄影：吴景腾
Photography: Wu Jingteng

蔬果雕

　　台湾是一个盛产水果的宝岛，土质、气候和环境条件无一不宜，常在乡间路旁随便一个空地便能看见自行从泥土里冒出的果树，而且还果实累累。乡下小路也常可看到以果树当行道树的，每当水果成熟，迤逦十里不见尽头，树上水果简直采都采不完。加上近几十年来果农的努力，水果质量益见提升，许多来自世界各地的观光客发现台湾水果又便宜又好吃，总是连连惊呼天堂到了。

　　水果本身便是美食，而近年来水果更被提升功能，化身为美化美食的角色。水果和蔬菜被相互搭配，巧妙刀工加上创意拼排，创造出千变万化的蔬果雕艺术，大大提升了饮食文化之美。而巧师在一展手艺之余也不吝分享手艺，除了在厨房里慷慨传授绝学，也在高中、高职、大学、学院以及各地小区大学开起专班，系统性引领学员深入钻研，使之成为有深度及厚度的新兴热门学识。更进一步的是近年来国际上厨艺美食竞赛连连，一些拥有好手艺好创意的年轻人携着他们的刀具东征西讨，夺标连连，为台湾水果的名气更添光彩。

　　台湾乡下流行外烩办桌，厨师率领他的助手，用卡车运来炉灶厨具及桌椅，直接开到主人家，往往晒谷场或是骑楼下搭个篷便成为施展手艺之处。乡下地区甚至于经过简单申请还能封路办桌，特大号的篷子就搭在农村马路上，宾客在绿油油的田野中享受美食。而在这样的办桌场合，

文化篇 Culture

宾客最容易近距离观赏厨师烹调手艺，想看蔬果雕花正是最好时机。

只见师父随手拿个地瓜，或是胡萝卜、白萝卜、芋头、黄瓜，随手切上几刀，翻个方向再是几刀，然后加上不同颜色的以辣椒、瓜果皮层切成的小小饰物点缀，瞬间一只只小白兔、小乌龟、小猫小狗就蹦出来了！上菜时摆在大盘子上，往往比一整盘的美食更加吸睛。

这是蔬果雕的小饰物，小饰物只是配角，遇到更大的场合，须有更大的排场，这时师父们便有了一显身手的好时机。材料仍然是地瓜芋头萝卜青椒之类不起眼之物，只见手起刀落，忽然间就组合成一组壮观而又精致的作品，龙凤呈祥栩栩如生、天鹅比翼无限缱绻、猛虎张口如闻吼声、牡丹国色若闻清香飘逸……如此精彩作品，往往引得观众目瞪口呆。了不起的是师傅们总是手法利落，疾如闪电，不消片刻已然完成。观赏者的赞美，也正是他们继续努力钻研的原动力，说不定下一回再来，又推出更惊人的作品！

中国传统历史人物、神话故事，常常成为果雕大师的"入门款"，忽而关公提着大刀威风凛凛站在桌上，忽而三太子足踩风火轮奔行于前，或是八仙过海、牛郎织女、水淹金山寺……这些题材，人们耳熟能详，非常容易与作品产生共鸣，也是果雕达人引以为傲的创作灵感来源。

蔬果雕的难度在刀工，其实只要掌握几个诀窍，人人都可学着做。大部分的水果

蔬果雕师刀下完整呈现的大熊猫家族的天伦之乐。
摄影：吴景腾
Using his knife, this fruit sculptor is able to realistically portray a family of pandas.
Photography: Wu Jingteng

101

或是蔬菜都可以利用，挑选时注意新鲜，水分饱满但不要过熟，刻起来不易软烂变形的。刀具要选择刀锋尖锐又锋利、刀刃较长者。由于蔬果容易变软，影响美观，做完后可以用保鲜膜包起来，或是喷水再以湿纸巾盖住。如果雕苹果，刻完后要用盐水泡一下防止氧化变色。

这里介绍几位台湾蔬果雕达人：

高世达老师，2016德国IKA奥林匹克世界厨艺竞赛双金牌得主，是一位努力不懈、勤奋学习的人。高老师自己当老师也常去旁听别的高手的课，往往学得比别人更认真，切配炒菜洗锅都抢着做，付钱来学习，完全没架子。他在德国拿下的双金牌，包括餐饮艺术类展示组金牌，和蔬果雕刻现场动态组的金牌，作品巧夺天工，得奖实至名归。

黄铭波老师，2012第十三届中国美食节食材造型艺术金奖、第二届海峡两岸美食文化论坛十大名厨、2013德国电视频道ProSieben来台专访甲壳雕塑、五星级饭店首席果雕师、高雄餐旅学院兼任讲师、1996年新加坡国际美食厨艺竞赛蔬果雕金、银牌、2002年中国烹饪世界大赛蔬果雕组特金奖、第一届教育百人团得奖者。他介绍的蔬果雕诀窍是一定要运用联想力，例如菠萝可联想成凤凰尾巴和龙鳞，长型冬瓜变身为长颈鹿脖子，绿色西瓜皮再挖几个圆洞就成为瓢虫，还可用小玉西瓜做成释迦牟尼佛身体，莲子做成头顶与佛珠项链。

台糖长荣酒店的杨顺龙，凭自修苦练将寻常瓜果雕成奇花异兽，在国际美食展上拿奖拿到手软。他从高中毕业便到台北餐厅当学徒，头一次参赛就抱回个人静态组金牌。几年来征战各大美食展，前后拿了20面金牌，其中包括2面香港HOFEX国际美食大展的"超金牌"，还有人开玩笑要他效法金曲歌后江蕙："不要再比了，让别人有机会拿奖。"

蟹壳制作的"将官首"，让人惊叹其巧夺天工。摄影：吴景腾
An ancient general made of crab shells.
Photography: Wu Jingteng

Vegetable and Fruit Sculptures

The island of Taiwan abounds in fruit. Alongside country roads, one can often spot saplings sprouting up from the earth, bearing fruit. Every year, when the trees that line the streets of rural villages come into season, a proliferation of ripe fruit extends as far as the eye can see.

In a popular art form, fruit and vegetables are cleverly sculpted and arranged into creative displays. Fruit sculptors have even begun to give classes in high schools, universities and colleges, as well as participating in international culinary arts competitions as a means of increasing the prestige of local fruit.

In Taiwan's villages, it is a popular practice to hire chefs for a private banquet. Accompanied by their assistants, the chefs drive in a truck carrying their kitchen appliances, as well as tables and chairs, directly to their client's home. Very often, they will choose to show off their culinary skills in a tent outdoors, near where grain is dried, or under a covered passageway. Villagers can also acquire a permit to set up an enormous tent in the street, allowing guests to enjoy a meal in the resplendent countryside. At these venues, guests can appreciate up-close the diverse artistry of the chefs, including fruit and vegetable sculptures.

The chef takes a sweet potato — or a carrot, radish, taro, cucumber — gives it a few artful slashes on both sides with his knife, and adds little embellishments cut from chili peppers and melon skins. In an instant, the vegetable is

蔬果雕师将中国童话"拔萝卜"生动地雕刻出来。摄影：吴景腾
A master fruit sculptor brings to life the Chinese fairytale *Ba Luobo* (*Pulling Out Radishes*). Photography: Wu Jingteng

transformed into a little white rabbit, a turtle, a cat or a dog. Paired with delicious dishes, these fruit sculptures render banquets all the more alluring to guests.

The grander the occasion, the bigger the sculptures. Using ordinary fruits and vegetables, master sculptors are able to craft scenes such as flying dragons and phoenixes; a flock of swans spreading their wings; a ferocious tiger baring its teeth; or a bouquet of peonies in bloom. With their dexterous hands, they are able to assemble these sculptures in a matter of moments, leaving spectators dumbfounded.

Many fruit sculptors begin by learning how to carve Chinese historical figures or myths — for instance, the General Guan Yu wielding a great sword (from *The Romance of the Three Kingdoms*); the folk deity Nezha, riding on the "wind-and-fire wheels"; the Eight Immortals crossing the sea; the Cowherd and the Weaver Girl; the legend of Madame White Snake... These are all stories that Chinese people have been grown up hearing, and therefore find particularly relatable.

The difficulty of vegetable and fruit sculptures lies in the knifework, although anyone can learn to make basic sculptures by mastering a few simple techniques. When selecting the fruit, one must pay particular attention to its freshness. It must be juicy, but not too ripe, so as to ensure that it doesn't spoil or change shape after it is cut. The preferred cutting implement is a knife with a long, sharp blade. Once the sculpture is complete, one can keep it fresh using cling wrap, or by spraying it with water and covering it in damp tissue. If the sculpture is made of apples, it may be soaked in salt water as a means of preventing oxidization.

According to Huang Mingbo, the chief fruit sculptor of a five-star hotel, the trick to making fruit and vegetable sculptures is to use one's imagination. For instance, a pineapple can remind us of the tail of a phoenix and the scales of a dragon; a long wax gourd may transform into the neck of a giraffe; and, by carving a few round holes into the green skin of a watermelon, one can create a ladybug. One could even use a yellow-fleshed melon known in Taiwan as a "little jade watermelon" to make a statue of Buddha.

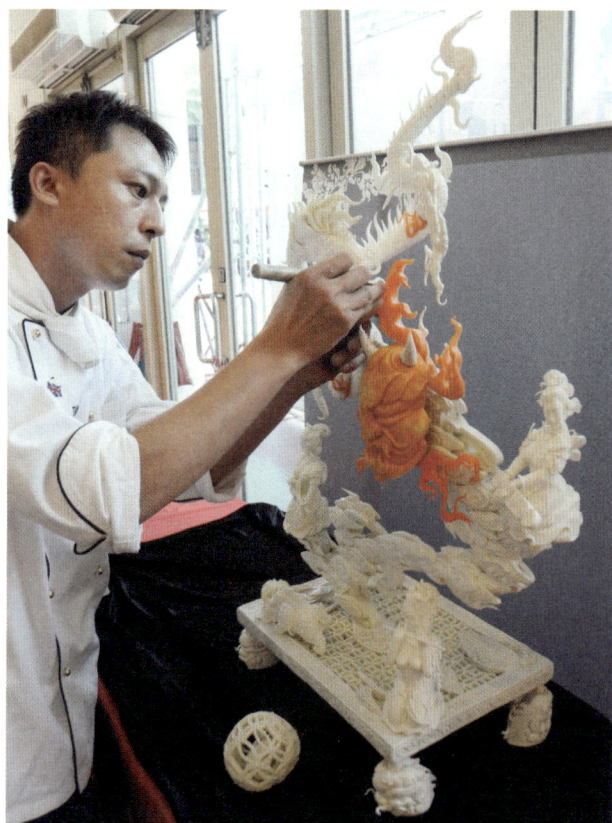

各种蔬果巧妙雕刻出中国传统神话故事。
摄影：吴景腾

Various vegetables and fruits are ingeniously carved into Chinese myths and legends.
Photography: Wu Jingteng

民俗篇
Folk Customs

过新年

台湾民众的过年民俗礼仪几乎完全传承自中华传统文化,虽然人人都在埋怨年味越来越淡,却也有许多期待,至少可以放个长长的年假。

什么是年味呢?说不出,却有几个观察指标,因此年味其实是可以营造出来的。

例如,家里可有年糕、发糕这一味?

家里可有贴春联?不是门口贴一张某某首长某某机关署名相赠的印刷春联,而是根据不同张贴位置一张张手写,并依古制逐一张贴在正确位置的春联。

大年初二嫁出去的女儿要回娘家,这是多么古老的传统,当爸当妈的一大早认真准备,巴巴望着路口,女儿可有带着女婿、外孙和外孙女回来?

然后,过完年,收心喽!

过年之后最大的收心操便是开市,各行各业从这一刻开始恢复常态,又要认真打拼啦。开市,可有认真选定一个良辰吉时,认真准备一份牲礼,规规矩矩祭拜祈求,请求老天爷赐给来年平安顺心、财源广进?

从这几个指标来检视,其实台湾还是有年味的,只差家主人没有头戴瓜皮帽、身穿长袍马褂而已。

年味真的可以营造,与其埋怨年味淡薄,何不反躬自省,你为这个

民俗篇 Folk Customs

社会增添了多少年味呢？倘若发动一条小街，拜托小街人家过年时家家户户都要在门口贴春联，在几乎已快要找不到春联的今日台湾，一定会被记者发现，会被传播媒体热烈报道，喻为最有年味的地方，这不就引出我们期待的氛围来了？

自己的年自己过，我们总不能期待老外来帮我们创造过年的气氛吧！

年糕和发糕

一切求简的今天，过年什么都可以省略，年糕和发糕却省不了。这两道传统年节必备美食，缺了它们几乎就不像过年了。

过年从农历十二月二十四日开始，这一天是家中的灶神升天的日子，灶神要回到天庭向玉皇大帝禀报一年来驻在这一家的所见所闻，人们为了希望灶神多说好事少提坏事，总得准备一些好料诚心相送，这时奉上香甜可口的年糕发糕让灶神爷甜甜嘴最

年糕是过年必备的应景食品，商家以传统竹制蒸笼炊蒸年糕，场面壮观。摄影：吴景腾

Nian gao is an indispensable dish on Chinese New Year. Local businesses produce *nian gao* in the traditional fashion, using steamers made of bamboo. Photography: Wu Jingteng

是适宜,所以送灶之日,就得实时蒸好这两道过年好滋味了。

年糕以糯米蒸出来,称作甜粿,在台湾有俗话说吃年糕"吃甜甜,好过年",就寓有"年年高""步步高升"的含义。

发糕一样以米为材料,只是在糯米与在来米的混合比例上稍做调整。年糕以米浆置于方形或圆形蒸笼中隔水蒸成一整块,祭拜或食用时再分切,发糕则加入酵母粉,倒在碗或盆之类容器,同样隔水蒸熟,酵母的作用使得蒸成的粿呈膨松并且裂开状,这样的现象象征着"发"的好运,裂纹越大,家庭主妇的嘴巴往往也笑得越大。

年糕的口感黏而稠,甜而不腻,常以切片油煎为传统吃法,有些还卷上咸菜等佐料以增加口味的变化,也有人喜欢原味而单纯将之蒸软了食用。冷掉的年糕变得坚硬密实,方便多保存几天。但因台湾气候往往潮湿高温,还是得三天两天便将之重蒸一遍以免发霉。

相对于年糕,发糕因发酵膨胀,口感膨松,油煎又是另一番滋味。下锅油煎时油放多些,半煎半炸,发糕香甜中带着酥脆,更是好吃。

年糕和发糕之外,这里过年有时还多几道米食,例如红龟糕(印成乌龟并着上红色的米食,内馅分甜咸两大类)、芋糕(糯米中掺入芋头制作)、菜头糕(糯米中加入萝卜,萝卜被称为菜头,与彩头同音,象征好彩头)、菜包(糯米包着肉丝、萝卜丝、虾米而捏成龟壳状)……,种类越是繁多,越能突显家庭主妇的好手艺。只惜现代社会家中多半已无大灶,炊蒸不易,家庭主妇多半前往卖场买块年糕回家应应景,闻不到蒸年糕的香味了。

年糕已有2000多年历史,相传源自于春秋战国时期。吴王阖闾命伍子胥筑城,建成后吴王大喜,称为"阖闾大城",大宴群臣。但独有伍子胥闷闷不乐,认为吴王骄奢而不知防备越王勾践和范蠡,国家危矣。

伍子胥令手下以糯米制作大量年糕,埋于城墙之下,并密嘱随从:死后如国家遭难,民饥无食,可往相门(苏州6个主要城门之一)城下掘地三尺得食。

伍子胥后来遭诬陷身亡,吴国被越军歼灭,都城断粮,饿殍遍野。随从想起伍子胥生前嘱咐,便带领百姓前往相门拆城掘地,这才发现原来相门下的城砖不是泥土做的,而是用糯米磨成粉做成的年糕,城里的百姓因此得以年糕充饥获救。此后苏州人民为了纪念伍子胥,春节家家吃年糕,而流传至今,这是祭灶传说之外的另一个年糕典故。

民俗篇 Folk Customs

过年吃发糕象征发财、高升，发糕外形发得越大、裂痕越深，即代表新的一年运势越好。摄影：吴景腾
Fa gao (literally "rising cakes") symbolize rising to prosperity as well as earning promotions. The higher the pudding rises, and the wider it splits, the luckier the client will be in the year to come. Photography: Wu Jingteng

写春联

写春联似乎也是越来越难被坚持的春节习俗了。地方要人为了讨好民众，过年前总会大量印制"现代版"春联，上面写一句吉祥话，签上自己姓名，免费发送给大家，于是贴春联变得有如穿制服般刻板而缺变化。幸好还有一些人家或是公私机关行号，仍会请来书法家规规矩矩写标准春联贴上大门，为呆板的春联新文化添上几分古意。

在台湾过年贴春联贴了多久啦？当中原文化传抵台湾，春联文学也随之移入，应已有三四百年了。

春联是一种文学吗？毫无疑问，乃文学之一种呈现方式。

标准的春联本身便是以一副对联作为主结构，必须对仗工整，且还必须依着张贴者的身份、行业、期望等条件书写，标准的"客制化"作业。只是客制化之余也有套装联，甚至有春联题库，毕竟三百六十行再多也就那么多种，年复一年书写，古来累积好联已多，无人主张著作权，就老实不客气来个"天下好联一大抄"了。

贴春联过年的习俗起自何时呢？考据上五代十国时期已开始发展，明清两代尤为兴盛，至今已传承一千多年。

相传上古时代有两个英勇的兄弟，一个叫神荼，一个叫郁垒，住在东海度朔山，两人常在大桃树下击退许多恐怖野鬼。秦汉时期人民常悬挂两块桃木大板，书写"神荼"和"郁垒"的名号，用以避邪驱鬼，这是春联的前身，即是"桃符"由来。

五代后蜀国君孟昶突发奇想，认为桃符太单调，于是提笔写了两行字"新年纳余庆，佳节号长春"贴在门前，众人叫好又叫座，最早的春联于焉出现。明朝时期因崇尚红色而用红纸取代桃木板，加上明太祖朱元璋大力提倡，新年期间贴春联的风气大兴，传续至今。

朱元璋有多喜爱春联呢？说他不但亲书春联赐给文武百官，有一次微服出巡，遇到一位阉猪人，竟还御笔书就"双手劈开生死路，一刀割断是非根"赏赐，一时成为举国佳话。

类似的春联故事多得不胜枚举。

春联故事多，春联笑话也不少，贴春联可不能乱贴的。据说有人把六畜兴旺这个

台湾农家彩绘墙壁、贴上新的春联迎接新的一年。摄影：吴景腾

A family of local farmers paint their walls and hang up new *chun lian* to usher in the new year. Photography: Wu Jingteng

民俗篇 Folk Customs

在新的一年，小朋友们聚集写春联，祈求新年新愿望。摄影：吴景腾
In the new year, children gather together and write *chun lian* that express their wishes for the new year. Photography: Wu Jingteng

贴在猪舍的联贴上了卧室的门，在厕所前贴了黄金万两，这绝对是贴错位置了，而最常犯的错误还是上下联错置，如果记住一个原则就不会犯错。切记直幅之大小边（即左右边）的判断可由其最下方一个字的平、上、去、入声韵来判断，上声（第三声）、去声（第四声）、入声（短促声）者，贴于右边（大边），平声（第一声、第二声）者，则贴左边（小边），例如：

"天增岁月人增寿"（右边）（大边）

"春满乾坤福满堂"（左边）（小边）

若两幅之最后一个字皆为汉语的第一声或第二声，则需用台湾闽南语发音来判断，短促而重者，视为入声，贴于右边。声音较轻者，视为平声，贴于左边。例如：

"门迎春夏秋冬福"（右边）（大边）

"户纳东西南北财"（左边）（小边）

民众通常会在除夕前一天子夜酬神、敬拜天公，春联也会在拜拜之前贴好，一直到自然脱落为止。有些人家贴得牢，年头到年尾都留在墙上，来年贴新，重重叠叠也是一道风景。

大年初二回娘家

在许多有趣有味的过年习俗中，最不合时宜者可能是初二女儿回娘家这一项了。为什么回娘家非得在大年初二这一天？为什么必得当天去来，且还得早早离开不得久留？女人家从年尾忙到年头，忙得昏天暗地，还得准备带着夫婿孩子赶路赶车回娘家，这是多么折腾人！所有的人都得在同一天赶着办这同一件事，弄得交通打结，塞车塞得苦不堪言也就罢了，妈妈健在者妈妈自己也要回娘家，年轻的第二代姑娘侍候老妈妈回娘家那自己还要不要回娘家？要等待到何时自己才能和别人一样欢天喜地大年初二回去看爹娘？女人们往往提起初二回娘家就有满肚子怨。

有一首老歌回娘家，唱得多么浪漫优雅，幸福感浓得都要溢出来了，对许许多多女人而言，这首歌教她们听了更是哀怨伤感。

可就是没几个人胆敢勇于挑战这个根深蒂固的老规矩，过年连大庙都可以不去朝拜了，娘家却仍是不敢不乖乖回一趟。

根据习俗，嫁出去的女儿要在初二回娘家，为什么"回娘家"必须是初二，而不能是初一呢？推测乃是老祖宗"重男轻女"的观念作祟，认为凡是出嫁的女儿都已经是不折不扣的"外人"，除夕初一拜祖宗，已逝的祖宗在除夕或初一回家看到这个"外人"，就会不愿进家门来了，这还真是让人听不进耳的说法。然而除此之外，竟再也翻不到第二个典故了。

出嫁的女儿被当外人也就罢了，初二回娘家还有许多禁忌不能触犯。第一是绝对不许在初一回娘家，理由是女儿如果在初一就回娘家，没有在夫家围炉，代表婚后不幸，才会迫不及待跑回娘家求助；更让人难受的是"嫁出去的女儿，泼出去的水"，如果女儿在初一回娘家，会让娘家变穷或把娘家吃穷。

其次是回娘家必须准备伴手礼或红包，红包内的金额必须是"双数"（传统的观念认为只有发生不吉利的事情才会包单数），否则娘家就会变得不幸，或是穷一整年。

回娘家还必须早去早回，但目前社会形态改变，女儿回了娘家住下来一天两天也不以为忤啦，算是进步了一小步。

再一个怪规矩是如果无法回娘家必须寄回旧衣代替，台湾习俗认为女儿出嫁后，如果连续3年都没有回娘家，就是背叛祖先，之后便永远不得再回家，因此有此一说是如果女儿无法在大年初二回娘家，就要寄回穿过的旧衣代替，象征已回来啦。

民俗篇 Folk Customs

许多人憎恶过年的繁文缛节，尤以回娘家这一套最是爱不了，因而近年来台湾民众时兴过年时利用年假出国旅游小玩一趟，避过亲友往返酬酢之苦，避过塞车挤车回娘家的烦恼，这使得旅行业者和航空公司大发利市，春节不但公路上塞车，连空中也"塞机"，机场里外更是处处挤了个水泄不通，这是台湾的新年景！

挑个良辰吉日好开市

台湾民众的过年口诀：初一早、初二早、初三困到饱，初四接神，初五隔开，意思是初一要早早起床拜天公、拜祖先，到大庙小庙烧香祈福。初二要起个大早准备回娘家或是准备迎接女儿回来娘家，初三大致没什么事，可以安安稳稳睡晚一点，初四迎接财神爷，初五隔开的意思是这个日子将年节假日和正常工作日一切为二，从此人人各就各位，上学或上班，不得再偷懒。

新春台北股市开盘，证券公司请来财神及招财童子跳加官，希望股市长红。摄影：吴景腾
When the Taipei Stock Market reopens in the new year, securities companies pay their respect to the Lord of Wealth and the Child of Wealth. Photography: Wu Jingteng

初五因而变成一个关键角色。

但是，民间却也有更讲究的说法，初五固然是传统开工开市日，还得依照当年历书推算，有时偏偏就要把开市日提前或延后个一天两天。民俗学者的说法是口诀中所称的开市、开工，跟一般民间正式的开市开工并不一样，年初五的开市是指"神职兵将"的开市、开工，而民间的开市开工，要另外找农（黄）历上的良日吉时来办。

民间传说，过年前的十二月廿四日人民将"神职兵将"等众神送回天庭，让他们也放年假，直到年初四才将他们接回凡间，这才是黄历上开市的意义。年初四接了神明，初五是众神明上班的第一天，新年的太岁也新上任，民间自然要准备一些供品迎接致敬。同时也要贴张开店大吉或开市大吉、开工大吉、开车大吉的红纸，向众神明求个吉利。

讲究的规矩是开市时得祭拜土地公、五路财神，在土地公的神龛前祭拜，如果自家没有供奉土地公，便在公司或店门口祭拜。祭拜时以三牲、水果、糕饼、三杯清茶、三杯酒为供品，点蜡烛，献茶酒，焚香祈祷，烧三色金（寿金、刈金、福金）和元宝船，礼毕时还要将酒洒在纸灰上。

仪式上的开工开市完成后，实质上依着历书排定的开工开市也有另一番程序，得准备花生粩或土豆粩（传统敬神点心）、麻糬，领着店员或工厂员工在店门口或工厂大门前祭拜，拜完放一串长长的鞭炮作为结束。

近代人讲求一切从简，虽然古训"新例不设，旧例不除"（意思是尊重传统而不任意改变传统），在通晓旧俗而喜欢指指点点的长辈人物逐渐老去之后，年轻一代继起接棒，常有将两个开工开市合而为一的。毕竟此事由一家之主、一厂之主说了算，轮不到旁人说三道四。

民 俗 篇 Folk Customs

Chinese New Year

       The traditions for ringing in the new year in Taiwan are virtually all derived from traditional Han Chinese culture. Although many people lament that the "atmosphere of the Spring Festival" is dying out, they continue to look forward to Chinese New Year — if only because they can take a long holiday. Just what is the atmosphere of the Spring Festival? Truth be told, such an atmosphere can be easily created.

       For instance, families can start by making a *nian gao* ("year cake") and hanging *chun lian* ("spring couplets") — not mass-produced *chun lian*, but unique works of calligraphy hung in the correct places around the home. On the second day of the lunar new year, married daughters are to visit their mothers in keeping with an ancient tradition. Parents begin preparing for this day early in the morning, periodically peering out at the street as they eagerly await the arrival of their daughter — accompanied, they hope, by their son-in-law and their grandchildren.

       Once the new year has passed, businesses all return to their regular schedules in an event known as *kai shi* ("opening the market"). If they are to ensure harmony and prosperity in the new year, managers must choose an auspicious time to reopen their businesses, as well as preparing offerings and performing rituals in strict adherence to ancient customs.

       If these customs are anything to go by, then Taiwan's New Year atmosphere is still very much alive — the only thing that has really changed is

过年前的台北市迪化街总是人山人海！摄影：吴景腾
On Chinese New Year's Eve, Dihua St (a historic street in Taipei) is a dense sea of people. Photography: Wu Jingteng

that the heads of households no long wear the traditional *guapi mao* ("melon-skin hats") and *magua* ("horse-jackets") of the Qing Dynasty.

With a little effort, one can easily create an atmospheric New Year's celebration. Sometimes, creating the desired atmosphere is as easy as asking one's neighbors to hang *chun lian* in their doorways; if you live in a tight-knit community, you can imagine that this proliferation of banners creates quite a scene.

New year's pudding: *nian gao* and *fa gao*

The traditional rice puddings, *nian gao* and *fa gao*, are indispensable to any Chinese New Year's celebration.

Local people begin to celebrate the Chinese New Year beginning on the 24th day of the 12th lunar month. This day marks the Kitchen God ascent to heaven, where he informs the Jade Emperor of each family's behavior throughout the year. As a means of encouraging the Kitchen God to mention only positive things to the Jade Emperor, households must lay out some delicious offerings to accompany him on his way back to heaven. The sugary and fragrant rice puddings, *nian gao* and *fa gao*, are a sure-fire way to satisfy the Kitchen God's sweet tooth.

Nian gao ("year cake") is made by pouring glutinous rice paste into a rectangular or round steamer and cooking it into a solid pudding that may then be cut into slices — either to eat or to use as offerings. In order to make *fa gao* ("rising cake"), yeast is added to a paste made from a combination of glutinous rice and long-grain rice. This mixture is then poured into a receptacle and steamed until solid. The yeast causes it to expand and split open — a symbol for rising to prosperity. The wider the split in the pudding, the wider the smiles of the heads of the family.

Nian gao have a thick and sticky texture; they are sweet without being too rich. They are traditionally cut into slices and fried in oil. Some people like to add ingredients such as salted vegetables for extra flavor, while some prefer to simply steam them and enjoy their original flavor. *Nian gao* become compact and stiff when cooled, and can be stored for a few days. However, due to Taiwan's humid and hot climate, *nian gao* should be re-steamed every few days to prevent them from growing mold.

Due to the addition of yeast, *fa gao* have a fluffier texture. Frying *fa gao* in oil brings

民众购买年糕准备过年。吃年糕还有取"年高"长寿之意。摄影：吴景腾
Locals buy *nian gao* in preparation for Chinese New Year. *Nian gao* is a homonym for "higher year", and therefore symbolizes longevity.
Photography: Wu Jingteng

out their sweet spices while making them crisp.

In addition to *nian gao* and *fa gao*, local people sometimes prepare other rice dishes to ring in the new year. These dishes include "red turtle puddings" (rice puddings made in a turtle shell mold with red food coloring), taro pudding (where taro has been added to the sticky rice paste), white radish pudding (where white radish has been added, as its name in Minnan dialect is a homophone of "sign of good fortune"), as well as sticky rice buns — also shaped to look like turtle shells, and filled with ingredients such as shredded meat, strips of radish, and diced shrimp. Some households will make a variety of different puddings to show off their culinary skills. Unfortunately, most modern households don't have the wood-fired stoves that are traditionally used to make these puddings, and very often buy them at the store. This means that one can no longer smell the sweet fragrance of *nian gao* wafting through the kitchen as they are cooked in bamboo steamers.

Nian gao are said to originate from the Spring and Autumn period, over two thousand years ago. King Helü of Wu ordered Wu Zixu, a politician and military strategist, to lead the construction of a protective wall around the Wu kingdom's capital city (modern-day Suzhou). Wu Zixu instructed his subordinates to make a large number of sticky rice puddings and bury them underneath the city wall. He gave a secret directive to his entourage: if, after his death, a disaster occurred and the people had nothing to eat, they could find these rations buried three feet under the wall. Wu Zixu was later framed and forced to commit suicide. Not long after his death, the Kingdom of Wu was conquered by King Goujian of Yue's army, leaving the capital without food. Zixu's former entourage recalled his directive and led the civilians to the city wall. As they demolished the wall and began to dig underneath, they discovered that the bricks at the bottom were not made of clay, but of *nian gao*. Thanks to Wu Zixu's efforts, the city's inhabitants were saved from famine. Since then, the people of Suzhou have eaten *nian gao* in commemoration of Wu Zixu.

Chun lian

These days, during Chinese New Year's celebrations, it is rare to see traditional *chun lian* ("spring couplets"). Most people buy printed *chun lian* in stores, which by comparison seem homogenous and bland. Fortunately, some people still invite calligraphers to write spring couplets with a brush on red paper. When hung in doorways, these handwritten *chun lian* immediately add a sense of history to the occasion.

The custom of hanging *chun lian* was introduced to Taiwan from the mainland three to four hundred years ago. *Chun lian* is first and foremost a type of literature. The two lines of the couplet have to feature a certain degree of parallelism and conform to certain stylistic conventions and at the same time reflect the identity, profession and hopes of the person posting it. Companies that print *chun lian* do not write their own original texts; instead, they choose from an immense database of couplets for all types of professions. Given how long the tradition has endured, it is not surprising that people have run out of ideas for new couplets.

When did the tradition of hanging up *chun lian* begin? According to an ancient legend, there were once two heroic brothers named Shen Tu and Yu Lei who lived on Dushuo Mountain in the East China Sea, and who spent their days fending off demons underneath a giant peach tree. During the Qin and Han dynasties, people would often write "Shen Tu" and "Yu Lei" on separate planks of peach tree wood and hang them up in their doorways as a means of scaring off demons. It is from this practice that the tradition of *chun lian* emerged — hence *chun lian* were formerly referred to as *tao fu*, or "peachwood charms".

Deciding that the *tao fu* were too bland, the last emperor of Later Shu during the Five Dynasties and Ten Kingdoms period, Emperor Meng Chang, chose to hang up an original poem instead. "May the good deeds of our ancestors bring us good tidings in the new year/ And may this magnificent celebration call in an everlasting spring." These couplets were greatly appreciated by the people, thus beginning the tradition of *chun lian* as they are known today.

小朋友参加迎春写春联活动。摄影：吴景腾
Children help writing *chun lian*. Photography: Wu Jingteng

During the Ming Dynasty, people began to write *chun lian* on red paper rather than peachwood, as red was believed to signify joy. This change in material, combined with Emperor Hongwu of Ming's fervent advocation, led to a surge in the popularity of hanging *chun lian* on Chinese New Year, and the practice has remained popular to this day. Just how fond was Emperor Hongwu of *chun lian*? He not only personally wrote *chun lian* to give to court officials; once, during an imperial excursion, he penned a *chun lian* for a man who castrated pigs for a living: "With both hands, he splits open the path between life and death/ Severing the root of reason in one fell swoop." This couplet was appreciated across the nation for its wittiness.

When picking *chun lian*, one must carefully consider their content and placement: while a well-placed *chun lian* can be flattering, a misplaced one can have embarrassing implications. I have heard of people hanging up couplets intended for pigsties and barns above their bedroom doors, or hanging wishes of prosperity outside their bathrooms — both definite *faux-pas*. The most commonly made error when hanging *chun lian* is placing them back-to-front. One can determine the correct order of the couplet based on the pronunciation of the final syllable of each line.

Chun lian are generally hung up at midnight on Chinese New Year's Eve, as people pay their respects to spirits and deities. Afterwards, they remain in place until they naturally fall down. Some families stick the *chun lian* down so firmly that it still hasn't fallen down by the next year. In this case, a new *chun lian* is simply stuck over the top. These overlapping *chun lian* create quite a sight.

Married daughters visiting their mothers on the second day of the lunar new year

Out of many interesting New Year's customs, the most outdated is perhaps the one where married daughters must return on the second day of the lunar new year, rather than the first. Women are already frantically busy on lunar New Year's; but on top of everything else, they must also prepare a journey back to their mother's home, accompanied by their husband and children! What's more, this journey has to occur on a specific date, which inevitably leads to bumper-to-bumper traffic. The custom becomes particularly complicated in families with great-grandmothers, in that, just as their married daughters and grandchildren come to visit, grandmothers themselves must visit their own mothers.

民俗篇 Folk Customs

台湾大年初二是女儿女婿回娘家日。娘家常以丰盛的外烩（办桌）迎接他们回来团聚。摄影：吴景腾

On the second day of the lunar new year, married daughters must visit their mothers, accompanied by their husband and children. The mother often welcomes them with a sumptuous feast. Photography: Wu Jingteng

However, few people dare challenge this deeply engrained tradition. At New Year's, one can be forgiven for not paying one's respects at a temple — but no married daughter would dare skip the annual visit to her mother.

Why is it that married daughters must return on the second, and not on the first? I presume that it is due to our ancestors' patriarchal notions, according to which women were thought to have left their original families and become "outsiders" upon getting married. If this "outsider" is present when the ancestral spirits return home on New Year's Eve or New Year's Day, they will refuse to come inside. These days, such a mentality is unthinkable.

Furthermore, when returning to their mothers' homes, married daughters must also bring a gift or a red envelope containing an even sum of money (as, in traditional culture, odd numbers are inherently inauspicious); otherwise, the mother's home may be struck by poverty or misfortune for the year to come.

It was traditionally important to arrive and leave early when visiting one's mother, but society has changed; these days, it's no longer thought of as strange for a daughter to spend a whole day or two at her mother's — a sign, perhaps, of some progress.

Another strange custom is that, if a married daughter has no means of returning home to see her mother, she must send her some of her old clothes instead. In tradition, it is believed that, if a married daughter doesn't return to see her mother for three consecutive years, she has betrayed her ancestors and may never return home again. If the daughter sends old clothes, however, she is considered to have returned.

Many people loathe the endless succession of rituals associated with New Year's — in particular, the custom of making married daughters return to see their mothers on a particular day. As a result, a number of local people have chosen in recent years to go on vacation during New Year's, thus saving their friends and family the hassle of coming to visit them. This trend marks a new era in the celebration of Chinese New Year in Taiwan.

"Opening the market" on an auspicious day

Local people have a saying at New Year's: "On the first and second day, you must get up early; on the third day, you can sleep in until lunch; on the fourth, you welcome the gods; and on the fifth, you must put the celebration behind you." The meaning of this saying is that, on New Year's Day, one must get up early to pay respects to spirits and ancestors by burning incense and praying at the temple. On the second day of the new year, one also has to get up early for the journey back to the maternal grandmother's home. On the third day, there is little to do, so one can sleep in a little; while on the fourth day, people welcome the gods of prosperity into their homes. Finally, the fifth day marks the end of the celebration, when people must return to their academic or professional duties. From this day onward, no one is allowed to laze about — it's back to work as usual!

The fifth day has, in this way, come to play a unique role in New Year celebrations. According to popular belief, on the 24th day of the 12th lunar month, people send deified soldiers and generals off to spend the holiday in heaven, and then welcome them back into the mortal world on the fourth day of the new year. On the fifth day, as both mortals and deities return to work on Earth, the people naturally must prepare certain offerings to welcome the deities back. Meanwhile, they also post red posters that ask the deities for blessings as they re-open their stores and return to their own jobs.

As people "open the market", they must pay respects to the Lord of the Land and the Lord of Wealth. If one hasn't laid out offerings for the Lord of the Land in one's home, one may pay one's respects to him at the entrance to one's store or company. These offerings include the three sacrificial domestic meats (beef, lamb and pork), fruit, pudding and flat cakes, as well as tea and wine. In addition to praying, families also light candles and incense, as well as burning paper money in three colors, and origami boats. At the end of the ritual, wine is poured onto the ashes of the burnt paper.

Managers must also prepare either a pudding made of potato or peanuts, or mochi, and lead all their employees in paying respects at the entrance to their businesses. A long firecracker is set off to mark the end of the ritual.

新春开工前老板、员工一起拜拜、放鞭炮，希望在新的一年都能够财运亨通、财源滚滚。
摄影：吴景腾

Before returning to work in the new year, bosses and their employees pay their respects to deities and set off fireworks so as to ensure prosperity throughout the year to come.
Photography: Wu Jingteng

欢喜元宵节

在台湾，农历正月十五元宵节是一个重大的节日，通常人们总得过了元宵才算是正式过完年，要收心，好好回到工作岗位了。

元宵在台湾算是过年之后一个熔吃喝玩乐于一炉的节庆。汤圆、元宵是少不了的应景美食。除了提灯笼、赏花灯、逛灯会，更有所谓北天灯、南蜂炮，外加台东的炸寒单等重头戏分头举行，民众绝不可能同一天连赶这三大元宵盛会，唯有分年分次赶场。而这三场活动，台湾民众是不能错过的，越来越多的老外也不辞路远专程前来，往往被场景吓得目瞪口呆，连呼疯狂。

元宵活动随时代而变化，例如从前时兴提灯，小朋友或是从街头小店买灯笼，或是自己动手做灯笼，元宵之夜人手一只提得好不快活，但提灯游戏已逐渐被小朋友抛弃了，现在取而代之的是大型灯会，全岛各地都有灯会，还有由全岛轮办的大型重点灯会，各县市热烈争取主办权，争到最后在"输人不输阵"（即使可以输给一个人，也绝不容许输给一群人）的心情下无不铆上全劲去办，也因而近年来逛灯会取代了提灯笼，成为元宵不可少的活动。而灯会往往持续半个月到一个月，连春节也包括进展期之中，把过年的氛围更加提升了许多。

元宵提灯、吃元宵、放天灯，乃至被炸的寒单爷，无一不传承自祖国大陆，台湾民众因恋旧而代代传承。为什么蜂炮非在台南？天灯非在平溪？寒单爷非在台东？这是有趣的话题。最简单的理由无非是：移到别的地方去，就不像了。

元宵提灯笼

提灯笼是以前广受欢迎无分城乡的元宵活动，虽然逐渐不再时兴，却仍是这一代中老年人最怀念的儿时记忆。

由于"灯"谐音"丁"，提灯、闹灯也就是被当作人丁兴旺的佳兆，也就是说，灯节愈热闹，人丁就愈昌旺。庙宇每逢元宵佳节会举办盛大的闹灯会活动——"钻灯脚"，就是一个祈求添丁的民俗。

元宵提灯的缘由众说纷纭，台湾民间传说是两千年前，佛教传入我国，当第一次月圆的时候，人们隐隐约约可以见到月光下有一群天神在翩翩起舞，有一年浮云遮蔽了天空，人们突然不见天神踪迹，十分恐慌，纷纷点起火把，照亮天空，找寻天神。

小朋友自己绘制灯笼庆祝元宵节。摄影：吴景腾

Children make their own lanterns on Lantern Festival. Photography: Wu Jingteng

自此以后，虽然看不见天神，却仍年年点燃火把，逐渐演变成一种风俗了。

另一个说法是古时候凶禽猛兽很多，常常攻击人。有一次一只神鸟因为迷路降落人间，却被不知情的民众给猎杀了。天帝知道后十分震怒，下令天兵于正月十五下凡放火，烧尽大地上的人民。由于天帝之女心地善良，不忍看百姓受难，便偷偷地下凡把这消息告诉人们，并且要人们在正月十四、十五、十六日这三天家家户户张灯结彩、燃放爆竹烟火。正月十五日这天，天帝看到凡间一片火红，以为是烧出来的大火，就不再命令天兵放火了。

还有传说唐代私塾从农历过年后要到元宵节才开课，开学时学生皆要从家中带一盏灯笼，请老师点燃，再提着灯四处走，象征日后前途一片光明，之后逐渐普及成为元宵节提灯笼的习俗。

依照道教的观点，上元节是沿袭道教的旧习而来的。唐代以后有所谓的"三元日"，即上元日（农历元月十五天官赐福日）、中元日（七月十五地官赦罪日）、下元日（十月十五水官解厄日）。人们为了祈求天官赐福，纷纷在上元日悬挂花灯，敬拜三官。

历史上元宵夜挂灯笼的风俗源起于西汉，盛行于唐朝。历代帝王为了夸示天下太平，大力倡导人们垂挂灯笼。明太祖朱元璋在位期间，命百姓自正月八日夜晚即开始挂灯笼。永乐帝朱棣命百姓彻夜挂灯笼，鸣乐到天明。并让王妃、宫女们在正月十五日出宫看花灯，营造举国同欢的气氛。

其实元宵节也是东亚地区人们共有的节庆，同样过农历正月十五，只是庆祝方式不同而已。日本、朝鲜半岛都有烧塔的习俗，中国山西省的旺火、陕西省榆林地区神木县的火塔塔，到了朝鲜半岛称为烧月屋，日本则称为左义长。无非都是元宵种种与火有关的民俗活动。至于灯笼这类的用物，早在古埃及时就已经出现，在东亚地区，灯笼除了用来照明之外，还是一种工艺品，传统的灯笼是利用竹条或木条作为主结构，外面再粘上一层纸，而光源则是灯笼中央插的蜡烛。

种种与火有关的习俗，其实隐含大自然四时运作之意义。古人在春耕之前将田里的杂草烧掉以除虫害。除了驱除害虫、猛兽外，传统上人们认为灯火具有驱魔降福、祈许光明的象征意义，所以燃灯又具有避邪平安的意义。也有把一盏灯挂在竹竿上插放于田间，用火势颜色预测来年水旱情况，称为照田蚕。火色偏红预示有可能会干旱，火色偏白则表示可能有水灾。后来用于照田蚕的彩灯愈益讲究和精致，是后世挂灯笼闹花灯的起源之一。由于点蜡烛较危险，现代灯笼早已改用小型灯泡或是LED作为光源，传统纸灯笼更早已被塑料制品取代。

民俗篇 Folk Customs

元宵汤圆皆美味

元宵节民间有吃元宵或是汤圆的传统习俗。

汤圆和元宵有什么差别呢？外观上两者大小不同，内容则以是否包馅来区分。大致上台湾传统本来是吃汤圆的，用糯米制成和龙眼一般大小的圆子，沸水汤煮，调上甜咸口味，称为"汤圆"，而后才从大陆传入北方人吃的体型较大、里面包馅的元宵。

元宵又依包馅的方法分为两大类。大致上内馅分甜咸两味：甜的内包豆沙、芝麻、花生、枣泥、桂花、白果等等；咸的内包猪肉、火腿、虾仁、咖喱等。一种做法是以馅沾粉，用筛子一层层滚出来，这便是所谓的摇元宵；另一种不是用摇的，而是像做汤圆那样先捏出一颗颗糯米小球，在小球中央包馅，再用手将之搓圆成型，因此称作包元宵。台湾民众非常幸福，各种口味、各种做法皆能随心所欲，吃得痛快。

"元宵"作为食品，由来已久。早在南朝时代，当时人们吃的是拌和肉和动物油熬煮的豆粥或米粥，元宵尚未成型。唐代人改吃一种蚕状的面食和烤饼，一直到宋朝才出现用糯米粉加果糖做成的元宵，不过当时不叫元宵，而是称为"浮圆子"或是"汤圆"。后来，由于这种食品专在元宵节吃，因此才被称为"元宵"。

关于提灯和吃元宵，来源另有一说。汉高祖死后由吕后掌权，等到吕氏之乱被平定，汉文帝即位，令定农历元月十五张灯结彩提灯上街庆元宵。到了武帝时代，又出

元宵节吃元宵或汤圆，小朋友也跟着学习搓汤圆。
On Lantern Festival, children also learn how to roll *tangyuan*.

元宵节一到，市场内的商家忙着摇出各种不同口味的元宵。
When Lantern Festival arrives, merchants at the market hurry to whip up different varieties of *yuanxiao*.

摄影：吴景腾
Photography: Wu Jingteng

现了与元宵和提灯有关的故事，说是精通天文地理的大臣东方朔，在御花园赏梅遇见一位叫作元宵的宫女，因思亲太甚正要跳井自杀，东方朔将之制止，并费了好一番努力，不但让武帝亲自下令上元之夜人人提灯上街，连宫女也要出宫与民同欢，并同享元宵美食，这不但圆了那位元宵姑娘会见亲人之愿，竟也开启了元宵之夜提灯民俗，还让元宵成为过节最应景之物。

时至今日，无论元宵或汤圆早已不限元宵之夜才能享用了，每一家超市或便利商店从年头直到年尾随时都能买到包着各种口味馅料的"大汤圆"，这也混淆了元宵和汤圆的界定，让年轻人几乎傻傻分不清两者的区别了。与此同时，没有包馅料的"正港"汤圆，则逐渐在百姓生活中扮演起不同的角色：一是在结婚的好日子中端上桌，款待嘉宾，同贺团团圆圆；二是在敬神祭祖的庄严仪式中敬奉甜汤圆，祈求神明和祖先福佑；三是在街道食坊中，作为一道足以供人饱足的美味料理。

天灯，矛盾中的梦幻

2008 年 DISCOVERY 将之评选为"世界第二代节庆嘉年华"，2013 年 FODOR'S 将之列为"全球 14 大此生必游的经典节庆"，接下来 CNN 也将之推荐为"世界上 52 件最值得参与的年度新鲜事"，而去年《国家地理》杂志也将之列为"全球十大冬季最佳旅游首选"。究竟是什么活动，赢得三千宠爱于一身呢？

那就是在台湾北部一个默默无闻的小村承袭了一两百年之久的元宵节活动——平溪天灯。

平溪位于新北市十分寮地区，当地位处基隆河上游。据十分寮地区父老前辈的口述表示，前清年间十分寮曾闹过土匪，由于地处山区，土匪一来村民都向山中逃跑，等到土匪走后，留守在村中的人就在夜间施放天灯作为信号，告知山上避难的村民可以下山回家了，这是村民间彼此报平安的古老方法。有一回土匪闹得凶，走后放天灯的日子正逢农历正月十五元宵节，从此以后每年的元宵村民便以放天灯庆祝，且向邻村的村民互报平安。也因此天灯又被称为"祈福灯"或"平安灯"。久而久之，这个习俗竟不知不觉绵延至今长达一两百年之久。

天灯另称孔明灯，相传为三国时期诸葛亮的发明，也被公认为热气球的始祖。三

民俗篇 Folk Customs

放天灯是台湾北部在元宵节时最热门的活动。摄影：吴景腾
Releasing sky lanterns is one of Northern Taiwan's most popular events. Photography: Wu Jingteng

国时诸葛亮被司马懿困于平阳，为求脱困制作天灯，系上求救信息，算准风向放上天空，最终得以脱险。后人为纪念诸葛亮，放孔明灯逐渐变成节庆仪式。孔明灯也成了祈求收获与功名之物。

  天灯由铁丝或竹子制作底部框架，粘上纸，形成底小顶大而中空之物，底架中间放置油纸，点燃之后由于里面的热空气较外面冷空气轻而冉冉上升。台湾的天灯外部以宣纸糊成，宣纸上往往写满许多祝福祈福之语，施放者看着自己的愿望飘向高空，内心充满喜悦。

  向夜空中放天灯本身充满了浓浓幸福感，可是随着环保意识抬头，放天灯衍生的问题也逐渐暴露出来。放天灯曾引发过数起火灾，未烧完的天灯掉落地面可能造成交通事故。天灯由竹框、铁丝、宣纸、金纸与煤油等材料制作，其中有一大半不会在天空中烧完而直接掉落地面，过去几年的统计发现每年的天灯节过后都会有大量的垃圾掉落在平原、村落、山林，需要人千辛万苦地清理出来，造成的环境污染真是不可言喻。此外，天灯还会破坏生态，几年前曾发现一只猫头鹰在飞行过程中遇到天灯缠勒，最后跟着天灯残骸一起坠落。英国防止虐待动物协会发布了照片，天灯顿时成为国际关

台湾天灯师傅以铁丝或竹子当底部,框架糊以宣纸做成灯身。摄影:吴景腾

An artisan makes sky lanterns using metal wire or bamboo slats for the base frame, with high-quality paper from Xuancheng (Anhui) overtop. Photography: Wu Jingteng

切的生态杀手。此外,有些天灯掉落河川,也被质疑煤油污染河水。为了解决这些问题,现已明定施放天灯的管理办法,机场四周、储油槽、弹药库、可燃性气体储槽及基地内、高速公路、化学工厂、住宅区、商业区及港区都已被禁止施放天灯。

疯蜂炮,不怕蜇

盐水蜂炮号称世界三大民俗庆典之一,每年都吸引海内外众多游客前来台南盐水小镇,享受万炮齐发的震撼,以及疯狂声光刺激之快感。蜂炮,这个名称取得贴切,谁能想象万蜂倾巢而出的惊人场面?唯有亲自体验了。

台南市的盐水区是个靠海小乡镇,居民多为讨海为生的渔民,相传蜂炮的活动起源于清光绪十一年,当年小镇突发瘟疫,居民向当地武庙供奉的"关圣帝君"祈求平安,并依占卜结果在元宵节晚上请出庙中的周仓爷做开路,关圣帝君殿后,一路燃放炮竹,通宵达旦绕镇，果真瘟疫渐平。此后元宵彻夜放炮竹游行成为地方传统。初期全镇各村都在元宵节前后放三天炮竹，后来改为各村轮流放。

由鞭炮变身为蜂炮是一个重大的改变，这是鞭炮放到后来，有人改用刺激度更高的冲天炮取代鞭炮，年年改良，越放越是震撼。基本的做法是以木条钉制一个个大型支架，名叫炮台或炮城，再将冲天炮连接整齐排满在木架上，有些木架高达两丈，摆置上万支冲天炮，外观贴纸彩绘，组成各种形状，争奇斗妍，蓄势待发。

蜂炮游行路线依例由武庙广场开始，绕过整个盐水区。原本绕境定在元宵节当日，为期一天，后因绕境时间过长而划分为几个区域，安排两天行程，因此目前的盐水蜂炮活动时间为农历正月十四日上午八时开始，至隔日元宵节午夜过后方全部结束。在绕境活动当中，当神轿抵达信众门前的一刻，民众才从大厅里推出自家的炮台，拉开红布，撕下炮台上"恭祝关圣帝君圣诞千秋弟子某某某叩谢"等字样的红纸，在神明面前与金纸共同焚烧祝祷，之后便正式引燃炮城，让绕境神明点收蜂炮。这便是一场场刹那间涌现的万箭齐发，场景令人难忘。

盐水蜂炮火光四射，瀑布般的烟火美得令人惊叹。摄影：杨锦煌
The beehive fireworks of Yanshui set off in all directions as a cascade of sparks stuns festival-goers with its beauty. Photography: Yang Jinhuang

2017年盐水蜂炮主炮城名"金鸡报喜庆元宵",由3座主题炮城串起40米鞭炮长城;武庙庙埕广场则放置一座移动式陆上水舞,配合全城超过200座的炮城,整个盐水充满了硝烟弹雨,处处都能感受到刺激的蜂炮体验。而如果要追求更大的刺激,可以尾随在神轿后面,一时之间群"蜂"四面八方而来,教人躲无可躲,逃无可逃,个中滋味足以教人毕生都忘不了。

看蜂炮难免被冲天炮命中,称作被蜇了,而那种疼痛恰如被蜂蜇了一针。事实上,每一位游客都早有准备,穿戴防护周全无比,一套标准配备是里里外外多层衣物,全身包得密不透风,手、脚、脸更是重点防护部位,着装之后几乎难辨彼此,个个都成了航天员。但尽管防护周到,终还是难免百密一疏,每年蜂炮炸过,总有小伤大伤,救护车的警笛声在如雷蜂炮声中共鸣,这也为观赏蜂炮添加了更多一分的刺激。

寒单爷不怕炮炸

没有人不怕鞭炮炸的,无论大人小孩,放鞭炮总是点了引信就跑得远远的,但台东的寒单爷却朝鞭炮里冲,在四面八方投过来的鞭炮中挥挥手中一把榕树枝叶,继续昂然前行。恐怖的是这位寒单爷由真人装扮,而且上身完全赤裸!

相传,寒单爷是掌管钱财的财神爷,出巡就表示为地方带来吉利,由于传说寒单爷生性怕冷,天寒时即心痛,因此,当寒单爷出巡时,信众皆以火炮为财神爷驱寒取暖,这是台湾元宵夜特有,又称"走佛"的"迎玄坛爷"游街习俗。

扮演寒单爷的人,头上扎上头巾,穿着红色短裤,赤裸着上身,站在轿子上接受民众用鞭炮轰击,据说轰得越是猛烈,这位肉身寒单本人会除去越多的噩运,也会赢来越大的好运。对信众而言,更猛烈的轰炸则代表更伟大的愿力,是对寒单爷致上最大的敬意。有了这项说法,使得台东元宵炸寒单爷几乎陷入疯狂状态!

寒单爷的称呼繁多,有:邯郸爷、玄坛元帅、玄坛爷、赵玄坛、银主公王、赵元帅、赵府元帅、武财神等。有关寒单爷的传说,起源得很早,最早是记载于晋干宝所撰《搜神记》之卷五,赵公明(寒单爷)被视为上帝派往人间督鬼取人命的三将军之一;而梁朝陶弘景在《真诰》中,则称他为"上下冢中直气五方神",在最初时期,赵公明原被归类为冥神、瘟神。隋唐时期,隋文帝封赵公明为"感应将军"。在元、明时期,

民俗篇 Folk Customs

赵公明逐渐演变为道教的护法天神，在台湾被称为"玄坛爷"或"玄坛元帅"。

另有一说是，道教的财神神像是商朝武官"赵公明"，因为很会理财而富有，人民奉他为武财神。原为峨眉山罗浮洞的炼气士，黑面浓须、顶盔披甲，一手执神鞭、一手执元宝，胯下黑虎，随身携带百发百中的定海珠与缚龙绳法宝，武艺高强，在"封神演义"中为商朝勇将，后来死于姜子牙七箭封喉的法术，死后被封为"金龙如意正一龙虎玄坛真君"，功成圆满，成为职司禳灾保安、买卖生财之神，御位中路财神，又受玉皇大帝玉旨敕封为三十六天官之首，职司掌管天下四方财库，迎祥纳福，统管凡间之祸福，被奉为"武财神"，道家称之"赵元帅"。

每年炮炸寒单爷都在南京路广场上，并在主要道路游行，现场总是鞭炮声响彻云霄，炮硝烟雾弥漫。许多人就像去盐水看蜂炮，也是全副武装，只希望能一睹寒单爷精彩的表演。寒单爷的神像牢牢绑在竹椅子上，椅脚另外绑上两根长竹竿，由四名身材彪形矫健的轿夫抬着上身赤裸的肉身所扮寒单爷上阵，只见他手持一枝榕树枝叶，用以保护眼睛免受炮击，所经之处无不炮声如雷！当然扮寒单爷的并非一人，大致上总有三五位随行，轮流上阵。

炮炸寒单爷的习俗在台东传承已半世纪，游行所经之处，家家户户事先备好供桌和香炉祭品恭迎，有些还祭出赏金大战肉身寒单，总把准备的大量鞭炮轰光才过瘾。五十多年来，扮演者似乎也多能平安挨过炮袭。

元宵节台东特有的炮炸寒单爷行，相传越炸越旺。
摄影：杨锦煌

Taitung's unique Lantern Festival celebration, "Bombing Lord Handan", grows in popularity and scale each year.
Photography: Yang Jinhuang

Lantern Festival

In Taiwan, the Lantern Festival, which takes place on the 15th day of the first lunar month (coinciding with the first full moon), is a momentous occasion. Most people feel that Chinese New Year isn't truly over until they've celebrated the Lantern Festival. After the Lantern Festival, they are ready to get back into a serious frame of mind and focus on their jobs.

The Lantern Festival celebrations comprise food, alcohol and entertainment. *Tangyuan* and *yuanxiao* are two indispensable delicacies. In addition to the time-honored traditions of carrying lanterns, admiring local lantern spectacles and attending lantern gatherings, Taiwan also boasts three large-scale festivals: the Sky Lanterns of Pingxi, the Beehive Fireworks of Tainan, and the "Bombing Master Handan" event of Taitung. As it is impossible to see all of these festivals in the one day, people generally alternate between them from one year to the next. Unfazed by the distance, an increasing number of tourists from all around the globe have specifically come to enjoy these jaw-dropping spectacles.

In the past, on the Lantern Festival, people would make their own lanterns and carry them through the streets. Nowadays, celebrations take place in the form of large-scale lantern gatherings. Gatherings are held all over the island and usually take place over the course of two weeks to one month.

All of all these traditions — carrying lanterns, eating *yuanxiao*, and the three great festivals — were all derived from the mainland. Local people have carried them on, from one generation to another, out of nostalgia.

民 俗 篇 Folk Customs

庆祝元宵节的灯笼与远处 101 大楼相互辉映，让台北的夜晚越发美丽。摄影：吴景腾
In celebration of the Lantern Festival, a sea of lanterns glitter in harmony with the Taipei 101 skyscraper in the distance.
Photography: Wu Jingteng

Lanterns

Nothing makes local senior citizens more nostalgic than the memory of carrying lanterns in their youth. As the word for lantern, *deng*, sounds somewhat like *ding* — a word used to refer to male descendants — lanterns have come to be seen as a sign that one will have a large family. Lanterns were traditionally made by building a frame out of bamboo or wooden slats, applying an outer layer of paper, and placing a wax candle in the center.

According to legend, on the first full moon of the lunar year after Buddhism was introduced to China, two thousand years ago, people could faintly see a group of divine spirits dancing in the moonlight. One year, it was too overcast to make out the full moon — or the divine spirits. Afraid that the spirits had abandoned them, people lit torches to illuminate the sky and find them. Since then, although the spirits are nowhere to be found, people continue to light torches on the first full moon, year after year, in order to illuminate the night sky.

Another theory is that, in ancient times, people were often attacked by ferocious beasts. Once, a divine bird lost its way and fell down to the mortal world. Fearing that the bird would attack them, the people slayed it. When the celestial ruler learned of its death, he ordered his soldiers to descend to earth on the first full moon and light a fire that would destroy humanity. His daughter, a kind-hearted woman, couldn't bear to see innocent people suffer. She surreptitiously visited the moral world and informed the people of her father's plans, as well as urging every household to light lanterns, hang colored streamers, and set off firecrackers on the 14th, 15th and 16th days of the first lunar month. On the 15th — the day of the first full moon — the celestial ruler saw that the mortal world was seemingly ablaze and called off his soldiers.

According to another version, private schools in the Tang Dynasty would begin the academic year on the 15th. On this day, students would take a lantern to school, ask their teacher to light it for them, and then carry the lit lantern through the streets as a symbol of their bright future prospects. This tradition would gradually be adopted by the rest of the population, marking the beginning of the Lantern Festival as we know it today.

The first full moon of the year is commonly celebrated throughout East Asia, but the way it is celebrated varies from one place to another. Japan, Korea, as well as Shanxi and

民俗篇 Folk Customs

灯笼工艺师制作传统灯笼。摄影：吴景腾
A talented artisan makes traditional lanterns.
Photography: Wu Jingteng

Shaanxi in China, share the custom of burning makeshift pagodas. The fire-related customs on the 15th day of the lunar year are likely related to the beginning of the spring plowing season in ancient times. Before plowing the fields, one first had to burn off weeds to kill any pests. Traditionally, people have also believed that fire served to dispel demons, summon good fortune, and instill harmony.

Tangyuan and Yuanxiao

On the Lantern Festival, Chinese people eat *tangyuan* and *yuanxiao*. The two are virtually the same in terms of their outer appearance — however, *tangyuan* are not stuffed with a filling, while *yuanxiao* are.

Eating *tangyuan* is a tradition. Dough made of sticky rice is rolled into a ball, boiled, and then dipped in sweet or salty flavoring.

台湾民众在元宵节当天都要吃元宵或汤圆，象征着团圆吉利。摄影：吴景腾

In Taiwan, everyone eats *yuanxiao* or *tangyuan* on the Lantern Festival, as these delicacies represent unity and good fortune. Photography: Wu Jingteng

Yuanxiao originate from northern China, are relatively large, and have fillings. *Yuanxiao* fillings are either sweet or savory. Sweet fillings include bean paste, sesame, peanuts, jujube paste, osmanthus flowers, and ginko; while savory fillings include pork, ham, shrimp and curry. *Yuanxiao* are made by applying sticky rice starch to the filling in layers.

Nowadays, eating *yuanxiao* and *tangyuan* is no longer limited to the night of the Lantern Festival. At any time of the year, at virtually any supermarket or convenience store, one can buy this delicacy with a variety of different fillings. Although the addition of a filling means that they are technically *yuanxiao*, they are sold as *da tangyuan* ("large *tangyuan*"). Authentic *tangyuan* — i.e. those that are not stuffed — have gradually come to play an important role in the lives of ordinary people. First of all, they are eaten at traditional weddings, as their round, dense form symbolizes cohesiveness and unity between the newly married couple. Secondly, they are presented as offerings when praying to local deities and ancestors for their wisdom and good fortune.

Pingxi Sky Lanterns

In a village named Pingxi in Northern Taiwan, locals have celebrated the first full moon in the same way for the last 100-200 years: by lighting sky lanterns. In 2008, Discovery Channel named the Pingxi Sky Lantern Festival the "World's Second Largest Nighttime Carnival", while in 2013, Fodor's listed it as one of the "14 Festivals to Attend Before You Die".

Pingxi is located in Shifenliao, New Taipei. According to local elders, at the beginning of the Qing Dynasty, the village was overrun by bandits. Every time the bandits sieged the town, most of the villagers would flee for the hills. When the bandits finally left, the villagers who had stayed behind would release sky lanterns into the night sky as a signal to the others that they could return from the mountains. One such occasion just so happened on the night of the first full moon. Since then, the villagers of Pingxi have celebrated the first full moon by releasing sky lanterns. Because they represent a return to safety, sky lanterns are also called "blessing lanterns" or "peace lanterns".

Another name for them is "Kongming lanterns" — Kongming being the courtesy name of Zhuge Liang, a strategist from the Three Kingdoms period, who is thought to be their inventor. It is generally acknowledged that these lanterns are the predecessor of hot-air balloons. When Zhuge Liang was trapped in Pingyang by Sima Yi, a rival strategist, he successfully sought salvation by tying messages to makeshift sky lanterns. Later generations would gradually develop the custom of releasing sky lanterns in Zhuge Liang's memory. In this way, releasing sky lanterns has also become a means of praying for success.

The base frame of sky lanterns is composed of metal wire or bamboo slats; then, paper is glued on top. They have a small base that gradually widens into a broad top. The burning flame heats the air in the lantern, making it lighter than the surrounding air and causing the lantern to rise up through the air. People often write wishes and blessings all over these lanterns. As they watch their wishes soar up through the sky, their hearts fill with joy.

In recent years, the environmental issues caused by sky lanterns have become increasingly apparent. Sky lanterns have, in the past, been the culprit of many fires and traffic accidents. Every year, the sky lantern festival causes a large amount of litter to be strewn throughout the village, as well as its neighboring fields and mountain forests. Volunteers

游客在天灯四面写下满满祝福,祈求心想事成。摄影:吴景腾

Tourists write their wishes and blessings on all sides of the sky lanterns. Photography: Wu Jingteng

and workers must then go to great lengths to retrieve this litter, which seriously pollutes the environment. Furthermore, sky lanterns have disastrous consequences on local ecologies — a few years ago, it was reported that an owl fell to its death when it collided with and became entangled in a sky lantern. Some of these sky lanterns fall into waterways and pollute them with kerosene. As a solution to these environmental issues, the local government has begun to regulate the practice, with many regions banning the use of sky lanterns.

Beehive Fireworks of Yanshui

The Beehive Fireworks Festival is said to be one of the top three largest folk celebrations. Every year, the festival and its exhilarating pyrotechnics attract droves of tourists to the small town of Yanshui in Tainan.

Yanshui is a coastal town on the outskirts of Tainan City whose inhabitants are predominantly fishermen. According to legend, this event originated during the 11th year of Emperor Guangxu of Qing's reign. That year, when the town was struck by the pestilence, the locals prayed for salvation at the Emperor Guan Temple. Then, based on what they had learned during a divination session, they returned to the temple on the evening of the first full moon to call upon the services of the local deities, Lord Zhou Cang and Emperor Guan. After releasing these spirits from the temple, the locals led a night-long procession around the village, setting off fireworks as they went. In the next few days, the epidemic would gradually clear up. Since then, Yanshui villagers have held a three day-long event around the Lantern Festival, where they led a procession around the town and let off firecrackers.

Eventually, these firecrackers would be replaced by rockets so as to make the festival even more exhilarating. Before they are lit, these rockets are stacked on tall wooden frames. Some of these frames are up to 6.4 m high, carry thousands of rockets at once, and are decorated with colorful patterns.

The procession leaves from the Emperor Guan Temple at eight in the morning on the eve of the Lantern Festival, and winds around the entire town of Yanshui until the afternoon the next day. As the sacred palanquin at the head of the procession passes different houses, families push their own towers outside, pull the protective red fabric off, burn red paper covered in words of gratitude, and light the fireworks. In an instant, a swarm of rockets fly through the air, creating a thrilling scene.

In 2017, the three main towers, which had a combined length of 40 m, were given the thematic name Jinji Baoxi ("Golden Pheasants, Heralds of Joy"). Throughout the entire

蜂炮庆典中所有参与绕境的信众都要全副武装,参与蜂炮洗礼。信众深信经过这场震撼考验,可以将厄运解除。
摄影:杨锦煌

During the beehive fireworks celebration, tourists must wear armor from head to toe that will protect them as they are showered in sparks. Photography: Yang Jinhuang

town, there were over 200 towers, which showered the streets in sparks and created a dense haze. If standing on the sidelines is not exciting enough, one can truly experience the thrill of a lifetime by following behind the sacred palanquin as fireworks rain down from all sides.

Being hit by the sparks is called being "stung", as the pain is supposedly similar to being stung by a bee. That said, every participant is sufficiently prepared. With every inch of their body covered in fire-retardant clothing or protective gear, they can hardly tell each other apart. Be that as it may, there are still a number of people who are injured to varying degrees of severity each year. The wailing sirens of ambulances fuse with the crackling of fireworks, further adding to the excitement.

Bombing Lord Handan

No one is unafraid of being stung by firecrackers, but in Taitung, people willingly rush into the crossfire, their upper bodies completely exposed, in imitation of Lord Handan.

Lord Handan is said to be hypersensitive to the cold and would suffer heart pain on cold days. Therefore, during the procession, his followers throw fireworks at him to dispel the

民 俗 篇 Folk Customs

cold. This Lantern Festival tradition is unique to Taiwan.

Whoever plays the role of Lord Handan stands on the palanquin wearing nothing but a towel on the head and red shorts as the crowd launches firecrackers at him. This crowd acts without mercy, as they believe that, the more intense the barrage of firecrackers, the more effective it will be in dispelling Lord Handan's personal misfortunes. With this in mind, festival-goers feel free to let themselves go really crazy!

According to legend, Lord Handan's real name was Zhao Gongming. Initially he was thought of as a spirit of pestilence and the underworld. During the Yuan and Ming dynasties, Zhao Gongming gradually came to be seen as a Daoist deity of wealth and defender of justice. This deity is perhaps named Zhao Gongming because his image resembles that of the military advisor from the Shang Dynasty.

Every year, the Lord Handan procession weaves through the main arteries of Taitung, filling the streets with thunderous crackling and wafting blue smoke. People come to watch in droves, dressed from head to toe in protective clothing. The palanquin on which the actor playing Lord Handan stands is carried through the streets by four strapping volunteers. This actor protects his eyes from sparks with a branch from the banyan tree as firecrackers erupt from all around. Throughout the festival, Lord Handan is played in turns by three to five different actors.

Wherever the procession goes, it is welcomed by local households, both with offerings and copious amounts of fireworks. In over fifty years, most of the actors seem to have emerged unscathed.

也有传说寒单爷原是一个鱼肉乡民的流氓，受到点化后为表示忏悔之意，赤裸上身游街，让民众泄愤以减轻罪孽，最后演变成财神爷。摄影：杨锦煌

There is also another story that Lord Handan was a bandit who oppressed local villagers. After his enlightenment, as a means of repenting, he stripped down to his waist and paraded in the streets, calling on the people to vent their anger by attacking him. Afterwards, he would come to be recognized as a deity of wealth. Photography: Yang Jinhuang

三月疯妈祖

妈祖绕境

台湾民众常说"三月疯妈祖",妈祖是自福建湄洲传来台湾的神明,也是在台湾拥有最多信众和最多庙宇的慈悲之神,但怎么一到了三月就会发疯呢?

三月疯妈祖的意思是:一到了农历三月,因为妈祖娘娘的诞辰日就要到了,整个台湾岛从北到南,凡是有妈祖庙的城镇无不是盛大庆祝,有些庆祝仪式真可说是如火如荼,人们如醉如痴地陷入几近疯狂的状态。所以说是人疯了,而不是妈祖娘娘疯了。

台湾民众为妈祖做寿是怎么个疯法呢?全台湾规模最大,号称全球三大宗教盛会之一的大甲妈祖绕境进香活动,全程8天7夜,参加者成千上万,笔者30年前曾随队徒步采访,只见鞭炮根本来不及一串串放,而是集中成几个大大的鞭炮堆,引爆时有如炸弹开炸,一朵大大的蕈状云从地面冉冉升起。在一些狭窄的小街,进香队伍走进去,两旁人家争相掷放鞭炮,轰得见不到对街人家。走过之处,整条街铺满了鞭炮屑,惊人场景,30年都忘不了。

妈祖原为航海之神,来到台湾成了民众最重要的心灵依靠和守护神。

民 俗 篇 Folk Customs

因而每年元宵之后到三月廿三妈祖生日之间，各地妈祖的绕境进香活动便成为台湾民间最重要的宗教活动。

"绕境"是神明每年定期巡视其辖区的活动，"进香"则是信徒迎请神明前往外地庙宇进行拜会、联谊，借此巩固双方情谊。绕境进香队伍来自社会各阶层，无论男女老少、贫富贵贱，沿途相互扶持、关怀。参与的动机大多是为还愿、赎罪或祈求平安，借由长途跋涉以答谢神恩、祈福消灾或洗涤罪业。

台湾的妈祖进香绕境，全岛组团众多，各自择日举行。其中徒步进香绕境距离最远的首推苗栗通霄拱天宫白沙屯妈祖庙，规模最为庞大的是大甲镇澜宫绕境团，北港朝天宫妈祖绕境被认为是最震撼人心的，而基隆的妈祖参与海祭神轿直冲入海，桃园的隆德宫由年轻少女组成抬轿护轿队伍，澎湖妈祖出海进行海上巡境也颇具特色。

拱天宫白沙屯妈祖往北港朝天宫进香，进香时间约八九天，往返路程将近400公里。白沙屯是一个偏僻的滨海小村落，每年拱天宫妈祖往北港进香成为小村落一年一度的大事，借进香活动凝聚村民的向心力，许多离乡背井的子弟都会回乡参与盛会。进香前，信徒向妈祖"掷筊"决定日期及相关仪式的时辰。除了全程徒步，行程皆依

为了跟随大甲妈祖绕境，不少信众虔诚地跟着绕境队伍徒步八天七夜。天天都从白天走到晚上。
A number of devout believers follow the procession for the entire duration of the eight-day tour of Taiwan.

据称从大甲妈祖的銮轿下钻过可以带来一整年的好运，每当銮轿停驻，到处可看到跪在地上大排长龙等着"钻轿脚"的信众。
According to legend, passing under Mazu's palanquin will ensure good luck for the entire year to come. Every time the palanquin stops, one can see a long line of followers kneeling, waiting to crawl underneath.

摄影：于志旭
Photography: Yu Zhixu

大甲妈祖的绕境活动，銮轿到达折返点嘉义县新港乡时，街头挤满了迎驾信众。摄影：于志旭
As the palanquin arrives in Chiayi County, the streets fill with followers who anxiously await the procession. Photography: Yu Zhixu

妈祖銮轿的"踩轿"而定，神轿经常突然穿越马路，走进田野小径、涉水过溪，时而无预警休憩于民宅、市场、学校、工厂等，妈祖銮轿成为全团人马的最高统帅，每当妈祖銮轿改变前进方向时，头旗必须秉持"只前进不后退"的原则，快速绕道再回到进香队伍的前哨。

大甲妈祖绕境进香起源于清代，当时每隔12年前往湄洲朝天阁进香，后来一度转向北港朝天宫"割火进香"。1988年起改到新港"绕境进香"，8天7夜的绕境进香，行程经台中、彰化、云林、嘉义等二十几个乡镇市。往返300多公里，参与人数众多、规模盛大。主要仪式有祈安、上轿、起驾、驻驾、祈福、祝寿、回驾及安座等八大典礼。进香期间，沿途信众除了摆设香案迎驾，义务供应餐饮，还要由执事人员提供货柜沐浴车全程随行，让信徒免费洗澡，甚至还提供免费让信徒将脏衣服宅配送到家的服务。

还有许多流传于民间可祈求平安、增加运势的习俗，例如以抢轿方式挽留妈祖、钻轿脚求平安、向妈祖求敬茶治病、向报马仔拿红丝线求姻缘、与三太子交换奶嘴祈求孩子好摇饲（平安长大）、触摸执士队的文昌笔求考运等。从这些现象可以发现，只要是与妈祖进香有关的器物,都会被赋予"神圣性",而每一年妈祖进香团所经之处,常常可见跪地迎接妈祖的信众在神轿出现的时候崩溃痛哭,无论有什么委屈,仿佛这一刹那都得以纾解。

北港朝天宫是台湾最具影响力、分灵最多的妈祖庙。清康熙三十三年(公元1694年),树璧和尚自湄洲屿朝天阁奉请妈祖来台,航途中遇暴风雨漂流至北港,树璧和尚认为此乃神意,遂将妈祖奉祀于笨港街,仿湄洲朝天阁取名"朝天宫"。起初仅以茅草建造,至1700年始建庙奉祀。

北港妈祖绕境除了活动场面浩大外,其"艺阁"及"炸轿"更具特色。艺阁是以真人扮演,乘坐花车之上,早年以人力抬阁,之后改成牛车或板车装阁,现则为声光俱有的大型花车装置。绕境时信徒会用大量的鞭炮轰炸神轿,希望事业"愈炸愈发",炸轿疯狂的程度几乎可与台东炸寒单爷及盐水蜂炮相比拟。彰化市妈祖庙有内妈祖与外妈祖之分,以彰化城内外作为区分,南瑶宫为外妈祖,天后宫则为内妈祖。南瑶宫往笨港进香曾是全台规模最盛大的进香活动,目前南瑶宫仍有庞大的信众组织,早年信徒约每四年一次前往笨港天后宫进香,但在嘉庆年间笨港天后宫被水患冲毁后,信徒改往新港奉天宫进香至今。

彰化地区有"大妈四爱吃鸡,二妈五爱冤家,三妈六爱潦溪"之谚语,冤家在台湾闽南语中是争执之意,潦溪则是涉溪。"南瑶宫妈祖潦溪",源自西螺大桥兴建之前,往笨港进香须渡过浊水溪,故称"爱潦溪"。白沙屯妈祖和南瑶宫妈祖都有妈祖显灵分开浊水溪之溪水,让进香客安全通过的传说。据说某一年进香团往北港进香,返回途中大雨造成溪水暴涨,当神轿行至河边,浊水溪忽然从中分为两半,让进香团顺利穿越,待进香队伍通过之后,才又恢复滚滚洪流,这是《圣经》摩西故事的妈祖版,"妈祖潦溪"也就成为南瑶宫绕境进香最让人津津乐道的妈祖传奇。

台澎地区年代最久的妈祖庙坐落在澎湖,号称开台澎湖天后宫,成立之确切年代已不可考,由其保存的"沈有容谕退红毛番韦麻郎等"古碑可推测,最迟于明万历年间妈祖庙便已存在了。澎湖天后宫的元宵节乞龟及妈祖海巡两大活动,是天后宫最具特色的盛会。澎湖四面环海,岛屿罗列,陆上绕境并不符合环境现实,1986年首度举办妈祖海上出巡,以盛大的船队安奉妈祖神像和妈祖令旗,并迎请众神参与一同搭船绕巡澎湖群岛各港口,然后再回到陆上绕境。这项庆典方式一举震动全台,成为全台湾最吸睛的妈祖寿诞活动。

道光年间台中地区稻作发生严重病虫害,农民深以为苦,迎请乐成宫"旱溪妈"

绕境赐福，神轿所到之处天降大雨，害虫消失无踪，当地十八庄民欣喜之余，传出一句民谚："旱溪妈祖荫外庄"，意思是不论是本庄或是外庄信徒，只要笃信妈祖，都能得到"旱溪妈"一视同仁的庇佑。

乾隆年间台中梧栖创建浩天宫妈祖庙，初期当地人烟稀少，不久之后外来移民快速迁入而日趋繁荣。妈祖庙遂成梧栖、沙鹿、龙井、大肚等乡镇的信仰中心。100多年前浩天宫信众组团前往北港朝天宫进香，此后相延至今，成为中部地区重要进香活动之一。

新社妈祖庙供奉的九庄妈也是起源自清代，原奉祀于土城庄（今月湖村），后来改由新社地区人口较集中的新社、山顶、畚箕湖、大南、水底寮、土城、马力埔、摆头店及鸟铳头等九庄依序轮流迎请祭祀，在炉主家中设坛祭拜，遂名"九庄妈"。由于九庄妈信仰无固定庙宇祭祀，轮庄方式反而增进新社乡各村庄之间民众的情感，也促进地方团结。每年轮值的村庄都必须全体总动员、家家户户参与，扛旗、抬轿、阵头均由村民自己担任，小区参与成为九庄妈绕境特色。

基隆港庆祝妈祖诞辰，由渔家壮汉扛着神轿，喧天鼓声中连人带轿逐一冲进海港，这种震撼场面也是紧扣人心，每年专程前往参与祭典，观看神轿冲海的民众，无不惊呼连连，誉为最刺激的庆贺方式。

祖庙妈祖巡游台湾

在台湾精彩万分的迎妈祖、疯妈祖活动中，最让信众难忘的一场应是1997年的祖庙金身渡海来台的千秋盛会了。妈祖的家乡福建省湄洲建有一座妈祖庙，被视为全世界妈祖信仰的最高圣堂，分住全球各地的信徒无不以能亲临祖庙为妈祖进香为一生最重大也最荣耀之事。而在两岸信徒一致期盼下，祖庙妈祖金身竟然史无前例地跨海来台，环游全台各大庙。那一年，台湾妈祖信徒得以沐浴祖庙妈祖驾临的慈晖之中，为世代传承的信仰见证了神圣的一刻。

祖庙金身起驾前湄洲地区连续风雨三天，3万居民像是迎接新年般兴奋准备，也深知这乃妈祖大喜之庆必然出现的天候现象。果真起驾吉时一到，瞬间天朗气晴，顺利成行。这一趟行程，除了祖庙正殿金身供奉的软身妈祖，另有一尊元代石雕妈

民 俗 篇 Folk Customs

祖，这尊石雕妈祖身高约30厘米，名列国家级重要文物，以往鲜少公开，被安奉于一座特制的强化玻璃神龛内，两尊妈祖并由台方主办单位投保1000万元人民币以策万一。陪侍大队簇拥着神轿经澳门转机，随即登上长荣公司747豪华客机直达桃园机场。

莅台行程共达102天，安排环绕全岛巡游。但台湾妈祖庙多达2000余座，经登记者700座，其中名列古迹者也有20余座，为了绕境行程能够充分满足热情民众之期待，主办单位真是伤透了脑筋，幸好最后也算功德圆满，顺利完成千载盛会。

湄洲祖庙妈祖搭乘长荣专机，从厦门飞往台湾进行102天的巡游。
The Mazu statues from Meizhou were transported by private jet from Xiamen to Taiwan, where they were carried on a 102-day tour all throughout Taiwan.

湄洲妈祖首次出游台湾。两岸媒体高度关注，纷纷随行采访。
The Mazu statues from the ancestral temple in Meizhou toured Taiwan for the first time. Various media outlets flocked in droves to cover its journey.

摄影：何叔娟
Photography: He Shujuan

Mazu March Mania

Mazu Pilgrimage

The culture of veneration surrounding Mazu originated in Fujian Province and was later introduced to Taiwan. Mazu was originally a goddess of the seas, but after she came to Taiwan she became the people's most important spiritual support and protector. Local people often speak of "Mazu March Mania". In the third month of the lunar year, around the time of Mazu's birthday, there is not a single town or city with Mazu temples that doesn't organize a grandiose ceremony in her honor. At certain festivals, the crowd's enthusiasm is palpable, with some spectators entering an almost manic state.

The largest religious festival in Taiwan and the third largest in the world, the Mazu Pilgrimage of Taiwan takes place over the course of eight days and seven nights, with hundreds of thousands of people taking part.

Thirty years ago, I once took part in this pilgrimage. The pace of the procession was so hectic that there wasn't even enough time to let off individual firecrackers — instead, people would gather them into great piles and let them off all at once. When they were lit, it was almost like bombs exploding, with great clouds of smoke billowing up from the ground. As processions weaved through some of the narrower streets in the city, families on both sides would compete to set off the most fireworks, filling the street with blue smoke and leaving a sea of confetti on the ground. In the thirty years

民 俗 篇 Folk Customs

since then, I still have not forgotten this stunning scene.

During this pilgrimage, referred to in Chinese as *raojing jinxiang* ("touring the realm and offering incense"), processions carry a statue of Mazu from one town to the other, visiting temples and bringing locals together. The processions are made up of people of different identities and backgrounds — whether they are young or old, rich or poor, they support and care for one another along the way. Most of the pilgrims take part to redeem vows, repent for past sins, or to pray for peace.

Different Mazu temples throughout Taiwan have their own processions and determine their own schedules for the pilgrimage. Some of them even go out to sea and tour the island by boat. When on land, however, processions complete their entire journey by foot. The palanquins that lead these processions must cross busy streets, weave through countryside roads, and traverse rivers. Along the way, they rest in private homes, markets, schools and factories. For many villages, the pilgrimage serves as a means of bringing their community together. Many people who have left their hometowns to pursue studies or a career elsewhere continue to come home during the third month for the great celebrations.

The Dajia Mazu Pilgrimage originated during the Qing Dynasty. Initially, pilgrims would make the journey from Zhenlan Temple, in Dajia, to the Chaotian Pavilion of

大甲妈祖绕境活动，大批信众随着队伍走过田间小路。摄影：于志旭
A procession weaves their way through the countryside. Photography: Yu Zhixu

the Ancestral Mazu Temple in Meizhou (Fujian Province) every 12 years. Later on, the destination of this pilgrimage was changed to Xingang (in Chiayi County, Taiwan). It takes place over the course of eight days and seven nights, passing through over 20 towns and villages. The journey from Dajia to Xingang and back is over 300 kilometers long. Countless people take part, both in the pilgrimage and in the large-scale celebrations that occur along the way. During the celebrations, in order to welcome the palanquin, followers in villages located along the pilgrimage route set up incense altars as well as providing food and beverages. Mobile shower units also follow the procession so that pilgrims may wash free of charge.

Among the people, there are a number of customs that serve to instill harmony or bring good fortune. These include holding the palanquin and praying for peace; serving tea to Mazu in the hope that she will cure your illness; holding red string in the hope that she will lead you to your future spouse; exchanging a pacifier with her in the hope that she will ensure a peaceful life for your child; and touching her brush in the hope that she will help you to pass an upcoming exam. From these customs, it is easy to see that all objects that are in some way related to Mazu have been attributed sacred significance. Wherever the Mazu procession leads, one can see fervent believers welcoming her on their knees. When the palanquin appears, it is not uncommon to see people breaking down and crying, as, in that very moment, they seemingly obtain salvation from whatever afflicts them.

Some palanquins are designed to look like large carnival floats. During the "tour of the realm", believers barrage the palanquin with countless firecrackers, as they believe that "the greater the explosion, the more prosperous one will be". The degree of mania is comparable to that of the "Bombing Lord Handan" event and the Yanshui Beehive Fireworks Festival.

Apparently, one year, a procession was held up by the surging tide of a brook. However, when the palanquin reached the shore, the brook abruptly forked into two streams, allowing the procession to cross unimpeded. After the procession had crossed, the brook closed up again — a Mazu take on the story of Moses, if you will. This legend also caused the Mazu temple nearest to the brook to become famous.

The oldest Mazu temple in the region of Taiwan and its surrounding islands is located on archipelago of Penghu and is estimated to have been built as early as the reign of Emperor Wanli of Ming (1573-1620). In 1986, the Penghu Islands began to organize a maritime version of the pilgrimage, where an immense fleet of ships carries a statue of Mazu on a tour around the islands, coaxing out other deities on their way. This event has gradually become the most eye-catching celebration of Mazu's birthday in the whole of Taiwan.

Meanwhile, on Mazu's birthday, one can witness a similarly stirring scene in the port of

"快快快！快来不及了！"一群彰化县庙宇的神祇，由执事人员用摩托载着，赶着要去迎接妈祖銮驾。摄影：于志旭
Local clergy members pack vehicles full of Mazu idols and hurry off to welcome the palanquin. Photography: Yu Zhixu

Keelung City: a team of fit fishermen carry Mazu's palanquin on their shoulders and charge into the water, accompanied by the thunderous rumble of drums.

Mazu leaves her ancestral temple to tour Taiwan

One of the most unforgettable celebrations of Mazu occurred in 1997, when the golden statue of Mazu located at her ancestral temple in Meizhou was sent across the Straits on a tour of Taiwan. Meizhou, in Fujian Province, is the birthplace of Mazu, and the temple there is considered to be the most sacred site in the world for Mazu's followers. Any devout follower of Mazu would consider personally offering incense to the golden statue at this ancestral temple to be the honor of a lifetime.

Therefore, the statue's unprecedented tour of major Mazu temples all throughout Taiwan was greatly anticipated by followers on both sides of the Straits. Prior to its departure, it had rained in Meizhou for three consecutive days. The people, however, knew that such a great celebration of Mazu would inevitably be preceded by inclement weather. As they expected, on the day of the statue's departure, the clouds suddenly parted, and the procession unfolded as planned. For this tour, the golden statue of Mazu from her ancestral temple was accompanied by a smaller stone statue in her image, dating from the Yuan Dynasty. The two Mazus were insured by the tour's main organizer for RMB10 million, and were escorted by plane to Taiwan via Macao.

Over the next 102 days, they toured throughout the entire island. There are as many as 2,000 temples consecrated to Mazu in Taiwan, 700 of which have been registered. The main organizers of this tour racked their brains in order to come up with a tour schedule that wouldn't leave any of these temples disappointed. Ultimately, the tour was a success.

湄洲妈巡游台湾各地妈祖庙，所到之处无不受到信徒热烈恭迎。摄影：何叔娟

The statues of Mazu from Meizhou were taken to temples in the goddess' honor all throughout the island, where they were welcomed passionately by her followers. Photography: He Shujuan

清明节习俗

清明节是华人世界传统三大节之一，是一个满怀感恩、慎终追远的日子。

清明节习俗由来已久，相传源自春秋时代（公元前770至476年），晋国发生内乱，公子重耳被迫流亡国外，有一天与随从在山区迷了路，好几天没有食物。贤臣介之推默默离开，从自己的腿上割下一块肉，煮成肉汤后，送给重耳充饥。流亡19年后，重耳返国就大位，成为春秋五霸之一的晋文公。

晋文公登基后论功行赏，加封随他流亡的大臣，介之推淡泊名利，还乡探母，错过了晋文公封赏。晋文公经他人提醒，内心感到羞愧，连忙赶到介之推老家绵山探访，介之推在山林中隐而不出。随员献了一个馊主意，认为介之推是个孝子，只要放火烧山，介之推为了母亲，一定会逃出来。晋文公果真下令放火烧山，大火延烧三天三夜，还是见不着介之推。等火熄灭后，才发现介之推和母亲在一棵柳树下被活活烧死了。

晋文公十分伤心，将介之推被烧死的那天定为寒食节，每年这一天禁止生火、全国上下一律吃生冷的食物，以追怀介之推的情操。

清明节要为祖坟扫墓，有些地方民俗还要荡秋千、拔河、登山踏青、在门上插柳树枝、吃润饼……各有各的寓意。

吃润饼

润饼不但是清明时节家家户户之所爱，在有些地方还成为专卖店的招牌商品，随时想吃便上门点一卷，配上一碗四神汤，真是太好吃啦！

2016 年，桃园市派了一支小团队，携带一道美食前往日本小豆岛，作为国际美食交流的秘密美味，让各国嘉宾大大惊喜，这就是润饼。

润饼，简单一张面粉皮摊开来，铺上任何你想吃的食材，卷起来就可以吃个痛快，简便、健康，而且食用时连碗筷刀叉等餐具都不必，直接动手就好，难怪叫人食指大动。

说来简单，其实是有窍门的。

一般人做不出润饼皮，大部分都得前往专卖店买现成的回家。润饼皮是用面粉加上适当比例的盐拌匀，打成一个糊糊的面团，然后备好烧热了的平板，面皮朝平板上一抹，很快受热熟成，轻巧一揭便是一张。熟练的师傅可以同时摆上好几块铁板，依序抹去，再回头一一挑起，看得人目不暇接。虽然动作迅速无比，往往等着买的人还是大排长龙，遇到热门日子，队伍往往排上好几条街。

润饼皮买回来，开始准备馅料，馅料包括烫熟切细的芹菜、切好的肉条或肉片、生菜、红萝卜……一道道摆满一桌。不能忘了的有两样：一是花生粉，一是白糖。摊开润饼皮，一道道菜肴自在添加平铺其上，撒一层花生粉和白糖，仔细卷好，一条肥嘟嘟的润饼便已成型。老饕可以连吃三卷，吃得万分饱足。

吃润饼令人想起介之推先生那凄美的故事。寒食，润饼果真是凉凉的饼皮卷着凉凉的馅料，冷冷地享用，这也成为公认的润饼来源典故。而在历史上则另有多种叙述，唐朝就有立春日吃春饼的习俗，杜甫诗："春日春盘细生菜"。《四时宝镜》也提到："立春日，食芦菔、春饼、生菜，号春盘"。春饼传至闽南，居然变成了清明节的应景食品润饼。

另外还有一说，据说清末太平天国运动，蔓延到闽南泉、漳一带，清明时节却逢兵荒马乱，人们无法从容准备祭品，干脆把所有食物切细一一卷进面皮里，携之上坟祭扫，演变成了清明吃润饼。

还有一个说法，金门出身的一位叫蔡复一的人，曾官拜兵部右侍郎，总督贵州、云南、湖广军务，兼贵州巡抚，因为整日忙于公务而无暇顾及三餐，夫人看在眼里，疼在心里，就想出个法子，将鱼、虾、猪肉、香菇、冬笋、胡萝卜、豆干等食材，切

民俗篇 Folk Customs

民众排队买润饼。润饼皮内只要包上豆芽菜、红萝卜丝、笋丝及肉丝、豆干丝、蛋皮等，再撒上花生粉及糖粉，卷成圆筒状即可食用，相当可口。摄影：吴景腾

Locals line up to buy popiah. All one has to do to enjoy this delicacy is spread the desired ingredients on a popiah wafer, sprinkle some peanut flour and powdered sugar, and wrap it up into a tube. Photography: Wu Jingteng

丝后炒香成为馅料，再用面粉制成薄饼皮包卷馅料，每到用餐时，直接捧着这款"薄饼卷"喂丈夫吃。蔡复一一面批阅公文，一面一口接一口把卷饼吃了，这样饭也吃了，也不影响办公，真是方便又可口。这也是润饼来源的另一种出处。比起介之推丧母的悲情、兵荒马乱过清明的无奈，这故事相对甜蜜多了。

祭祖

清明节祭祖，台湾最主要的两大族群有相当不一样的祭祖方式。

台湾河洛人习惯于孩子长大后分家而住，各自独立打拼。神主牌位也各自分香而祀，形成所谓的"一人一家代，公妈随人立"的现象，清明一到，才集合各房子孙一同上坟祭祖。而客家人则习惯不分伙不分香，因此祖塔往往建得规模庞大，祭祖日一到，再远的"派下子孙"也要回来参加祭祖大典。例如桃园新屋的叶姓宗祠，每逢清明节，

祖塔和祖庙前汇聚的子孙达八九千人，往往使得途为之塞，成为新闻媒体报道的题材。

清明上坟祭扫，除了审视一下祖坟是否完整，如有水淹、坍塌，须得立即动手修整，也要趁机清理墓冢上的杂树杂草，这就是扫墓的重要用意。扫墓时还要"挂纸"，称为"压墓纸"。坟墓上的野草清除完毕，随手捡些小石块小土块把一种特制的纸钱一一压在坟冢上，用意是表示这个坟是有后嗣的，避免被误以为是无主孤坟而受到破坏。墓纸分为白色、红色、黄色的古仔纸以及五色纸（红黄蓝白黑）两类。客家人挂纸，如果依照传统规矩要先用锄头挖一块草皮，把带来的一叠滴有鸡血的黄纸用草皮压在坟上，然后在坟地四周摆上十二张银纸，除了挂墓纸的目的外，还有血祭的象征。

清明祭扫要供奉牲礼（三牲或五牲）、刈金、寿金、烛等，或十二道菜蔬（韭菜、鱿鱼、春干、甜菜、甜芋、肉脯、蒿菜、莲子、枣子、竹笋、猪肠、苣头）和各种粿类（红龟粿、鼠曲粿或草仔粿）。若为新坟，则必须供奉五牲（如猪头、鸡、鸭蛋、面粿、红龟粿）。祭品摆好后，点香向后土（坟墓的守护神，即土地公）祭拜，礼拜完毕，先烧刈金、寿金给后土，再烧银纸等给祖灵，纸钱烧完后，在纸灰上洒酒（称为奠酒），还要鸣炮。

祭拜完毕要离开前，还要将祭拜所用的鸡蛋、鸭蛋在墓碑上敲碎，将蛋壳洒在坟上，象征"脱壳"或"蝉蜕"，表示新陈代谢。早年还会将祭品中的红龟粿、面粿分送给围拢而来的当地小孩子享用，称为"猜墓粿"（又称乞墓粿、印墓粿），但现在再也没有小朋友围着讨要东西吃了。

现在许多人将祖先牌位或灵骨送往公私经营的灵塔，各自前往上香、探视，传统式墓园及传统扫墓风俗已逐渐减少。即使仍然上坟扫墓，方式已经大为简化，大多以鲜花水果为祭品，上香鞠躬，礼节简单隆重。

祭祖起源于商朝，传承至今已近四千年。祭祖是对祖先和圣贤念念不忘，慎终追远，传的无非就是四个字：不能忘本。

民俗篇 Folk Customs

黄帝陵是中华民族始祖黄帝轩辕氏的陵墓，也是炎黄子孙共有的精神家园，海内外华夏儿女情感、精神、心灵的寄托，维系、凝聚中华民族的精神纽带。

The Mausoleum of the Yellow Emperor is the resting place of Xuanyuan, who is said to be the father of Chinese civilization. In this way, this landmark is of profound significance to the Chinese people's shared cultural identity.

陕西省黄陵县桥山黄帝陵祭祀广场，一年一度的清明公祭轩辕黄帝活动，一条五六米长的中华龙腾空而起，象征传统文化同祀共仰的精神。

On Qingming Festival, in the commemorative square of the Mausoleum of the Yellow Emperor (in Huangling County, Shaanxi Province), there are annual events in the Yellow Emperor's honor. A five- to six-meter-long dragon soars in the sky as a symbol of reverence towards traditional Chinese culture.

摄影：陈柏亨

Photography: Chen Boheng

Qingming Festival

Qingming Festival (also known in English as "Tomb-Sweeping Day") is an important occasion where descendants express gratitude and pay dues to their deceased ancestors. Qingming Festival has far-reaching origins. According to legend, it originated during the Spring and Autumn period (770-476 BC), when Chong'er, an heir to the throne of Jin, was forced into exile as a result of turmoil in his kingdom. One day, when he and his entourage lost their way in the mountains, they were stuck without food for several days in a row. Chong'er's sage courtier, Jie Zhitui, quietly snuck away from the group, cut a slice of flesh from his thigh and boiled it into a soup, which he then gave to Chong'er to prevent him from starving. After 19 years of exile, Chong'er returned to his kingdom and was installed as Duke Wen of Jin, thus becoming one of the five overlords of the Spring and Autumn period.

After ascending the throne, Duke Wen of Jin rewarded the courtiers who had followed him during his exile by conferring additional titles on them. Unswayed by prestige, Jie Zhitui declined this reward and returned to his hometown to take care of his mother. Later, when Duke Wen was reminded of Zhitui, he felt terribly ashamed, and immediately set out to track him down. However, Jie Zhitui and his mother had long since become recluses in the mountain forest and were nowhere to be found. One of the Duke's aides put forth a lousy idea: he suggested that the Duke set the forest ablaze, as Zhitui was such a pious son that he would surely abandon his hermetic dwelling and carry his mother to safety. The Duke of Wen heeded this advice, ordering his subordinates to set fire to the mountains. The blaze raged for three days and three nights, but Jie Zhitui was still nowhere to be seen. Once the fire went out, he discovered that Jie Zhitui and his mother had both burned to death underneath a willow tree. The Duke was utterly bereft and declared the day of Jie Zhitui's death to be the Cold Food Festival. On this day, in commemoration of Jie Zhitui, it was forbidden to light fires of any kind — everyone throughout the nation, regardless of status, was only allowed to eat raw or cold food.

On the Qingming Festival, people express reverence towards their ancestors by sweeping their tombs. There are also certain regional customs, such as playing on swings, holding tug-of-war contests, going for hikes in the mountains, hanging willow branches in one's doorway, and eating popiah ("thin wafers"). Each of these traditions have particular significance.

Eating popiah

In Taiwan, popiah ("thin wafers") are an essential addition at any familial celebration of the Qingming Festival. One simply lays out one of the wafers, adds whatever one wants to eat, and wraps it up into a delicious, hassle-free and healthy meal.

Popiah wafers are quite difficult to make, meaning that most people simply buy them at the market. The batter used to make these wafers is a precise combination of flour, salt and water. One spreads a thin layer of this batter on a heated iron board and allows it to cook for a short instant before peeling it off, creating a light, paper-thin wafer. Consummate chefs are able to spread out several wafers on the iron board and pick them up one after the other. Although popiah chefs' movements are lightning-fast, the popiah are in such hot demand that there's still enough time for a line of customers to form.

After bringing popiah wafers home from the market, families lay out an array of fillings on the table, including finely chopped and properly blanched celery, strips of meat, lettuce, and carrots. The popiah wafers are laid out and fillings are added one by one. Then, roasted peanut flour and white sugar is added for extra flavor before the popiah wafer is wrapped up tightly.

Eating popiah often reminds people of the tragically beautiful tale of Jie Zhitui. In keeping with the ancient customs of the Cold Food Festival, popiah are served cold. There are many recounts of this tradition throughout history; as early as the Tang Dynasty, it was

A merchant demonstrates great agility and coordination as he makes popiah wafers. Photography: Wu Jingteng

customary to eat "spring wafers" during the first solar term of the lunar year. When, towards the end of the Qing Dynasty, the army of the Taiping Heavenly Kingdom staged a revolt that spread to Fujian Province, the people of Fujian were no longer able to prepare sacrificial offerings at their leisure. Instead, they had to hurriedly chop up all of the offerings and roll them up in a wafer, which they would present to their ancestors after sweeping their grave. This would later evolve into the custom of eating popiah on the Qingming Festival.

There is also another explanation of how popiah came into being. In Kinmen, there was an official named Cai Fuyi, who was so busy with paperwork that he didn't have time to prepare or even eat — three meals a day. His wife, who couldn't bear to see him go without food, had an ingenious idea: she could chop up and stir-fry ingredients (such as fish, shrimp, pork, mushrooms, bamboo shoots, carrots and dried tofu), and wrap them up in a thin wafer. Whenever it was time to eat, she would simply hold this wafer up to her husband's mouth as he worked. In this way, she could make sure her husband ate without disrupting his affairs. This alternative explanation is considerably more heartwarming than the tragic tale of Jie Zhitui and his mother, or the story of a tradition born of war and turmoil.

民俗篇 Folk Customs

Venerating one's ancestors

Taiwan's two predominant ethnic groups have different customs for venerating their ancestors on the Qingming Festival.

Hoklo parents generally don't live or worship with their adult children. Once their children fly the coop, they worship a separate set of ancestral tablets in their own home. The only time of the year when different households of the same family get together to pay respects to their ancestors is on the Qingming Festival. On the other hand, in Hakka families, several generations often live under the same roof and worship the same ancestral tablets. On days of ancestral worship, every descendants — no matter how far away they live — must return to take part in their clan's celebrations. Every Qingming Festival, eight- to nine-thousand descendants gather at the Ye-Clan Ancestral Temple in Xinwu District, Taoyuan, drawing the attention of numerous media outlets.

When worshipping and sweeping the ancestral tombs on the Qingming Festival, one must check to make sure that it hasn't been damaged or flooded — if it is not in top condition, it must be immediately fixed. It is also important to clear any weeds and debris. After sweeping the tombs, families also leave paper money — a practice known in Taiwan

清明节是一个怀念先祖、祭祀祖先的日子，扫墓也是表达对先祖怀念、感恩、孝顺的方式。

Qingming Festival, also known as "Tomb-Sweeping Day", is an occasion on which the Chinese people remember and worship their ancestors.

台湾人的传统坟墓，墓碑上方都会刻上祖籍。

On traditional tombs in Taiwan, the deceased's ancestral home is always engraved on the tombstone.

摄影：吴景腾

Photography: Wu Jingteng

165

as *ya muzhi* ("pinning grave money"). Using small stones or clumps of earth, notes of joss money are pinned down to the tomb one by one as a sign to others that the ancestral tomb is guarded by descendants. In this way, descendants can prevent the grave from being destroyed by someone who mistakenly believes that it has been abandoned.

During this ritual, families also traditionally left arrangements of either three or five typical sacrificial meats, as well as joss money and candles. Alternatively, they would leave 12 dishes and various types of *kuih* (glutinous desserts). They then offered incense to the Lord of the Land and burned joss paper for their ancestors. Then, once the flames went out, they would pour wine on the ashes and set off firecrackers. Finally, before leaving, they would crack a chicken or duck's egg on the gravestone and scatter the shell on the grave as a symbol for the new superseding the old. In the past, worshippers would often give their *kuih* to little children, who would hang around the graveyards in the hope of satisfying their sweet tooth. However, these days, this rarely — if ever — occurs.

Traditional graveyards and tomb-sweeping customs have gradually disappeared over time. Although people still sweep their ancestors' tombs, the general procedure has been greatly simplified. Most people leave flowers and fresh fruit as offerings, as well as lighting incense and bowing in reverence in a simple, yet solemn ceremony.

The practice of venerating one's ancestors originated during the Shang Dynasty, close to 4,000 years ago. These customs are a means of demonstrating loyalty to one's roots and unending appreciation of one's heritage.

端午节习俗

端午节,也称为"五月节",也有叫作"五日节"的。但无论如何称呼,大家都非常明白,那就是"肉粽节"。

台湾民众如何过端午节呢?无论是插菖蒲、榕叶或艾草,还是吃肉粽、扒龙舟、打"午时水"洗脸煮茶、围着蹲在地上把蛋立起来,看起来多彩多姿,细问缘由,竟然没有一样不是源自大陆老家。年轻人就算节日观念日益淡薄,提笔写作文时依然人人大谈屈原故事。端午不但是中华民族的传统节日,甚至许多受中华文化熏陶的邻近国家也传承了此遗风。

想知道台湾民众过端午有多疯吗?2012年新竹市在端午节举办千人立蛋活动,参加的民众超过5500位,成功立起4247颗鸡蛋,创下吉尼斯世界纪录!而在更早的70年代,在桃园大园这样一个滨海农乡,在海边举行的划龙舟比赛,连比三天,吸引数十万人参与盛会,通往海滨的路,塞车塞了几公里长。

端午是纪念爱国诗人屈原的日子,但是除了这个典故,其实还有多种说法。有的说东汉时代14岁的曹娥因父亲溺亡,而沿江嚎哭17天,最后在五月一日投江,5日后两尸合抱而浮起,乡人群而祭之。另有一说是白蛇传说中的白素贞为了报答许仙之恩,与他结为夫妻,没想到端午节当天喝了几口雄黄酒,差点现出蛇形,最后演出水淹金山寺的故事。还有说是伍子胥助吴伐楚越大胜,越王勾践请和,伍子胥主战,夫差不听,却听信奸臣言，赐伍子胥自戕，并于五月五日将尸体投入江中，此后人们于端午节祭祀伍子胥。说法虽多，却以屈原故事最为深入人心。

划龙舟

许多传统民俗文化活动在台湾不是式微了，而是随着时代变化，以另一种形式继续传承，深入到家家户户。

端午节划龙舟，便是其中一例。

50多年前，笔者还是一个少年，就跟着家人辗转搭车，千里迢迢去看龙舟竞渡。在台湾，划龙舟不叫作划龙舟，叫作飞龙船，或是扒龙船，应是河洛语（闽南语）之传承。

龙舟竞渡之前，必须依古礼举行祭江仪式。摄影：吴景腾

Before beginning the race, competitors must pay their respects to the river according to ancient customs. Photography: Wu Jingteng

民俗篇 Folk Customs

迎接端午节，布置在街头的花卉龙舟，有如与摩托骑士在雨中竞速，画面别有一番趣味。摄影：吴景腾
In celebration of Dragon Boat Festival, motorcyclists race each other in the rain down the streets, which are decorated with floral arrangements in the shape of dragon boats. Photography: Wu Jingteng

    当年交通不便，看飞龙船总得一大早出门。家乡靠海处有一座海水浴场，端午节全县便在海水浴场举办龙舟大赛，通往海水浴场道路蜿蜒，一路上挤满了行人、单车、摩托车，公交车在万头攒动的人群中成了被困的巨兽。

    海水浴场里更是人山人海，整个海岸线上人群如蚁。那几天海水浴场虽然无人下水弄潮，门票收入却翻了好几番。来自全县各地的龙舟代表队接力下水，人群疯狂呼喊助阵的加油声，大大盖过了浪涛声。

    县城里有一个湖，名叫辨天池，是全县另一个重要的龙舟赛场，直到80年代，海水浴场封闭而辨天池也被填掉兴建住宅，全县龙舟竞渡才移师到另一个乡的龙潭大池，延续至今。龙潭看龙舟也成了近年来桃园人过端午不可少的应景活动之一。

    海水浴场封闭以后，我们家乡随即有人推出了另类龙舟大赛，把载送货物的低底盘小推车略加改装，变成行走陆上的一架架小龙舟，行驶时人们一脚在上，另一脚在地上猛蹬竞速，这便是轰动台湾媒体的陆上龙舟大赛了，可见划龙舟这项民俗可真是深入人心。

    桃园如此，全台湾各地也是如此，即使不能挤到现场观赏，拜今日科技之赐，只要是地方上的大型龙舟赛，无不通过电视实时转播，直接将现场实况传送到家，甚至传送到人手一部的手机上。划龙舟的观赏者，或许比当年还要多上好多倍。

走在台湾大街小巷，随便找一个小学生、幼儿园小朋友一问：端午节为什么要划龙舟呢？标准答案不会有错：纪念爱国诗人屈原！

出个画画题目给小朋友，画张端午节为主题的画吧！除了粽子，或许十有八九画的都是龙舟。

流传最广的划龙舟典故便是屈原自沉于江后，当时有人想要找寻屈原的尸体，就划着船在汨罗江上找，逐渐演变成划龙船的习俗。

台湾各地的龙船赛大同小异，宜兰县二龙村的龙舟比赛，因为一项相传有两百年历史的赛事闻名。他们只有两队：上二龙村的淇武兰和下二龙村的洲仔尾，他们各自拥有一条都绘有太极图案的龙舟，淇武兰以绿色为底，洲仔尾以红色为底。比赛规则是两村的居民都是选手，从午后到黄昏，反复在二龙溪比赛达数十次，选手累了马上换同村的人上场，最后以胜的次数多的队伍为赢。比赛虽然竞争激烈，但两村民众甚为友好，赛完握手相拥互祝，完全是君子之争。

吃粽子

端午节为什么要吃粽子呢？想必此题一出人人都会争相抢答：为了纪念屈原，让他的亡魂也有吃的。这也可以从粽子无分口味，均以耐水性高的竹箨或竹叶包装看出。

据说早年纪念屈原并不是包粽子，而是将各种食材装在竹筒里投入水中，此举用意也不是给屈原的灵魂吃，而是用以喂食水中鱼虾，让他们吃了这些东西，不要再去啃食屈原的身体，一直到后来才逐渐演变成粽子的形状。

而随着时间推移，各地民情不同、口味嗜好不同，粽子也出现了数不尽的种类。光是台湾至少就有北部粽、南部粽两大类，再细分甚至多达十余种。

北部粽是先将米泡于水中，沥干后调味炒香成半熟，包裹馅料后蒸熟。也有人先炒后蒸，直接用油将米粒炒至全熟才包裹馅料进笼蒸食。南部粽则为投水煮食，做法是用纯白糯米浸泡后加瘦肉、三层肉、香菇、鸭蛋黄、红葱头，亦有添加花生、栗子、萝卜干者，较特殊的还加入鱿鱼、虾米，馅料须先行腌制。填馅后以竹叶包裹，入大锅中以大火水煮。另外还有中部粽，做法南北融合，先将糯米浸泡再沥干，配上佐料

民 俗 篇 Folk Customs

端午节快到了，市场里摊商全家总动员现包粽子，供民众抢购。摄影：吴景腾
As Dragon Boat Festival approaches, merchants at stands all throughout the market make sticky rice dumplings on the spot and sell them to eager customers. Photography: Wu Jingteng

炒到三分熟后加入卤肉、虾米、萝卜干、鸭蛋黄、花生、香菇、栗子，再蒸至全熟，米粒口感有弹性，软硬适中。由于粽子制作费工，年轻人已经不愿意动手包粽子，端午节想吃直接到便利店、超市买，使得会包粽子的人日益减少。

肉粽之外，台湾还有一种碱粽，以糯米和碱剂混合后包妥下水蒸煮而成，蒸出来的粽子呈透明的金黄色，非常漂亮。食用时佐以糖浆或直接蘸白砂糖，也有红豆内馅等，口味多样。这种粽子具有独特的略带微苦的香气，夏季吃来特别爽口。

台湾少数民族也有不同的粽子做法，称为"阿拜"（排湾语：avay或qavay；鲁凯语：abay；卑南语：avay），流行于鲁凯、排湾、卑南等部落。用的材料是芋头粉、小米、糯米或高粱粉。内层包肉馅、外缘先包上假酸浆叶，再以月桃叶包覆外层，风味独特。而在马祖有所谓的马祖粽，把糯米泡软加碱，再加豌豆或花生粒，填装进粽叶中包封后水煮。成品为鹅黄色、口感有弹性，且内馅极具黏性。因造型如同甜筒冰淇淋，又名"甜筒粽"。马祖属闽北系统，粽子大大有别于台湾岛的闽南风。

台湾有一种习俗，如果家有丧事，年节应景食物一律不得自备，所以过年不能蒸年糕、元宵不能搓汤圆、端午也不包粽子，自有亲戚朋友源源送来。这样的礼俗一方面代表家有哀痛之事，不宜存有逸乐心依常例过年过节，一方面则借着亲友赠送及探望，带来亲情友情之慰藉，冲散丧亲之痛，这是非常具有人情味的习俗。另外，因"粽"与"中"音近，近年来在每逢考试季节或是选举季节，粽子成了热门应景之物，人人相赠粽子以预祝高中、包中，也是非常有趣的新习俗。

立蛋

端午节家家户户在门上挂艾草、菖蒲和榕树叶，让小孩佩戴香包、打午时水、吃粽子，有趣的是还要立蛋。听说在端午节当天的正午时刻能将鸡蛋直立起来，人人都想大显身手，享受这种一年只有一两小时可以玩的趣味游戏。

端午立蛋源自何时呢？何以端午时分方得将蛋直立？许多人都认为是因为端午节正午阳气最重，鸡蛋才能被立起。也有说是端午节这天的中午地心引力较强，可以较容易将鸡蛋竖立起来。但是科学家已经驳斥此说，指出端午节中午的地心引力与平常相同，还更进一步说只要有耐心，随时都可以将鸡蛋立起。这样的说法，让人感到有如上了月亮没有遇到嫦娥小姐，太煞风景了！

随机选一个时刻来试试科学家说法如何？真有人去试了，发现立蛋果真是随时随地都可以玩的，只要是心情愉快、平静而不烦躁、耐心地去试，蛋真的可以立起来！关键是立蛋的动作是很细腻的，手的平衡感要好，不能发抖，否则就不容易成功。如果在玻璃、光滑的金属板上蛋是很不容易竖起来的，水泥或柏油地面、石子地才容易成功。

新竹市在 2012 年端午节当天举办了一场千人立蛋活动，事先以为能吸引来 1000 人便算成功，没想到会场一下子涌进约 5500 人，主办单位紧急增购鸡蛋，结果有 4247 人现场立蛋成功，创下吉尼斯世界纪录！现场观察，果真心平气和而出手细腻者成功率高，心浮气躁弄得满头大汗的人，越是手忙脚乱，蛋就越是不会乖乖站直。

立蛋真的只是耐心而无任何科学上的依据吗？其实耐心之余，还是有诀窍可以拿捏的，有学者就认为"使蛋站立起来的因素是地球的引力，但重心必须低于蛋中部最大周长的曲线位置"。因而主张拿蛋的手只要保持一定姿势一直不动，直到蛋黄尽量往下沉落。蛋便相对容易立起。还有一位日本的物理教授也做过观察试验，发现蛋壳表面并不是完全的光滑，而是布满细微颗粒，只要找到适当的三个表面颗粒，就能像底盘一样托起整个蛋。

无论科学如何说，也无论是不是一年到头都一样容易立蛋，平常日子如果在街头有人围着尝试立蛋实在也是无趣之事，唯有端午节这一天的正午时分，一家人围聚着玩立蛋游戏才是应景，也才会是真正的趣味所在。小小一个点子，让人们在这个团聚的日子玩玩这古老的活动，也未尝不是增进家人间情谊和情趣之事。

下一个端午节就来玩一下吧，人生苦短，能逢得几个端午呢？

小朋友在端午节开心体验"立蛋"。摄影：吴景腾
Children on Dragon Boat Festival happily attempt to balance eggs. Photography: Wu Jingteng

Dragon Boat Festival

The Dragon Boat Festival is also called "Fifth Month Festival" in Taiwan. Whatever people call it, they all associate it with one thing in particular: *zongzi*, or sticky rice dumplings. Out of local people's various traditions on the Dragon Boat Festival — whether it be hanging mugwort, calamus, and fig branches in their doorways, eating sticky rice dumplings filled with meat, rowing dragon boats, or *li dan* ("balancing eggs") — not one doesn't originate from the mainland.

Although young people pay less and less attention to traditional holidays, it is still not uncommon for them to mention the legend of Qu Yuan when writing compositions. The general consensus is that the Dragon Boat Festival commemorates the patriotic poet Qu Yuan. However, aside from the story of Qu Yuan, there are a number of other explanations as to how the Dragon Boat Festival came into being. Some say that it commemorates Cao E, a young woman from the Eastern Han period. After her father drowned when she was 14, Cao E walked along the shore of a river, grieving. Ultimately, on the first day of the fifth lunar month, she committed suicide by leaping into the river. Five days later, her and her father's lifeless bodies floated to the surface, clinging on to one another. From then on, the people of her village would commemorate them on this day. Another theory connects the celebration to the legend of Madame White Snake. After transforming into a woman and marrying Xu Xian, the white snake spirit almost reveals her true form when she unwittingly drinks realgar wine on the Dragon Boat Festival. Finally, some suggest that the festival commemorates Wu Zixu. After Wu Zixu led the Army of Wu to victory in a battle against the Kingdom of Yue, the King of Yue requested a compromise. Although Wu Zixu had suggested that the King of Wu take no mercy and destroy the Kingdom of Yue, the king would not heed his advice. Instead, he listened to the advice of a treacherous courtier and ordered Wu Zixu to kill himself. On the fifth day of the fifth lunar month, Zixu's body was thrown into the river. Although there are many different explanations, the one that has most resonated with local people is the story of Qu Yuan.

Rowing dragon boats

Over 50 years ago, when I was still a young man, my family and I would take a number of coaches and trains from one place to another in order to see the dragon boat races that took place at the seaside resort of a coastal town located a great distance away from where

台北龙舟竞赛，选手使出全力，奋勇夺标。摄影：吴景腾
At the dragon boat race in Taipei, competitors row with all their might in the hope of snatching the banner at the finish line. Photography: Wu Jingteng

we lived. The road leading to this resort took many twists and turns and was packed with both vehicles and pedestrians. This was nothing compared to the beach, however, where one could hardly see the sand for all the spectators. Teams representing different places throughout the entire county took their respective dragon boats down into the water. As they set off, the cheers of the immense crowd of spectators were so loud that they even drowned out the crashing of the waves.

After the seaside resort closed down, people in the county came up with a unique variation on the dragon boat races. They modified low-suspension carts used to transport merchandise into land-borne dragon boats. Whoever controls the cart stands on the back with one foot and kicks off the ground with the other. This land-based dragon boat competition could cause a great stir in local media.

Thanks to the advent of various technologies, even those who are unable to squeeze through the crowds and witness the races in person are nonetheless able to watch them in real-time on satellite television. As a result, the number of spectators is perhaps several times greater than it was back then.

幼儿园小朋友组成"创意街龙"，兴奋参加踩街。摄影：吴景腾
Kindergartners are grouped into creative dragon formations and excitedly stomp through the streets. Photography: Wu Jingteng

Randomly ask any elementary student in Taiwan why people row dragon boats on the Dragon Boat Festival, and no matter who it is will invariably respond: to commemorate the patriotic poet Qu Yuan. The most commonly told story as to why people row dragon boats is that, after Qu Yuan drowned himself in the Miluo River, people rowed down the stream in search of his body. This would eventually develop into the custom of rowing dragon boats.

The dragon boat races in Erlongcun (an administrative district whose name literally translates to, "Two Dragon Villages"), Yilan County, are renowned throughout Taiwan due to a particular competition that has been held for over 200 years. At the time, the two villages of this administrative district only had one team each. From the afternoon until dawn the next day, each village will take turns competing in the dragon boat races until everyone has participated. The team with the most victories win the overall competition. Although the rivalry between the two teams is fierce, the two villages maintain an amicable relationship and a sense of sportsmanship: at the end of the day, they shake hands and exchange good wishes.

Eating sticking rice dumplings

Why is it that people eat sticky rice dumplings on the Dragon Boat Festival? Most people, having heard the basic story of Qu Yuan, would no doubt answer that these dumplings are offered to Qu Yuan so that he may have food to eat in the afterlife. This belief would be compounded by the fact that dumplings are wrapped in sheaths of bamboo shoots or bamboo leaves — relatively waterproof materials.

According to the legend, after Qu Yuan threw himself into the river, the villagers didn't cast sticky rice dumplings into the water, but rather bamboo tubes filled with different ingredients. The purpose was not to feed Qu Yuan in the afterlife, but to feed the fish and shrimp in the water, so that they wouldn't eat his body. It was only later on that the custom of eating sticky dumplings emerged.

Over time, communities in different regions would create a number of different types of sticky dumpling based on their local cultures and culinary preferences. Throughout the whole of Taiwan, one can find two main types of sticky dumpling — northern and southern although there are at least a dozen varieties in total.

In order to make northern sticky rice dumplings, the rice is first soaked and strained. Then, additional flavoring is added, and the rice is stir-fried until it is half-cooked. Finally,

民众到市场购买粽子，准备过端午节。
Locals buy sticky rice dumplings at the market in preparation for Dragon Boat Festival.

妈妈带着小朋友挑选香包。
A mother takes her child to pick out scent bags.

摄影：吴景腾
Photography: Wu Jingteng

it is wrapped around a filling and steamed. When making southern sticky rice dumplings, the rice is not stir-fried. The sticky rice is simply soaked before adding fillings such as meat, mushrooms, duck egg yolk, onion, peanuts and chestnuts. After these fillings are added, the sticky rice dumplings are wrapped up in bamboo leaves and boiled in a pot over a large flame. As sticky rice dumplings are particularly complicated to make, most young people simply buy them at the supermarket on the Dragon Boat Festival, rather than making them by hand. The number of people who know how to make sticky rice dumplings is dwindling at a rapid pace.

In addition to traditional pork-filled sticky rice dumplings, Taiwan also has a variant known as *xian zong* ("alkaline sticky rice dumplings"). The sticky rice is mixed with lye water, wrapped up in a bamboo leaf and steamed. This gives the rice a translucent golden hue that is very pretty to behold. People then dip these dumplings into syrup or white sugar. This type of sticky rice dumpling has a unique, slightly bitter fragrance that is particularly refreshing in summer.

The ethnic minority groups of Taiwan also have different ways of making sticky rice dumplings. These dumplings are made using taro starch, white rice, sticky rice or sorghum flour, and have meat fillings. Their wrapping has two layers: the leaf of the nicandra plant is used for the bottom layer, while shell ginger leaves are wrapped over top. This gives them a unique flavor and fragrance.

In Taiwan, there is a particular custom: should a member of a household pass away during the year, it is inauspicious for that household to prepare any of the delicacies for annual holidays. Whether it be *nian gao* for the Spring Festival, *tangyuan* for the Lantern Festival, or sticky rice dumplings for the Dragon Boat Festival, all of these delicacies must be provided by one's friends and relatives. This adds an extra layer of tradition and humanity to these occasions.

Li dan ("balancing eggs")

On the Dragon Boat Festival, households all over Taiwan hang mugwort, calamus, and fig branches in their doorways. There are also a number of customs that are often carried out by children. For instance, children help prepare scent bags to give to relatives, as well as pumping water from the well at noon, and — of course, eating sticking rice dumplings. The most amusing of these customs, however, is no doubt *li dan*: balancing eggs. It is said that, at noon on the Dragon Boat Festival, it is particularly easy to balance an egg on one end. People take advantage of this short window of only a couple of hours a year to try their hands at this amusing game.

Just why is it supposedly easier to balance an egg on one end at noon on the Dragon Boat Festival? Many people believe that this is due to *yang* energy being particularly heavy at this time. Others say that the pull of gravity is particularly heavy, making it easier to balance the egg. However, scientists have since proved that the pull of gravity at noon on the Dragon Boat Festival is the same as at other times of the year. The truth is that, with enough patience and concentration, one can successfully balance an egg at any time of the year. Balancing an egg also requires a certain amount of hand-eye coordination and steady hands. Balancing eggs is considerably more difficult on smooth surfaces such as metal or glass. Ideally, one should try it on porous surfaces such as concrete, asphalt or stone.

On the Dragon Boat Festival in 2012, the city of Xinzhu organized an egg-balancing event. Initially, they thought they would be lucky to have 1,000 participants. To their great surprise, however, over 5,500 people squeezed their way into the venue! The organizers were run off their feet as they struggled to distribute eggs among the crowd. Ultimately, 4,247 people succeeded in making their eggs stand on end, creating a Guinness world record. To those present, it was evident that participants who adopted a calm and subtle approach had a greater rate of success. Those who allowed themselves to get flustered quickly found that, the more they struggled, the harder it was to keep the egg steady.

In addition to pure patience, there are a few tricks to balancing the egg. One has a greater chance of succeeding by holding the egg in a particular way and maintaining one's hand in the same position until the egg is firmly planted on the ground. A Japanese physics professor discovered through a number of experiments that the shell of an egg is not completely smooth — rather, it is covered in microscopic bumps. One simply has to place the egg so that its gravity is centered between three separate points in the form of a triangle, much like a tripod.

Although one can play this game at any time of the year, it is only on the Dragon Boat Festival that people can truly enjoy it as a whole family.

客家义民节

　　义民爷信仰是典型的客家信仰，也称得上是台湾独特的客家祭祀。了不起的是，许多分散全球各地的客家子弟，到了祭祀时间，总是千里迢迢不辞远路专程赶回来参加盛会，客家人团结的个性表露无余。

　　义民爷信仰最早可以溯源到清乾隆五十一年（1786年），彰化林爽文举事反清于大里杙（今台中县大里乡），设府祖盟，建元顺天。新竹一带的客家人与之对抗，战死二百余人，死后由地方各界将其尸骨合葬，称为"义民冢"。同治元年，彰化又发生戴潮春之乱，新埔一带的客家人再组义勇军捍卫乡土，战死百余人，地方人士又拾取遗骸归葬，此即附冢之由来。事后，乡民在这些牺牲者的合葬之地觅得堪舆吉穴，就地建庙祭祀，称为义民庙。

　　义民庙坐落在新竹县新埔镇的枋寮，又称褒忠亭。大庙前后共修建三次，依据耆老口述，从前广场没有水泥、柏油，都是泥土、碎石，现在已经全改为水泥。甲午战争时因被烧毁重建过一次，20世纪60年代再修建，1994年第三次重建，方成今貌。庙广场外立有白马、麒麟、狮子，广场内则立有两座石牛、两座石象及两座麒麟，庙后方筑有花园，格局恢宏。目前全台三十多座义民庙皆分灵于此，而每年的义民节祭典，也成为客家人一年一度的盛事。

　　义民节办普度祭典起源于清道光十五年（1835年），桃、竹、苗附

根 图说台湾民俗文化
Roots: Customs and Traditions in Taiwan

三峡祖师庙神猪全景图。农家信徒们总会饲养神猪，来一分高下。他们普遍相信，神猪在一年一度的竞赛获得胜利，会为未来一年带来好运。摄影：林建荣

A full sight of the "Pigs of the Gods" event at the Zushi Temple in Sanxia. Farmers who venerate the Yimin Lords try their hand year after year in the hope of raising a prize pig. They believe that winning the event will bring them good fortune for the entire year to come.
Photography: Lin Jianrong

民众参加传统挑担奉饭踩街活动。

The people take part in a traditional parade where offerings are carried on shoulder poles.

神猪是义民节庆典的大型牲礼，摆在祭典供桌上表达对神祇的敬意。

The "Pigs of the Gods" event is a large-scale sacrifice. Believers place these tantalizing offerings on the sacred table to express reverence to the deified martyrs.

摄影：吴景腾
Photography: Wu Jingteng

近各大庄为了纪念义民们的义行，由各大庄轮值祭祀；每个村庄隔 15 年轮值一次，并定每年农历 7 月 18 至 20 日为祭典时间。

祭典第一天为"入坛"，庙前架起高达数丈的灯篙，招引孤魂，庙前供立鬼王大士爷坐镇。第二天于庙前的凤山溪施放水灯，引领水中孤魂浮上阳间。7 月 20 日是祭典的最高潮，乡民们献祭猪、羊、鸡、鸭等牲礼，摊贩群集，热闹非凡。

"神猪大赛"和"羊角竞长"的比赛是义民节的焦点。"神猪"的饲养者为了在比赛中争取荣誉，必须在三年前就物色具有潜力的猪来特别照顾。三年之间每天以饲料、奶粉、面皮和各种可口的新鲜野菜水果喂食，吃最好最新鲜的，猪舍又要通风、凉爽，有些人家甚至还让它吹电扇或冷气，夏天为它冲凉水降温，照顾得无微不至。为了让神猪平安长大，夺得大奖，还要祈求神明多多眷顾。

"神猪大赛"以重量计，获胜的前 20 名猪公，精心装在漂亮的猪公架上，浩浩荡荡运往义民庙广场献祭，这也是主人家最骄傲的时刻了。历年比赛中重达 900 公斤的超大肥猪屡见不鲜，形成特有的神猪文化。而羊角竞长是以角的长度为评比标准，参加比赛的羊往往饲养十几年，献祭时主人家会替它戴上墨镜、结上领结、口衔烟斗，打扮得有如一个高贵的绅士，为祭典带来让人捧腹的话题。

普度仪式大约在 20 日下午 4 点结束，此时庙前杂耍、卖艺的摊贩，看戏、进香的人潮逐渐散去；但轮值村庄举办的盛大宴席才刚刚开始，家家户户无不备好最丰盛的宴席款待各地涌到的亲戚朋友，吃吃喝喝一个晚上，直到午夜时分。大士爷像在熊熊火焰中化为灰烬，整个义民节盛典才告正式落幕。

客籍人士来说，义民庙不仅仅是一座办祭典的庙，更被视为客家精神凝聚的象征；而义民爷在他们的心目中就如同关圣帝君一般，忠肝义胆，为人人仰赖的守护神。因此，为了每年一度的义民节普度祭典，成千上万的客籍人士会怀着朝圣般的心情，不远千里赶到新竹县新埔镇的义民庙，向当年为捍卫家乡而牺牲的义民们表达最诚挚的景仰和怀念。

全台三十余座义民庙，也都会在同一时间举办祭典。其中桃园南崁义民庙据信为台湾最北的一座。有趣的是，这座义民庙因为附近已非客家聚落，由河洛民众管理并承续义民信仰，成为绝无仅有的河洛人主办义民庆典的特例。而在桃园平镇的另一座义民庙，规模宏伟，信徒众多，参拜者早已跨越族群而不分闽客，市政府将义民节活动与客家相关习俗结合并扩大举办，纳入桃园客家文化节之重点活动，也办得有声有色。

Hakka Yimin Festival

The veneration of the Yimin Lords (or "Lords of the Righteous") is unique to the Hakka people of Taiwan. On the Yimin Festival, many people of Hakka descent scattered all throughout the globe make the long journey back to their ancestral land to take part in the celebrations, demonstrating the sense of unity for which they are well known.

This system of folk beliefs can be traced back to the Qing Dynasty, when, in the 51st year of Emperor Qianlong's reign (1786), a man named Lin Shuangwen from Zhanghua staged a rebellion against the Qing rulers. The Hakka people from the region of Xinzhu joined him in this revolt, although over 200 of them ultimately died in battle. After their death, their bodies were gathered and buried in a mass grave, called Yimin Zhong, or "Tomb of the Righteous". In the first year of Emperor Tongzhi's reign, another uprising occurred in Zhanghua. Hakka people in the region of Xinpu reformed an army of volunteers to protect their soil. This time, over 100 people died in battle. Once more, their bodies were gathered and buried together. Later on, the villagers would erect a temple, Yimin Temple, at the burial site of these martyrs.

This temple is located in Xinzhu County. Currently, there are over 30 branches of the Yimin Temple throughout the whole of Taiwan. The first Yimin Festival took place in the 15th year of Emperor Daoguang of Qing's reign (1835). Since then, local villages have hosted this festival in "shifts" of

民俗篇 Folk Customs

民众兴奋参加阵头踩街游行。
The people excitedly join in the parade.

小朋友开心参加阵头踩街游行。
Children happily walk at the front of the procession.

摄影：吴景腾
Photography: Wu Jingteng

15 years each. The official dates of the festival are from the 18th to the 20th day of the 7th lunar month each year. On the first day of the celebration, villagers hoist up lampposts as tall as several meters in front of the temple to attract wandering spirits. On the second day, they shine lamps into the water to guide spirits back to the surface. The 20th day of the 7th month is when the celebration reaches its peak. On this day, the villagers offer different animals in sacrifice, such as pigs, goats, chicken and ducks.

The "Pigs of the Gods" competition and the "Goat Horns" competition are the two highlights of the Yimin Festival. In order to ensure their victory, competitors in the "Pigs of the Gods" event must find a promising pig to nourish and raise as soon as three years in advance. During those three years, they feed their prize pig regular pig feed, powdered milk, *mianpi* (a snack somewhat like flat noodles), as well as different types of fresh vegetables and fruit. It is also important that the pigsty be well ventilated and cool. Some people will even go so far as to install heating or electric fans, as well as hosing the pig down with cool water in the summer. The "Pigs of the Gods" event is judged based on weight. The 20 fattest pigs are sent to Yimin Temple, where they are sacrificed for the gods — an immense source of pride for those who raised them. It is not uncommon to see pigs as heavy as 900 kilograms at these events. This spectacle has contributed a unique culture to the Yimin Festival.

Meanwhile, the "Goat Horns" competition is judged based on the length of the horns. The goats that take part have often been raised specially for the event for over a decade. When they are sacrificed, their owners dress them up to look like distinguished gentlemen — complete with sunglasses, bow tie, and pipe. This adds an extra sense of novelty and humor to the event.

In the evenings, households all throughout the village prepare sumptuous feasts to welcome their friends and family, eating and drinking until late at night.

Yimin Temples are viewed as a symbol of spiritual cohesiveness among the Hakka people. In their hearts, the "Lords of the Righteous" are protective deities upon whom the people can rely.

舞狮和舞龙

舞狮

在台湾可以发现到处都建着庙宇,而无论大庙小庙,门口必定左右各站着一头威武的石狮。事实上古代四灵中并无狮子,而是麒麟、龙、凤凰和龟。麒麟为四灵之首,但在台湾的庙中常退居到庙门两侧的墙堵,被称作麒麟堵,门口最重要的位置被狮子占有了。从这里也可以看出在台湾狮崇拜是非常普遍的。

狮子占有如此地位,除了大小庙宇都要请它担任警卫,在生活中也与人联系紧密。遍布台湾的舞狮活动说明了这一点,开市开店开工要舞狮,建桥建屋建高楼大厦的动土典礼要舞狮,落成竣工通车启用也要舞狮,过年过节或是寺庙祭典更少不了舞狮。城市乡村,一年365天,处处常闻咚咚呛呛的醒狮出柙之鼓乐伴奏声。

为什么重要时刻总有舞狮呢?狮子是祥瑞的神兽,也是避邪的猛兽,故以舞狮来驱邪逐鬼;而舞狮集合音乐、舞蹈、特技表演于一体,带来的热闹欢乐气氛远非其他活动所能比,也因而大受欢迎,难以取代。

舞狮相传起源于南北朝至唐朝,舞狮在历史上最早的文字记载是在唐高祖登基后,为接待宾客而设计的活动,其中"五方狮舞"的表演被

根 图说台湾民俗文化
Roots: Customs and Traditions in Taiwan

台湾云林县四湖乡狮头制作工艺师陈保僮与友人合力打造一座世界最大的传统狮头。狮头直径 2.8 米，连同狮耳及狮须长近 5 米，重达 100 公斤，用卡车才载得动。陈保僮说，制作狮头要先用坯土打模后外层糊纸，晒干以后小心取下纸模进行彩绘，最后再装上耳、须；其中最困难的是纸张糊贴过程，因无法看清大狮头全貌与比例，只能凭经验和感觉，稍有差池，狮脸歪了或比例不对，就前功尽弃了。摄影：吴景腾

The artisan Chen Baotong and his friends join their efforts to create the world's largest lion head. The lion's head has a diameter of 5 meters, weighs approximately 100 km, and can only be transported by truck. Chen Baotong says that, in order to make the lion's head, they covered a mold from clay in papier-mâché. Once it dried, they painted the surface in different colors, and added ears and a beard. The most difficult part of the process, he explains, was applying the paper: as one cannot see the entire head at once, one must rely on one's experience and intuition in order to make sure that the proportions remain correct. The slightest error, and all one's labor will be lost. Photography: Wu Jingteng

民俗篇 Folk Customs

认为是今日舞狮的雏形。另一传说源自更早年代，这便是每年春节出来危害人民的"年兽"传说。古时候年兽作怪，农民便用竹子和花布做成怪兽模样，当年兽出现时，人造的假怪兽里面藏着的两个人立刻起而狂舞，大家也在一旁同时敲锣打鼓助威，年兽被吓得逃入山中不见了。以后民间每逢秋收或节庆，便以竹枝仿制年兽，并涂上鲜艳色彩，配以大锣大鼓到各家门前舞动，这便是舞狮的来源。

除了这两个传说，还有许多相关故事。其实舞狮除了在中国盛行，日本、朝鲜半岛、越南、琉球、印度尼西亚巴厘岛也都有此民俗。只是各地狮子造型不一，舞步及意涵也各不相同，都是对狮子的勇猛赋予的艺术诠译。

在台湾，舞狮被称为"弄狮"，就如称舞龙为"弄龙"，弄有戏弄耍弄之意，表达了戏耍的成分。以兽王之尊而由人们来驱之以为娱乐之物，似乎代表了人才是真正的万物之灵的骄傲感。

在台湾，狮子打造完成启用之前还要先行"点睛"，由法师或地方首长拿着毛笔在狮子眼部比划一下。这仪式就如同神明之开光，龙舟下水也须经此点睛礼，完成仪式便赋予了相当的神力，也象征给予生命。

台湾民间每逢神诞祭典或迎神赛会，都少不了舞狮表演。摄影：吴景腾
In Taiwan, lion dances are an essential component of ceremonies and processions dedicated to local deities.
Photography: Wu Jingteng

台湾狮的造型，狮头没有装饰皮毛而改以彩绘代之，色彩非常丰富，眼睛灵活有神，许多都刻意强调眼神之美而让它可以眨眼合眼。额上饰有粗眉、镜子或八卦。又以嘴巴有没有活动机关分为闭口狮和开口狮两大类。大致上北部以开口狮较盛行，舞着舞着嘴巴还能开口咬红包，或是吐出写着吉祥话的春联。南部狮俗称鸡笼狮，狮头一体成形，嘴巴固定不能随意张合，由于造型与古时农村饲鸡的竹笼相似，才有"鸡笼狮"之别名，但现在交通发达，地域特性已逐渐混淆而模糊了。

舞龙

据说舞龙起源于汉代，最先是为了祭祀祖先、祈求甘雨的宗教仪式，后来才逐渐成为一种娱乐活动。古人深信舞龙舞狮有驱邪镇妖之效、吉祥之兆，所以每逢春节便敲锣打鼓，舞龙舞狮，以消灾除害，预报吉祥。

舞龙在台湾闽南语中称为弄龙、舞龙的团队叫龙阵，龙阵包括随行的乐班和龙的本体两部分，龙的构造分龙首、龙身及龙尾三部分，另安排一名掷龙珠者为前导兼指挥。龙阵规模依龙的身躯多少节来组成，常见的龙大约是9到15节，最惊人的长达50多节。除了依长短配置，还要增配人员担任替换角色以防舞者过劳。

舞龙表演动作繁多而复杂，年轻一辈加入之后每每会有创新花招，挑战各种高难度表现。大龙炮、冲天炮、烟火弹、烟雾弹……穿插在舞龙过程中，简直无所不用其极。最近甚至还有直排轮龙队伍，全体舞龙人员人人穿着直排轮表演，行进更加快速，

舞龙是台湾庙会或大型庆典不可或缺的表演。
摄影：吴景腾

Dragon dances are indispensable to temple fairs and large-scale celebrations in Taiwan.
Photography: Wu Jingteng

南龙是江南一带发展出来的舞龙形式。舞南龙需要一人高举龙珠，龙身长约9米，需9人表演，大小适合小朋友学习。摄影：陈柏亨
The dancing dragon is led by a dancer who holds a "dragon pearl" on a stick. The dragon is approximately 9 meters long and is operated by nine performers. Photography: Chen Boheng

变化也更加丰富，往往看得观众如醉如痴。

舞龙常见的步法大致是：小跑步以S型进场叫作"龙形八步"出场式，出场后将龙身盘绕成圈，龙珠及龙头被包围在中间，龙头在龙珠引导下向主席台或主宾位行三叩首礼，称为"祥龙献瑞"。接着由龙首及龙尾穿过龙的腰部，叫作"龙尾穿龙"，再接着为穿尾与跨尾，仍延续上一动作，以反方向再绕一圈，称为"金龙摆尾""金龙跨尾"，然后是整条龙盘成一个8字形，前后反复追逐；再来是"金龙翻腾"，用快跑的方向绕圈，接下来还会有蟠龙、睡龙、直行、金龙缠身等等动作，表现龙的翻腾、飞翔、高攀、跳跃、快跑、慢跑等各种不同的动作，讲究的是团队合作无间、一气呵成的高度默契。

龙自古以来一直是权威和祥瑞的象征，也是古代天子的代表。在十二生肖中，龙是最受欢迎的生肖。每逢龙年来到，生育率总会向上攀升若干百分点。龙虽是人人耳熟能详之物，却只能从寺庙龙柱或一些绘画作品中欣赏而从来没有人见过真正的龙，也因此在人们心目中产生了神秘崇敬之感。人们把龙幻想成一种能飞腾也能潜水，还会呼风唤雨、来去无踪之物。在岁时节令，迎神赛会中舞龙为礼、舞龙为乐，大大拉近了龙与人的距离。

和舞狮一样，龙的造型虽有大致规律可循，体色彩绘则无所限制，因此各个团队无不卯足劲来求其鲜艳亮丽，出场吸睛。但诸种色调选择中唯有一个默契，忌讳用黑、白二色。民间的狮队、龙队团体往往也另备有黑白二色彩绘的狮与龙，平时深锁库房，唯有遇到有丧事阵头邀请才会将之抬出门。在丧仪之中，让黑白双色之龙与狮上场表演，作为对丧者的礼敬。

Dancing Lions and Dragons

Dancing Lions

Any visitor to Taiwan will quickly notice that, throughout the entire island, one can find countless temples — and that, outside these temples, regardless of their size, one can invariably find two stone lions. Evidently, local people universally revere lions.

With their privileged status in Chinese culture, lions not only keep guard over temples — they are also closely entwined with the daily lives of the local people. This fact is demonstrated by the numerous "dancing lion" events that take place all over Taiwan. Dancing lions are a fixture at opening ceremonies for markets and stores; at "ground-shifting" ceremonies that pay reverence to the land before the construction of bridges, houses and skyscrapers; and at ceremonies that mark the completion of construction initiatives, or the opening of new roads to traffic. Most importantly, they are an indispensable addition to Spring Festival celebrations and temple fairs. In both urban and rural areas, at any time throughout the year, one can hear the rumble and clash of cymbals and drums that accompany lion processions. This music is said to wake the lions from their sleep and mark their release from their cages.

Why are lion dances organized on important occasions? In Chinese culture, lions are an auspicious beast that exorcises evil. Lion dances are therefore organized as a means of chasing away demons. With their fusion of

民俗篇 Folk Customs

music, dance and stunts, the lion dances create an exciting atmosphere to which other events can only aspire. This makes them an extremely popular, irreplaceable tradition among locals.

The earliest written account of lion dances dates back to the reign of Emperor Gaozu of Tang, when it was invented as a means of welcoming and entertaining guests. A popular legend traces the tradition back to an even earlier point in history. Supposedly, a beast named Nian (literally "year") would come out to harm the people on the Spring Festival each year. One year, villagers had the idea of creating a disguise from bamboo and decorated fabric, which was operated from the inside by two people. When the beast appeared on the Spring Festival, the two people inside the disguise began to dance wildly as the villagers clashed cymbals and beat drums, scaring the beast off into the mountains. Since then, during the autumn harvest and on major holidays, the villagers would disguise themselves as Nian in costumes made of colorfully decorated fabric held up by bamboo rods, and dance in people's doorways to the sound of cymbals and drums. Thus began the tradition of the lion dances.

Local people refer to lion dancing as *nong shi*, or "teasing the lions", evoking a sense of playful mockery in the dances. By calling upon the so-called king of the jungle to entertain the people, the dances seemingly express man's sense of superiority over other creatures.

狮阵在台北市北投区街上绕境踩街。摄影：吴景腾
A formation of lion dancers dance through the streets in Beitou District, Taipei. Photography: Wu Jingteng

After the disguise has been made, a monk or local elder takes a brush and paints the eyes of the lion in a ritual known as *dian jing* ("adding the eyes"). This ritual symbolizes enlightenment and is also a necessary step prior to dragon boat races. It grants divine powers and life to the disguise.

In Taiwan, the lion costume has thick eyebrows, and its forehead is decorated with a mirror or the symbol of *ba gua* (the eight divinatory trigrams). It can blink and shut its eyes. The lions can also be sorted into two main categories: close-mouthed lions and open-mouthed lions. The former are able to open their mouths and "swallow" red envelopes or spit out auspicious spring couplets as they dance.

Dancing Dragons

It is said that dragon dances originate from the Han Dynasty and were initially a religious ritual that served to pay respects to ancestors and summon rain. Since their inception, they have gradually developed into a form of entertainment. In ancient China, people firmly believed that lion and dragon dances could dispel evil spirits and bring good tidings. Accompanied by the rumble of drums and clashing of cymbals, the people performed these lion and dragon dances as a means of preventing calamities and announcing good fortune for the year to come.

A dragon dance troupe is called a *long zhen* ("dragon battalion" or "dragon formation"), and comprises both a band and the dancers. A dancer holding a lantern representing the dragon's pearl (an object with which dragons are often depicted) leads the battalion. The size of the battalion depends on the number of "segments" that compose the dragon. Most dragons have 9 to 15 segments, although the longest battalions can have over 50 segments.

The dragon dancers' actions are complicated and varied, and every performance has unique and highly challenging choreography. These dances are interspersed with different types of pyrotechnics: *dalongpao* ("great dragon firecracker"), rockets, sparklers, and smoke bombs. In recent years, we have even seen dragon battalions moving entirely on rollerblades. These battalions move at a startling pace and feature a variety of transitions. During the dances, the dancers move in time so as to mimic typical dragon movements such as spinning, rolling, flying, climbing, jumping, charging and ambling. For these performances to be successful, the dancers need to move smoothly and seamlessly, as though they are the one entity.

民俗篇 Folk Customs

Throughout China's history, dragons have been seen as a symbol of authority and good fortune. In ancient times, they represented the divine emperor. The dragon is by far the most popular of the 12 zodiacs; on every Year of the Dragon, the birth rate skyrockets by several percent. As no one has ever seen a dragon in the flesh, they tend to inspire a sense of mystery and awe. In the Chinese people's collective imagination, dragons are a creature that can navigate the skies and the seas, summon the winds and rain, and come and go without a trace. At seasonal festivals and processions in honor of local deities, dragon dances fuse rites and music in keeping with Confucian tradition. These musical rituals have, over time, reinforced the link between dragons and humans.

摄影：吴景腾
Photography: Wu Jingteng

神秘的王船祭

烧王船是源自大陆而盛行于台湾西部沿海的重要庙会活动之一。澎湖、东港或小琉球每年都有烧王船或称为送王船的祭事。屏东东港迎王平安祭典,更被指定为无形文化资产,成为王船祭之最高荣誉与代表。

关于烧王船的由来,一般说法是源于"送瘟出海",台湾早期瘟疫猖獗,民众以作"王醮"来祭拜俗称王爷的瘟疫神,将瘟疫随祭典中送王船的仪式送走,东港三年一次的王船祭称得上是其中规模最大者。

东港人称此一祭典为"东港迎王",迎接"代天巡狩"的五位王爷神(千岁爷),前来扫荡瘟疫、驱除恶灵。在台湾民间信仰中,王爷神奉玉皇大帝敕令保境安民,东港除了在地的各府王爷、千岁爷(以东港东隆宫主祀的温府千岁为首),还认为每三年玉皇大帝会派遣五位千岁爷(称大千岁、二千岁、三千岁、四千岁、五千岁,以大千岁为领导者)到东港"代天巡狩",故要举行迎王祭典。由东港的造船匠师义务建造精美壮观的王船,作为迎王祭典中千岁爷押煞离境的交通工具。

迎王祭典前一个月开始"进表"、"设置代天府"。第一日举行"请水"仪式,请水当日,祀王、敬王后,必须在子时前将王爷神移到开基大清府嘉莲宫或者大清府旧嘉莲宫过夜,直到卯时才迎回东港。第二至第五日为"出巡绕境"、第六日为"王船法会"、"祀王、敬王",第七日"迁船绕境"、"宴王大典"、"添载"、"和瘟押煞",第八日"送

民 俗 篇 Folk Customs

屏东东港的王船信仰,是台湾最闻名、最有规模的王船祭典,每到迎王祭典,总是成为庙会文化与观光热潮的焦点。
Pingdong County boasts the largest Lords' Boat Ceremony in Taiwan.

屏东县盐埔乡新围慈天宫信众,在送王当日下午,会牵领王船绕境,男信众们遵行多年来的传统,将整座大型纸糊王船用肩膀扛起行进。

Believers in Pingdong County carry a papier-mâché lords' boat on their shoulders on a tour of the vicinity.

摄影:杨锦煌
Photography: Yang Jinhuang

根 图说台湾民俗文化
Roots: Customs and Traditions in Taiwan

台湾云林县土库地区的王船送王，通常是在台湾稻子第二期要收成前举行，王船缓缓经过田间小路时，形成一幅风调雨顺、收获满盈的动人画面。
In Yunlin County, the lords' boat is led slowly down country roads.

屏东县小琉球的王船在凌晨点燃送王时，信众们聚集在王船四周，伴随着王船燃烧五彩四射的火焰，场面非常壮观。
Believers gather on all sides of a lords' boat as it burns in the early hours of the morning.

摄影：杨锦煌
Photography: Yang Jinhuang

王"祭典中主事者会将五位千岁爷神位迎至"王船"之上,在仪式最终时堆栈寿金焚化,象征送神归天,完成万众瞩目的三年大典。

屏东茄萣乡的烧王船,仪式与内容虽一如各地王船祭,特色则是王船由数百名志愿为王爷服务的壮丁,手拉大绳索牵拉,沿滨海公路抵达海边,王船行驶的前方由消防水车洒水,先行"净街",象征为王爷开水路,之后由各阵头众、香客前呼后拥地"护驾"前行,所经之处,街道为之堵塞。待王船拖抵定位,信徒分工合作,将添载的金纸、柴、米、盐包、糖包及船上的贵重物品,推置在船上及船边,随即在神轿及诸多阵头卖力操演下,王船起火燃烧,恭送王爷保佑渔民在海上平安、丰收。

台南安定乡的烧王船始于同治三年,也是三年一办。王船信仰在台湾虽然南部热过北部,但北方也不乏王船故事。以桃园为例,2017年新屋区天后宫妈祖寿诞之庆举行净海祭,信众推着王船浩浩荡荡徒步前往永安渔港举行隆重的法会,并将王船焚烧。

另一则王船故事也发生在新屋,时间则跨越140年。清光绪二年间,新屋渔民许克明、许俊德兄弟在巡视石沪时,忽然发现石沪中有一条大船搁浅,隐约中见有人在船上朝他们招手。两兄弟出于好奇涉水登船,船上竟然有一头羊、一只狗,另有炊具和热腾腾的白米饭、菜汤。再往内舱探查,只见摆着案桌,供着鲜花水果,燃着香火,七位夫人和七位王爷神像端正排列,"灯烛辉煌,炉香四溢",两兄弟见状立即合掌膜拜。但查遍全船,不见一个人影,猜测应是一艘王船,检查全船,发现船帆缆索断了,船舵也坏了。他们接牢了缆索,却无法修复船舵,乃离船回到庄里,报告庄中父老。大批庄内民众闻讯赶来,蜂拥上了船,仔细查探,看到王船上有七顶红眠床、七架梳妆台,寝具桌椅一应俱全,另有白米、茶叶、油盐、鼎镬、薪材,甚至还有农具、雨具,以及各式神器,最大的发现则是有一本账册,书写有捐资打造王船及提供船上一切用品的捐献者名册。这本账册终于解开了王船之谜,它来自福建泉州府后府尾的鲎尾口。当地信众为了祈福,打造王船之后放洋而出,任由神明指示行往何方,没想到竟然直接进了新屋的石沪。

村民认为这是天意,立刻将七夫人及七王爷神像迎下船,船上物品也被分批卸下,暂时安奉在村民许加兴的一座罟寮里。两年之后集资动工建起福兴宫大庙,拆自王船船艏的一面咬剑狮木雕,如今安置于福兴宫正殿神龛正上方,成为这项传奇之见证。

澎湖县时里水仙宫在海边烧王船的那一刻，不分男女信众，为了要表达对王爷的依依不舍与敬重，都要以跪拜礼来恭送王爷升天缴旨，直到王船的中桅倒下才算功德圆满。摄影：杨锦煌

In the Penghu Islands, people burn lords' boats by the shore. As a means of expressing their respect, as well as their reluctance to see the lords go, believers kneel in prayer until the boat's middle mast collapses. Photography: Yang Jinhuang

民俗篇 Folk Customs

The Mysterious Lords' Boat Ceremony

"Burning the Royal Lords' Boat" is an important event at temple fairs along the western coastline of Taiwan that originated in the mainland. The most common theory concerning the origins of this event is that, early in the history of Taiwan, the pestilence was rampant. As a means of dispelling the pestilence, the people would burn boats carrying the Wang Ye ("royal lords", or divine emissaries who were known for their role in preventing and curing outbreaks of plague) at temples.

The townspeople of Donggang call this celebration the "Sacrifice to Welcome the Lords". In this ritual, they welcome five of the royal lords to clear the town of pestilence and dispel evil spirits. The celebration takes place over eight consecutive days. On the eighth day, the five lords are led to their boat, which is then burned over a bonfire as a symbol for the lords returning to the celestial realm.

A distinguishing feature of the "Burning the Royal Lords' Boat" event in Pingdong is that, before burning the boat, hundreds of volunteers first pull it with ropes along the coastal highway to the shore. In front of the royal lords' boat is a fire engine, which sprays the road with water so as to "purify" it. An immense retinue of people protect the boat as they proceed forward. Once the ship has been hauled to its final destination, the crowd places offerings (such as joss paper, firewood, rice, salt and sugar) on the boat before they set it alight. Their hope is that, by sending off the royal lords in this manner, they will be inclined

根 图说台湾民俗文化
Roots: Customs and Traditions in Taiwan

台湾屏东县小琉球的王船祭，信众牵引王船绕境时，依例在港区绕行，形成王船与众渔船并列的浩大场面。
At the Lords' Boat Ceremony in Pingdong County, Taiwan, believers tug the boat around the harbor.

东港烧王船的前一天下午必须牵引王船在市区绕境，各轿班人员穿着颜色不一的服饰，每个人手持一炷香，分工合作完成绕境市区的任务。
Townspeople of Donggang tug the lords' boat around the town center, accompanied by devout believers in different colored outfits, all of whom carry an incense stick in their hands.

摄影：杨锦煌
Photography: Yang Jinhuang

to protect the fishermen when they go out to sea, as well as ensuring an abundant harvest.

Another story concerning the royal lords' boat dates from 140 years ago. During the second year of Emperor Guangxu of Qing's reign, two fishermen discovered a large ship that had run aground on the sandbank. They could faintly see a person on deck, waving to them. Out of curiosity, they waded through the water and climbed aboard. To their great surprise, they discovered a goat, a dog, cooking utensils, cooked rice and vegetable soup on deck. In the cabin, they found a table, on which fresh flowers and fruits were placed, as well as incense — still burning — and neatly arranged idols of the divine emissaries. Upon making this discovery, they immediately joined their hands and prostrated themselves in prayer. Afterwards, people who had heard the news came in droves. Aboard the ship, they discovered an accounts book carrying the name of the person who had funded the ship's construction. As it turned out, the ship was from Quanzhou in Fujian Province. In the hope of obtaining good fortune, the locals of Quanzhou had built this ship and placed it in the sea, leaving it to be navigated by the deities. Little did they know, the ship had safely travelled all the way to Taiwan. Believing this to be the result of divine will, the villagers carried the idols off the boat, and built a temple where they could be worshipped.

云林县麦寮镇安宫的王船，属于台湾中部地区大型的王船，送王点燃游天河时，在蓝天白云的衬托下，画面甚是庄严浩大。摄影：杨锦煌

A large-scale lords' boat burns in Yunlin County, creating a stunning scene. Photography: Yang Jinhuang

生活篇 Lifestyle

台湾的茶文化

中国是茶的故乡,中国人饮茶,据说始于神农时代,少说也有将近四五千年的历史。而源自福建的台湾茶,经过茶农及研究单位通力合作,努力发展,也是异军突起,开出一枝奇葩。

在台湾桃园的大溪,有一个观光老茶厂,里头展示着近百年前从欧洲进口的揉茶机,迄今仍在运作。在当年的全盛时期,这座茶厂所有的制茶机器一字排开,火力全开,日夜不曾熄火,工人则是分成三班接力操作。当时所产的红茶除了供应全岛,还外销世界各地,成为全球四大名茶之一。而在这座规模惊人的百年老茶厂附近,还有一座年岁也近百年的老茶厂,也是至今依然维持着传统的制茶方式,努力生产出质量高滋味好的茶叶。

台湾 300 多年前就发现了野生茶树,但直到 200 年前才正式由福建武夷山引进茶种进行大规模种植。根据台湾农委会的资料,2016 年台湾茶叶种植规模为 11780 公顷,年产量约 14000 吨。产量虽大,却因近年来茶饮以多种面貌全面进入人民生活,连自产自销都不够,何况还有相当的外销需求。怎么会消费那么多的茶呢?几乎每户人家都有一组以上的茶桌和全套茶具,生活中从早喝到晚,客人来了更是一泡换一泡好茶连连,喝个痛快。

生活篇 Lifestyle

每年清明节前后是采春茶最佳季节。
Prior to and after Qingming Festival are the best times to pick spring tea.

台湾乌龙茶以茶树顶端最尖嫩的"一心两叶"制成。
Local oolong tea uses only the delicate, thin twin leaves from the very top of the tea plant.

摄影：吴景腾
Photography: Wu Jingteng

　　年轻人从便利商店买各种瓶装茶饮料，最喜欢的是不带甜味的原汁好味，逛夜市或是上班上学则几乎人手一杯泡沫红茶、珍珠奶茶，连咖啡店也供应茶品，这是台茶内需市场度过一段漫长的低潮期之后惊人的大改变。

　　台茶在质量上持续精进，已经跻身观光客必买、出游者必备的热门伴手礼品。海外游子若是拿到家乡托人携来的一罐好茶，不为之飙泪也难。在台茶日益热门，供不应求的情况下，许多山区几乎全面性开垦而变成茶园，知名风景区阿里山、溪头、瑞里等地迤逦数十里山道两旁都是茶园，就这样似乎依然不敷市场需求。台湾的茶叶进口最近创下了一年26,000吨的纪录，远远超过自己的产量。根据一项统计，2016年台湾进口茶叶的平均价格为每公斤2.38美元，出口价格则高达每公斤11.9美元，这是台湾茶农最引为自豪的事。

　　源自福建安溪的台湾名茶乌龙茶，原料取自青心乌龙、大冇乌龙、大叶乌龙等品种，偶尔也使用金萱、翠玉、四季春或其他品种制作。乌龙茶是台湾最受欢迎的茶品，以南投鹿谷所产最负盛名。而所谓台湾十大名茶指的是：冻顶茶（乌龙茶）、文山包

茶农将采摘后的茶叶进行日光萎凋，摘下的茶心先要放在日光下轻晒，逼走露水。
After picking the leaves, tea farmers leave them to dry in the sun.

褪去露水的新茶被移送到室内二次晾晒并发酵，称作室内萎凋。
Once the dew has evaporated, the tea leaves are taken inside, dried for a second time, and allowed to ferment in process known as "indoor wilting".

摄影：吴景腾
Photography: Wu Jingteng

种茶、东方美人茶、松柏长青茶、木栅铁观音、三峡龙井茶、阿里山珠露茶、高山茶、龙泉茶和日月潭红茶等。龙泉茶指的桃园龙潭所生产者，鹿谷的冻顶山则是乌龙的生产基地。

各种茶品有各自的粉丝群，以产自新竹、桃园、苗栗一带的东方美人茶为例，这种茶对农药有严格的排斥特性。它靠着一种名叫小绿叶蝉的微小昆虫啃咬留痕，留下特殊香气，方孕育出最佳风味。如果喷洒农药，农药歼灭了小虫，好茶也做不出来了。东方美人之名源自它外销时获得的赞美，有趣的是，它还有另一个名称叫作膨风茶，膨风二字在当地方言中是吹牛之意。相传有一位茶农挑了被虫子咬得千疮百孔而带着微腥味的茶到外地去卖，不但很快卖光了，还卖得了从未有过的高价钱。他返乡告知乡人，乡人纷纷报以嘘声，骂他膨风吹牛，此后这个茶也有了膨风茶的昵称。

东方美人茶的口感的确带着一点淡淡的微腥，但更大的特点是它还兼有果香之甜味，被喜爱者视为无上之美味。更因它无农药的特性，消费者在品啜时也多了一分安心。

台湾茶叶依采收季节分为春茶、夏茶、秋茶、冬茶。不同采茶时节，对于茶叶质量影响很大，价格也有很大影响。大致而言，春茶采收期是在清明至谷雨期间，这时的茶无论采收量和质量都居全年之冠。接下来在立夏之前采收的是夏茶，秋茶则在立秋、白露，冬茶采收期为立冬前后。各地经常举办年度茶叶大赛，在激烈竞争中脱颖而出者立刻身价百倍，成为当年抢手的茶叶圣品。茶农也视获奖为毕生之荣耀。

Tea Culture in Taiwan

China is the homeland of tea. It is said that Chinese people began drinking tea during the rule of Shennong (the "God of Agriculture") at least 4,000-5,000 years ago. Meanwhile, local tea, which is made from plants originating from Fujian Province, has developed a worldwide reputation, thanks to painstaking cultivation by tea farmers and research institutes.

Over 300 years ago, tea trees were found growing wild in Taiwan. However, it was only a century or so later that Taiwan began to cultivate tea on a large scale, using plants imported from Wuyi Mountain in Fujian Province. According to official statistics, the scale of Taiwan's tea plantations in 2016 was 11,780 ha, with an annual output of 14,000 tons. While this output could be considered large, it is nonetheless unable to satisfy the demands of the market. Virtually every household in Taiwan has at least one tea table and set. They drink tea from morning until sunset, and it is customary to welcome guests with one cup of tea after the other.

Young people buy various types of pre-made tea beverages from the store, and most prefer those that are unadulterated by sweeteners. At work and in schools, virtually everyone holds a cup of froth-topped black tea, or a tapioca bubble tea. Even specialized coffee shops offer tea beverages.

Local tea has been continually refined in order to become an essential souvenir, both for visitors to Taiwan and for local travelers going elsewhere. Many of Taiwan's mountainous regions have been brought under cultivation and converted into tea fields. Be that as it may, the tea industry is still unable to totally quench consumers' thirst.

Oolong tea leaves originating from Anxi in Fujian Province are Taiwan's most popular tea product. The most famous producer of this type of tea is the township of Lugu, in Nantou County. Taiwan's "Ten Famous Teas", as they are known, are: Dongding ("Frozen Peak") Oolong, Wenshan Baozhong Oolong, Oriental Beauty Oolong, Songbai Changqing Tea, Muzha Tieguanyin, Sanxia Dragon Well Tea, Alishan Zhulu Tea, High Mountain Tea, Longquan Tea, and Sun-Moon Lake Tea.

Different teas have their own fanbases. For instance, Oriental Beauty Oolong tea has a solid base of faithful drinkers due to its strict rejection of pesticides. Its leaves are partially eaten by a small insect, which give them a unique fragrance and palette. The slightest use of pesticides wipes out the insect, depriving the tea of its coveted flavor. Legend has it that Oriental Beauty was discovered when a tea farmer took tea leaves that were riddled with holes and had a slightly fishy flavor to sell to a market out of town. Not only did they sell out of leaves — they were able to sell them at an unprecedented price.

Local tea leaves can be divided into four categories based on the season in which they were harvested. The harvesting period for spring tea is from Qingming to Guyu (the fifth and sixth solar terms). This season surpasses the others in terms of both the volume and quality of the harvest. Summer tea is harvested during Lixia (the term that officially marks the beginning of the season); autumn tea is harvested in Liqiu and Bailu (the first and third terms of the season); while winter tea is picked prior to and after Lidong (the first term of the season).

茶艺师仔细亲尝不同茶叶的香气与口感，以一分高下。
摄影：吴景腾

A tea specialist carefully appraises and compares the fragrance and palette of different brews.
Photography: Wu Jingteng

台湾的中药故事

呷中药卡温和啦!

这是台湾民众常有的吃药观,意思是遇着生病而必须服用药物时,如果要求速效,赶紧找西医打针吃药去,如果要靠着身体的自我调理本能,从调整体质变好来治病就得有耐心,使用中药慢慢来帮忙,急不得。

西方近代医学从日本侵占时期大量被引进台湾,迅速发展为主流,一度还被视为科学疗法的代名词,但传统中医中药迄今依然根深蒂固、深植人心,百年来台湾民众已然巧妙地将两者结合而各取其长以保健身心。中药在台湾的使用,仍然普遍存在于社会每一阶层、每一家庭。

在台湾生活,无论住在城市或乡村,中医的医院诊所总是离家不会太远;除了中药药局和中医诊所,还有更多的历史悠远的中药房、汉药房设立在小街上。中药草店也往往站立在街头街尾,默默服务人群。甚至在偏乡僻壤,蜿蜒村中小径深处,小小三合院里,也有一些所谓祖传秘方的提供者隐居其中。

台湾健保制度企图让中西医疗平权,因此中西医院诊所能够平等地通过核准,被纳入健保体系。中西医疗院所都实施医药分业,也就是在医师诊间之外另设药局。不管中药还是西药,一律需要在药局通过药师提领后才能领药。这是健保体制内的中医药存在现状。

在健保体系之外,常见的中药供应中心便是中药房了。中药房往往

生活篇 Lifestyle

台北市的"青草巷"。青草店内外摆放着野外采集回来的中草药,散发出阵阵天然青草香。摄影:吴景腾
Qingcao Alley in Taipei. *Qingcaoyao* stores overflow with herbs that have been carefully picked in the mountains and transported back to the city. The heady aroma of natural herbal medicine wafts through the alleyway. Photography: Wu Jingteng

　　布置得古色古香,成排的精致磁质药罐整齐排列,置放药物的木制橱柜用工整的毛笔字写上药名,另外还有用玻璃罐、锡罐、铁盒盛装的;走过药房门口,便闻得一阵浓浓的中药香。这些药房常常是祖传多代,古老故事说不完。只可惜新规定不准药房像一般商店般世代沿袭,而且经营者必须通过证照考试。给药房设置的规矩日严,其用意虽在于保障全民健康,但这样下去传统药房恐怕就将逐渐淡出了。

　　中药草店则持续漫步在法律的边缘,通常青草药都以民间偏方为营业主流,有需求者通过某些管道取得药方前来寻觅药材,一把一把将晒干或是已被切片的药用青草买了去,回家用陶罐熬煮,现代化的自动煎煮器具更是方便,大大造福了有需求的人家。

　　一般而言,炮制过的药材叫作中药,以成株干草或是单纯晒干切片的则叫青草药,青草药店常隐身于街道小巷,常是店面狭窄,各色青草堆栈得整个房子都是。

　　中药,顾名思义便是中华传统之药,药材无论取自动物、植物、矿物,还是化石,以往几乎百分之百来自中国大陆山南地北,也被刻意强调来源产地以确保纯正质量与可靠性。近年来也有产自台湾本地者,有些地方还开辟园区大量栽种药用植物,但由于药材多样多元,各有特性,极大多数都无法替代,仍需要仰赖大陆药材商供应,这是一条切不断的脐带。

西方现代医学不过两百年历史,中医中药究竟有多久的历史呢?中药的产生,应该初始于早期人类对药物的需求,这是全人类古来为免除病痛而摸索出来的智慧结晶。通过文字的记载,中国远自殷商时代,在金文中已经出现"药"这个字。《说文解字》训释为:"治病草,从草,乐声。"商之后的周《西诗经》及《山海经》中,记载了120余种药物产地、效用和治疗性能。这是最远古的药书了!

春秋战国时期出现的《五十二病方》,记载药方已达280则,所用药物逾240种。《汉书·平帝纪》出现了长期以来人们习惯的中药之代名词本草一词,现存最早的药学专著则是《神农本草经》,考证最后成书不晚于东汉末年。

隋唐时期,南北统一,经济文化日渐繁荣,医药学有了更大的发展。唐显庆四年(公元659年)朝廷颁行了由李绩、苏敬等主持编纂的《新修本草》(又称《唐本草》)。载药844种,这本巨书的完成依赖了国家的行政力量和人力物力,是中国第一部药典性本草;比公元1542年欧洲纽伦堡药典的出版还早了800年。而一直到今天还被视为无可取代的中医药大典《本草纲目》,于明代由医药学家李时珍历时27年编成,全书共达52卷,约200万言,收药1892种,附图1100多幅,附方11000则,此书一出,立时被奉为中医药无可取代的最高典籍。

有趣的是,生活中脱离不了的中药,一直以来并不称作中药,古来总是泛称作生药,一直到清朝末年,才将沿用已久的生药一词改为中药,这倒是很多人不太清楚的一段历史。

"松下问童子,言师采药去,只在此山中,云深不知处。"短短20字,道尽古人山隐生活及大自然与医药的绵密关系。而这首诗的创作时空,距台湾何其之遥,却是台湾的孩子们皆能朗朗上口的东西!

中药店店员按照药方为顾客配药。
摄影:吴景腾
An employee in a TCM pharmacy makes up a prescription for a customer.
Photography: Wu Jingteng

Stories of Chinese Medicine in Taiwan

In Taiwan, the general consensus concerning medicine is that, if you need a speedy recovery, then your best bet is to see a Western doctor and get a shot or a round of antibiotics; however, if you want to slowly and carefully address the imbalances in your body, then you should take Chinese medicine.

Modern Western medicine was introduced to Taiwan during the Japanese colonial governance (1895-1945), and rapidly developed to become the predominant school of medicine. That said, traditional Chinese medicine has remained profoundly anchored in local culture. Over the last century, local people have continued to use an ingenious fusion of the two schools of medicine to maintain their health and prevent disease.

The use of traditional Chinese medicine is ubiquitous at every level of society. Whether you live in the city or the countryside, you are always certain to find a clinic or hospital specializing in traditional Chinese medicine within the vicinity. Most streets have at least one store that faithfully sells traditional Chinese herbs to the local population. Even in the most secluded confines of the wilderness, one can still find purveyors of so-called "secret ancestral formulae".

TCM pharmacies are often decorated to look like traditional apothecaries. Exquisite ceramic jars with the names of each ingredient written in calligraphy are meticulously arranged in wooden cabinets. Other ingredients are kept in glass jars, tin cans, or iron boxes. When one walks through the door, one is

民众采买所需要的青草，回家熬煮，治病、养生。摄影：吴景腾

Locals buy the *qingcaoyao* (unprocessed medicinal herbs) that they need, take them back home, and boil them into concoctions that can prevent and cure their illnesses. Photography: Wu Jingteng

overwhelmed by the potent fragrance of different medicinal herbs. These pharmacies are often family businesses that have been passed down over several generations.

Generally speaking, herbs that have already been brewed into concoctions are referred to as *zhong yao*, or "traditional Chinese medicine", while unprocessed natural ingredients such as herbs or bark are called *qingcaoyao* (literally "green grass medicine"). *Qingcaoyao* tiptoes on the margins of the law; customers who buy it must, based on popular recipes, seek out each dried and sliced ingredient in store, and then infuse them in a ceramic jar at home.

Virtually all of the ingredients used in traditional Chinese medicine — whether they are animal products, plants, minerals, or fossils — are sourced from the mainland. In recent years, certain companies have begun to produce ingredients on Taiwan's soil, with some regions even mass-cultivating medicinal herbs in specialized parks. However, due to the diversity and specificity of the ingredients used in Chinese medicine, the vast majority still have to be sourced from suppliers on the mainland. In this sense, Taiwan's umbilical cord remains tethered to its mother.

The Chinese character for herbal medicine, *yao*, can be found on bronzeware inscriptions dating back to the Shang Dynasty (over 3,000 years ago). The oldest extant Chinese medicinal text is the *Shennong Classic of Herbal Medicine*, which, it has been confirmed, was compiled no later than the end of the Eastern Han Dynasty. *Bencao Gangmu* (the *Compendium of Materia Medica*, as it is often translated) was compiled by the pharmacologist Li Shizhen during the Ming Dynasty. The book indexes a total of 1,892 drugs and 11,000 prescriptions. It is looked upon as the most precious and essential text of Chinese medicine.

"Beneath the pine, I asked of the child. 'My master's gone for herbs grown wild; He should just be in the mountain there, Deep, way deep in the clouds somewhere.'" This famous poem evokes the inextricable relationship between Chinese medicine and the natural world. Although the context in which it was written could not be more distant (both in terms of time and space) from contemporary Taiwan, children are still able to recite it by heart.

中药皆以天然动植物、矿物为药材，无人工合成之化学品。摄影：吴景腾

Traditional Chinese medicine is composed of natural animal products, plants and minerals; it is free of any synthetic chemicals. Photography: Wu Jingteng

米食和面食

台湾称得上是美食者的天堂，爱吃米的有各种美味的米食，爱吃面的有五花八门的面食。米食制品中首推米粉，从米粉又衍生出许多米粉食谱，不同吃法各有滋味。有趣的是，你可以在路边摊吃一碗米粉汤，也可以在五星级大饭店吃一盘炒米粉，都能吃得齿颊生香，十分满足。而最值得称道的乃在米粉售价便宜，无论干炒或是煮成米粉汤，做法简便，却又因调理者的手艺高下而出现级别高低之落差。厨艺高明的，即使简单小露两手，也会教人回味无穷。

台湾本身不是小麦的产地，面食文化却从不缺席。在台湾的各种面食中，最具有地方色彩的有两种，一是关庙面，一是手工面线，这两种面食的产制需要配合日晒与和风两个环境因素，也因而出现了条件俱足的专属产地。如果不是特定产地的产品，质量就逊了一级，失败率也高。

台湾米粉常以地名作为附加商标，例如新竹米粉、埔里米粉等等。买关庙面，则直接便是关庙两字，即使在其他地方生产，也直接称为某某牌或某某厂关庙面，关庙面已成约定俗成的通用名称。

生活篇 Lifestyle

关庙面

关庙面望文生义，发源于台南关庙区。关庙区在早期是平埔族中西拉雅族的新港社垦地，汉人从台江登陆，并经明郑时代的屯垦而繁荣起来。康熙年间，先民在此设立一座山西堂，祭拜关公，形成以庙宇为中心的商街，后来立乡直接便以关庙乡为名，升格之后台南各乡镇市改制为区，关庙区沿用旧名，而小庙早已变成巍峨大庙了。

关庙人原来并不把他们的特产称作关庙面，原名叫作柳仔面，也有叫作大面，这种面条由来已久。走进关庙区，处处看得到制面厂，制面厂的规模可以从晒面场的大小判断出来。关庙面和关庙区，形成了密不可分的关系。

关庙产出关庙面的重要原因是当地水质清澈甘美，日晒充足。以前没有冰箱，食物要长久保存不外乎腌制或晒干脱水。关庙位于山区，日照强烈而山风常吹，产出的面条口感与风味俱佳，日晒关庙面成了闻名全岛的特产。好的关庙面至少要有四个要求：久煮不烂、纯手工制作、采用古早日晒法生产、无添加色素与防腐剂。标准的制作流程是：将面粉跟水依比例及当天的温度跟湿度搅拌均匀，经过重复多次压面，接着醒面，再经过最后一次压面后裁切，再将切完的面条，以手工折成扇形，依序排上

台南关庙面纯以阳光曝晒而成，久煮不烂，不易煮糊，入口又香又 Q，销路遍全岛。摄影：吴景腾
Guanmiao noodles from Tainan are purely dried in the sun. They can be boiled for a long time without falling apart or sticking together, and have a pleasantly slippery texture. Photography: Wu Jingteng

竹筛进行日晒。日曝阶段每两小时就要翻一次面线，使其均匀受热。依照标准工序，产品可以保存十二个月不变质。

关庙面被当地人用于待客与祭祀，与菠萝、竹笋并称"关庙三宝"。

米粉

为何米粉一定要在新竹生产呢？新竹的东北季风每年从 11 月吹到来年 1 月，东北季风在新竹被叫作九降风，常是强到人都站不稳，日晒加上强风是做好米粉的天然条件。传统米粉业者最讲究的是"三分日晒、七分风干"，古早新竹人充分利用了这个地利条件，加上当地丰盛的稻田产出，开启了新竹米粉这一扇大门。

新竹米粉究竟始于何时？目前许多老品牌都是四代经营，有些老厂创立于 20 世纪初，谈起过往辉煌年代无不眉飞色舞！可以看出至少百年之前，新竹米粉已是全台知名特产。早年订单以明信片书写传递，常像雪片般来自四面八方，每个米粉厂的信箱都是爆满的状态，产品供不应求。因为产品只能靠日晒，一旦老天爷不赏脸，连下

工作人员将米团挤压成丝。
A worker compresses a ball of gelatinous rice into vermicelli.

工作人员将蒸熟的米粉甩开避免黏成一团。
Freshly steamed rice vermicelli are tossed and spread out to prevent them from sticking together.

摄影：吴景腾
Photography: Wu Jingteng

几天的雨，交货就马上受到影响，也因而米粉的产出永远赶不上订单的交货日期。生产米粉除了仰赖老天出太阳，人工部分也是复杂无比。传统工法有17道工序，从洗米、泡米、磨浆，制成米粿后挤压成条，蒸、切段、拆丝成型，一个制程至少耗时将近20个小时。接着再拿到户外去晒，也得耗费七八个钟头以上。

为了抢日照，米粉人家必须天没亮就把米粉赶制完成，这样才能确保在当天晒干。全家大小合力将米粉摆在筛上，逐一抬上推车，一车一车推到广场，一片一片把米粉整齐放上铁架，直到日落。如果当天天气晴朗，风又大，很快就能晒干。如果忽来阴雨，米粉只好在室内堆栈起来，靠木炭炉子保护它不变质，再静待太阳出来补足日晒能量，耗的劳力至少增加了好几倍。

来一碗米粉汤吧！享用美食之余，可别忘了背后生产过程有多么艰辛。

手工面线

许多店家常会标榜手作，因而曾有人发出揶揄：不用手作？难道用脚踩出来？其实所谓手作，无非强调坚持人工而少用或不用机器去量产。吃得到手工面线的地方事实上也不多，台湾是少数吃得到这一味的地方。台湾的手工面线目前有福州派和泉州派两大门派，泉州派拉面工法比较单纯，属于单棍手握横向拉面线（单人拉也可双人对拉），估计约有100家仍在传承此一手法。福州派拉面比较复杂，属多棍手夹横向拉面线（单人拉面线），据说全台已经寥寥无几了。福州派店家强调的是每一条面线都是经由搓揉捏挤压拉甩，一个步骤一个步骤堆栈上来的Q度，绝不是加入顺丁烯二酸造就出来的Q度，更不会添加任何化学药剂来增加口感。业者还开发手工面线DIY活动，让客人自己动手做，从面粉揉成面团，面团揉成面条，再从面条拉成面线，尝到亲手做出来的好味道。

手工面线传说源自东汉时期，传统做法是由制面师傅手工拉甩，随天候、手感决定曝晒烘干时间，制面师傅在三十几度环境中使劲拉面，过程中不时洒上米糠、太白粉防止粘连，不一会儿便落得满头满脸，白发苍苍。如此前后耗时7至8小时换来的成品，这是爱面一族心目中的极品，绝非机器制面可比。

根 图说台湾民俗文化
Roots: Customs and Traditions in Taiwan

制作面线的师傅天未亮就要完成和面、割面、搓面等工序，以确保日照足够。

The *misua* chef must mix the dough, separate it and knead it before the sun rises so that there is enough time to dry the *misua* in the sun.

原本约 0.5 厘米粗的面线，经过甩、抛，变得又细又长，但这动作须掌握好力道及巧劲，面线才能拉得够细却不断。

The *misua*, which were originally around 0.5 cm thick, are tossed and thrown until they are long and thin. One requires a certain sense of coordination and dexterity in order to pull the noodles so that they are thin without breaking.

手工面线除了以手工去拉，还仰赖好天气曝晒烘干，需费时 7 至 8 小时才能换得 Q 滑好滋味。

It takes 7 to 8 hours to produce smooth and delicious *misua*: not only do they need to be pulled by hand, they also need to be dried in adequate sunlight.

摄影：吴景腾

Photography: Wu Jingteng

生活篇 Lifestyle

Rice- and Wheat-Based Dishes

Taiwan is a paradise for foodies — those who love rice can enjoy all types of delicious rice snacks, while those who crave noodles and other wheaten delicacies are also sure to find something to their liking. Among the vast repertoire of rice snacks, rice vermicelli are by far the first choice of local people. Rice vermicelli have gradually spawned a diverse menu of dishes and can be prepared in a number of ways. What is so appealing about these dishes is that they all have the potential to be delicious, whether it's a rice vermicelli soup at a roadside stall or a plate of fried rice noodles at a five-star restaurant. Most importantly, rice vermicelli is very cheap and simple to prepare — one can either stir-fry them or boil them into a soup. Be that as it may, the chef's level of expertise can make an immense difference to the taste of the meal. Consummate chefs can, with just a couple of simple gestures, leave diners with a lasting and pleasant taste in their mouths.

Although Taiwan is not itself a producer of wheat, wheaten delicacies are nonetheless an essential part of its culinary culture. Among Taiwan's many wheat-based dishes, two have particularly strong regional characteristics: Guanmiao noodles and handmade *misua*, or wheaten vermicelli. As these two types of noodle need to be dried in the sun and gentle breeze, they can only be produced in regions that fulfil these two climatic conditions. When produced elsewhere, these two delicacies are significantly inferior in terms of quality and have a lower output due to a greater rate of failure.

Brands of local rice vermicelli are often named after their place of production — such as Xinzhu vermicelli and Puli vermicelli. On the other hand, although Guanmiao noodles are named after their place of origin, they are still referred to as "Guanmiao noodles" even if they are produced elsewhere — one simply adds the name of the brand or factory at the beginning. In this sense, "Guanmiao noodles" has become a general term.

Guanmiao noodles

As their name suggest, Guanmiao noodles originate from Guanmiao District in Tainan. In the Ming Dynasty, Guanmiao District was settled by immigrants and subsequently experienced a period of great prosperity. During the reign of Emperor Kangxi, the settlers erected the Shanxi Hall, where they venerated Lord Guan. It is after this temple that the district was named: Guanmiao literally means "Guan Temple". Upon arriving in Guanmiao District, one can see noodle factories everywhere — the noodles are an inextricable part of the district's history and identity.

关庙面是以特高筋面粉与盐水精制而成。摄影：吴景腾

Guanmiao noodles are painstakingly made from salt water and strong flour. Photography: Wu Jingteng

The reason for their superior quality is that the local water is exceptionally clear and the region is sufficiently sunny. As there were no refrigerators in the past, the only reliable ways of preserving food were to marinate it or dry it in the sun. Guanmiao is located in the mountains, where the sunlight is intense and there is a constant breeze. This gives Guanmiao noodles an excellent texture and flavor. As a result, sun-dried Guanmiao noodles are renowned as a local delicacy throughout the whole of Taiwan. There are four fundamental criteria upon which the quality of Guanmiao noodles is judged: they do not fall apart after they boiled for long periods of time; they are entirely made by hand; they are dried in the sun; and they do not have any coloring or preservatives. This product can be stored for a whole year without spoiling.

Locals prepare Guanmiao noodles for guests as well as offering them to deities. Along with pineapples and bamboo shoots, they are known as one of the "three treasures" of Guanmiao.

Rice vermicelli

Why is it that rice vermicelli must be produced in Xinzhu? Xinzhu's northeastern monsoonal winds start blowing in November of each year until January of the next. The winds are so strong that one can hardly stand steady. Sufficient sunlight and powerful winds are essential natural conditions to making rice vermicelli.

Many brands of rice vermicelli in Xinzhu are four-generation family businesses; certain old factories were founded as early as the 1910s. Initially, people would send their orders on postcards. Every factory's mailbox was perpetually overflowing, and they could hardly keep up. As this product absolutely must be sun-dried, any inclement weather has an immediate impact on deliveries. For this reason, the factories' output never surpasses the demand. There are 17 steps involved in the production of rice vermicelli—from washing and soaking the rice, to grinding it into a paste and making it into a cake, to squeezing and compressing this cake into noodles, and finally, to steaming them, cutting them and removing imperfections—the entire process takes at least 20 hours. Next, the vermicelli are taken outside and dried in the sun, which takes at least another seven to eight hours.

To make the most of a day's sunlight, producers of rice vermicelli must hurriedly make them before sunrise. That way, the vermicelli are sure to dry on the same day. Different generations of the one family work as a team to place the vermicelli on a screen, lift the

新竹米粉早已成为台湾最知名的特色美食。
Xinzhu rice vermicelli has long since been Taiwan's most famous delicacy.

工作人员将蒸熟的米粉披在竹筛或竹席上送到户外，接受三分日晒、七分风干的完整洗礼。
The steamed rice vermicelli is draped over a bamboo screen or seat and placed outside, where it is to be "30% sun-dried, and 70% wind-dried".

摄影：吴景腾
Photography: Wu Jingteng

screen onto a truck, drive it to an open field, hang them up neatly on an iron rack and leave them to dry until sunset. If the sun is out in force that day, and the wind is blowing hard, the vermicelli will be dry in no time. If a storm suddenly strikes, the rice vermicelli must be prevented from spoiling by being stored inside over a charcoal-stoked stove. Once the sun reappears, the vermicelli are taken back outside. In this way, unexpected poor weather can double or even triple the effort and work involved in making vermicelli.

Order a bowl of rice vermicelli soup, and as you savor each delicious mouthful, take a moment to consider the labor that went into its production.

Handmade *misua*

There are no longer many places left in the world where one can enjoy a bowl of handmade *misua* — literally "noodle threads", or wheaten vermicelli. Taiwan is one of the few places where the delicacy lives on.

In Taiwan, there are currently two major schools of handmade *misua*: Fuzhou-style *misua* and Quanzhou-style *misua*. The Quanzhou style of pulling noodles is relatively simple. One simply wraps the dough around a single stick and pulls it out horizontally. Approximately 100 businesses have still carried on this technique. The Fuzhou style of pulling noodles uses multiple sticks. The dough is wrapped around multiple sticks and pulled horizontally. It is said that only a few businesses in Taiwan still use this method. Fuzhou-style *misua* producers insist that each *misua* must be carefully kneaded, pinched, pressed, pulled and tossed. Their supple texture must be slowly crafted by hand, rather than emulated with the use of chemical additives. Businesses have also developed DIY events where customers can learn to make the noodles themselves, from kneading the dough into a ball, to separating the ball into noodles, and finally to pulling the noodles into *misua* "threads". This gives customers the extra satisfaction of knowing that their delicious meal results from their own hard work.

It is said that handmade *misua* originates from the Eastern Han period. These noodles were traditionally hand-pulled and tossed by a noodle chef in an environment heated to over 30 degrees. Throughout this process, the chef continually sprinkles rice bran and potato starch to prevent the dough from sticking. Soon the chef's face and hair are snow-white. After seven to eight hours of labor, they are left with a product that lives up to the highest expectations of the noodle-loving Chinese people — a product that could never be reproduced by machine.

古老的三合院晾满面线，风吹摇曳，光影跳跃，美得像白色线海。摄影：吴景腾
An ancient *sanheyuan* ("three-sided courthouse") is filled with drying *misua*. The veil of white threads sways gently in the breeze. Photography: Wu Jingteng

迪化街：台北第一大街

走遍中国大江南北，老早就找不到迪化这个地名了。然而，台北却有一条知名度超高的迪化街，还号称地名源自大陆。这是怎么一回事呢？

在台北市民权西路、台北桥以南、忠孝西路以北、重庆北路一、二段以西，西临淡水河，介于北门和大龙峒之间的这一个区块，古来一向称为大稻埕，稻埕是晒稻谷的广场。大稻埕顾名思义，古早年代这里肯定盛产稻米，所以才需要一个大大的晒谷场。这个大稻埕地区在清末接替昔时台湾"一府二鹿三艋舺"（当时的台湾三大港市，一府代表台南府城，二鹿代表中部鹿港，艋舺则为今台北万华区）中的艋舺，成为台北最繁华的地方。直到日占时期，大稻埕在经济、社会，以及文化活动上都有傲视全岛的惊人发展。难能可贵的是，此地不仅商业活动频繁，也是人文荟萃之地。

1947年国民党来台之后，陆陆续续把台湾重要街道改了名，每个城市最主要的道路几乎都被改成中正路和中山路，另外也把历史上一些先贤先圣及中国各地重要地名拿来替换城镇街道之名。迪化是今天乌鲁木齐在当时的旧称，便成了大稻埕中一条最主要的街道之名。

迪化街大约初建于19世纪50年代，由于当时河海运输兴盛，大稻埕毗邻淡水河，很快就发展成为整个台北市的南北货、茶叶、中药材及

生活篇 Lifestyle

迪化街目前依然是台湾北部南北货、茶叶、中药材及布料的集散地。
To this day, Dihua Street is still an entrepot for Northern Taiwan's household supplies, tea leaves, traditional Chinese medicine and fabric.

农具、木桶、蒸笼等传统用品，今天到迪化街还是可以买得到。
One can still purchase traditional supplies such as farming tools, wooden buckets and steamers on Dihua Street.

摄影：吴景腾

Photography: Wu Jingteng

迪化街上的永乐布业商场是全台最大布料批发零售中心。摄影：吴景腾

The Yongle Fabric Market on Dihua Street is the largest fabric wholesaler in the whole of Taiwan. Photography: Wu Jingteng

布匹的集散中心。可以说台北的发展就等于大稻埕商圈的发展，而大稻埕的发展也相当于迪化街的发展。

18世纪中期，大量泉州移民与一些漳州人定居台北艋舺，在与当地平埔族通婚后人口大增，艋舺因而大为兴盛，于是产生了"一府二鹿三艋舺"的说法。1853年，艋舺发生严重的泉漳械斗，泉州同安人大败，先奔往大龙峒，但不受当地同安移民接纳，再转到大稻埕，沿着淡水河建起毗邻店屋，为地方神建造霞海城隍庙。这也造就了大稻埕的发展。

19世纪中期，尚未淤积的台北淡水河可航行来自闽南一带的戎克船。大稻埕码头成了商货集散中心，一时商贾云集，街道以南方码头为基准，逐渐向北扩展。1891年，台湾巡抚刘铭传首建经过大稻埕的全台第一条铁路，迪化街成为水陆兼具之商业枢纽。

二战爆发前，大稻埕发展到顶峰，迪化街及外围街道放眼皆为大户家族兴建的镌刻有家徽式浮雕装饰的富丽堂皇的巴洛克式建筑。一般商街也竞相仿效，成为全台精

生活篇 Lifestyle

致建筑群集中区之一。直到 70 年代，只有不到 1 公里长的迪化商圈，已难负荷台北市百万人口的商业需要，于是大多数企业总部纷纷移出，台北市商圈也逐渐东移，迪化街由此迅速没落。

近年来，经过有计划的辅导和规划，迪化街成为全台最重要的年货大街，颇具风情的古街上卖起了南北货、伴手礼、食品、中药食材、零食等。中盘商性质的迪化街转型成一般消费者都可前来的门市，短短 800 米的街道能在 15 天内涌入数十万人。迪化街成功地度过了衰败期而重现风华，它的精致建筑群一年到头更吸引了川流不息的访客。迪化街无愧当年台北第一街之美名。

台北市迪化街保存着镌刻有浮雕装饰的巴洛克式建筑群。摄影：吴景腾

Dihua Steet in Taipei has preserved a number of Baroque buildings that feature extravagant reliefs. Photography: Wu Jingteng

Dihua St: Taipei's First Main Street

In Taipei, there is a district that in ancient times was called Dadaocheng. Dadaocheng literally means "big rice-drying field", making it likely that the region was originally an abundant producer of rice. During the 1950s, as Dadaocheng is located along a freshwater river, it quickly developed into an entrepot for Taipei. One could say that Taipei's development is inextricably linked to that of the businesses in Dadaocheng.

Before the Second World War, Dadaocheng reached the peak of its development. Wherever one looked were magnificent Baroque buildings, which were engraved with emblem-like reliefs that spoke of the wealthy families to whom they belonged.

After the Kuomintang retreated to Taiwan in 1947, they renamed its streets after various places in Taiwan. Dadaocheng was thus renamed Dihua, after the then-prefecture of Xinjiang, today known as Ürümqi.

By the 1970s, all that was left of Dihua was a kilometer-long commercial loop that was no longer able to single-handedly satisfy the demand of Taipei's one million consumers. The vast majority of companies left as Taipei's commercial center gradually shifted east, and Dihua Street quickly declined.

In recent years, with the government's careful assistance and planning, Dihua Street has become Taiwan's most important New Year's Market. Now, along this quaint historic street, one can buy various household supplies,

生活篇 Lifestyle

souvenirs, food products, traditional Chinese medicine and snacks. Within a fortnight, this 800-meter-long street can attract hundreds of thousands of visitors. Dihua Street has successfully overcome a long period of adversity and resumed its former glory. Its exquisitely crafted buildings attract droves of visitors, year in and year out.

传统纸灯笼何处寻？逛一趟迪化街必然可以买到。
Don't know where to find traditional paper lanterns? Dihua Street is your best bet.

未婚男女到迪化街的霞海城隍庙向月老求姻缘，希望能找到好归宿。
Single men and women pray at the Xiahai City God Temple on Dihua Street in the hope that Yue Lao (lit. "the elder under the moon") will help them find their soulmate.

摄影：吴景腾
Photography: Wu Jingteng

下象棋

棋中不语真君子

起手无回大丈夫

这一副对联在华人世界里几乎人人耳熟能详，或许每一个刚刚学会下象棋的人，第一个见到的就是这两句了。短短两句十四个字，简明地昭告象棋规矩：无论下棋观棋，要当个真君子大丈夫，观棋者切记不要在旁边指指点点、窃窃私语，而下棋者一旦出手，手指头离开了棋子就不能"悔棋"，这就叫作起手无回。如果下棋时旁观人个个抢着当军师，当局者又一步一徘徊地反反复复，那这盘棋也下不起来了。

在台湾，象棋曾经在很长时间里都是"桌游"之首，无分南北、无分城乡，随处可见。象棋自大陆传入台湾的年代已无法考据，一般推测始于明代郑成功时期，甚至更久。台湾民众把象棋玩得非常多元活泼，在学府中有象棋社团、象棋大赛，各级地方政府也常举办各种不同层级的象棋竞赛，民间则有象棋社和各种社团推出的竞赛。在最基层的百姓活动中，公园、路旁、庙埕（庙前广场）等，处处都可以看到两个人默默捉对厮杀，或是一群人围观两个聚精会神的对手。这样观棋下棋，往往持续大半天。早年甚至还曾发生过一些歹徒故意设局路旁，引人参战而趁机诈赌的事情。

2017年元月，《台北自由时报》刊发一则由记者陈慰慈撰述的报道：

生活篇 Lifestyle

台湾微雕家陈逢显雕出"世界最小中国象棋",这个铜雕棋盘直径只有1厘米,上面摆放有32颗0.1厘米的小棋子,小棋盘中间还刻有"观棋不语真君子,起手无回大丈夫"等字,作品费时3个月才完成。摄影:吴景腾
The miniature sculpture artist Chen Fengxian carves out "the world's tiniest Chinese chess set". This copper sculpture is composed of a chessboard with a diameter of only 1 cm, on which 32 pieces each measuring 0.1 cm are placed. Inscribed in the middle of the chessboard are citations such as the famous couplet ("A true gentleman never makes comments while watching a game of *xiangqi*/ And knows, that, once one's fingers let go of the piece, one cannot move it back"). The sculpture took Chen all of three months to complete. Photography: Wu Jingteng

有一个82岁的魏姓老翁,自称跟他的一个吴姓友人对赌象棋,半年间赌输了1575万元,遂透过许姓代书,将老婆名下的一笔房产,设定1500万元抵押给吴男,魏妻发现后怒告老公、吴男与代书涉嫌诈欺。这条新闻引人侧目是因为下个象棋居然可以连房子都输掉。虽然象棋热度近年似已逐渐降温,没想到仍有爱好者为它着迷得倾家荡产也在所不惜。

其实"桌游"这两个字是新兴词汇,出现的历史也只有短短几年,一般是指在桌几上进行的游乐,象棋当然可以列入,只可惜象棋和桌游在历史的洪流中似乎是注定要擦身而过了。随着各种声光俱佳的电子游戏的兴起,象棋正在走向没落。年轻人的手机已成为桌游的最佳载体和游玩工具,连曾经风靡全球的大型电玩都有荣景难回之

小朋友在大棋盘上下象棋。摄影：吴景腾
Children play *xiangqi* on a giant set. Photography: Wu Jingteng

叹。当年轻世代琵琶别抱之后，象棋爱好者的年纪自然也随之日趋老化。

学术界和教育专家无不认为，下象棋可以培养学龄儿童、青少年学习思考，专注与耐力，也是成年人怡养性情、防止大脑老化的高尚娱乐，在对战中运用策略技巧进行攻防，是老少皆宜、寓教于乐的文化教育活动。至于发展源流，一般人只知源自中华文化，考据起来则有多种不同推测。

目前各种说法包括有黄帝创制说、神农氏创制说、舜创制说、战国兵家创制说、韩信创制说、北周武帝创制说等。但这些说法多出自秦汉以降的典籍，其可信度有待商榷。比较被多数人接受的说法认为象棋应该是不断演变而来的，而不是单一人士的发明。据《中国象棋史》作者张如安先生研究，象棋可能萌芽于北周（约6世纪），发展于唐宋，而定型于南宋。而有关演变过程，唐代象棋至少已有将车马卒四兵种，北宋末的象棋几乎已与现代象棋无异，而"包"的出现，一说为唐末，一说为宋初。包代表了投石之战（炮）和火炮之战（炮）两种军武的出现。俗称楚河汉界的"河界"，

生活篇 Lifestyle

则被认为出现于北宋。河界的出现早于楚汉相争，楚汉争端之初，项羽的实力远比刘邦强大，刘邦为了扭转局势，任用张良、萧何等人才争取缓冲及坐大机会。等到刘的势力大增，在公元前 203 年发动攻击，项羽粮缺兵乏，被迫提出了"中分天下，割鸿沟以西为汉，以东为楚"，汉界自此产生。这一道楚河汉界位于古代的荥阳、成皋一带，该地北临黄河、西依邙山、东连平原、南接嵩山，是历代兵家兴师动众的战场。至今荥阳广武山上还保留有两座遥遥相对的古城遗址，西边那座叫汉王城，东边的叫霸王城，传说就是当年的刘邦、项羽所筑。两城中间有一条宽约 300 米的大壕沟，相传为人们平常所说的鸿沟。象棋中原已存在的河界被赋予此一故事，大大增加了两方对峙的剑拔弩张之气氛。

　　台湾目前究竟有多少人玩象棋呢？虽然爱好者逐年递减，会玩象棋的民众总数依然可观，这一方面没有精确的统计，估计千万人是少不了的。至于全球象棋人口有多少呢？英国 BGN 智力运动网络公司曾经做过统计，估计世界各地约有 2 亿多人会下象棋，主要集中在华人与亚太地区。全球大约有二十几个国家有象棋协会。目前重要的世界级赛事当属世界杯与亚洲杯，每年交替举办，成为象棋界最受瞩目的年度盛事。

绿豆糕制成的象棋，让你吃子后真的可以把对手的棋吃掉。摄影：吴景腾

With this *xiangqi* set made of mung bean cake, the Chinese term for capturing an opponent's piece — *chi*, or "eat" — becomes quite literal. Photography: Wu Jingteng

Playing *Xiangqi* (Chinese Chess)

A true gentleman never makes comments while watching a game of xiangqi.
And knows, that, once one's fingers let go of the piece, one cannot move it back.

Virtually everyone in the Chinese-speaking world has heard this couplet before. Its two short lines succinctly summarize the etiquette of *xiangqi*, or Chinese chess. Should one violate this etiquette, the game cannot be continued.

In Taiwan, *xiangqi* was once the number one board game. From existent records, one can infer that *xiangqi* was introduced to Taiwan from the mainland following Zheng Chenggong's driving Dutch invaders away in the Ming Dynasty. There are many *xiangqi* associations throughout Taiwan, as well as a number of competitions — some held by the people, and others by the government. In parks, on the side of the road and in temple squares, one is almost sure to see at least two people silently battling it out over a chessboard as a ring of spectators look onwards. Spectators often spend the better part of their day watching these games.

In January 2017, it was reported in newspapers that a wealthy 82-year-old by the name of Wei claimed to have lost RMB1.5 million over the course of six months by playing *xiangqi* for money with his friend named Wu. In order to pay Mr. Wu back, Mr. Wei was forced to mortgage a property under his wife's name. This news item caused a stir throughout Taiwan as people were shocked to hear that one can even lose one's house all because of a simple game of *xiangqi*.

Due to the advent of videogames, *xiangqi* is slowly falling out of vogue. Children now consider their cellphones to be the best way to kill time. However, education experts believe that playing *xiangqi* can help children and young adults train their cognition, attention span and patience. Meanwhile, *xiangqi* is also a refined form of entertainment for adults that allows them to hone their personal qualities and prevent their brains from ageing.

According to research by the author of *The History of* Xiangqi, Zhang Ru'an, *xiangqi* perhaps germinated in the Northern Zhou Dynasty (approx. 600 AD). It then developed during the Tang and Song dynasties, assuming its current form in the Southern Song Dynasty. The term "Chu River and Han Border" describing a boundary on the *xiangqi* board is believed to be a reference to the battle between the kingdoms of Chu and Han. In 203 BC, King Liu Bang of Han launched an offensive against King Xiangyu of Chu. Xiang Yu's kingdom lacked rations and didn't have a sufficiently large army. Ultimately, he was forced to make a compromise. The two kings would "split the realm down the middle along the Hong Gou ('Geese Canal'): the west would belong to the Han Kingdom and the east would belong to the Chu Kingdom".

Although the community of regular *xiangqi* players in Taiwan continues to dwindle, the number of people who know how to play *xiangqi* is nonetheless considerable, at an estimated 10 million. Statistics show that there are approximately 200 million people in the world who know how to play *xiangqi*. These people are largely concentrated within Chinese communities and in the Asia-Pacific region.

象棋是中華傳統文化，學習者不僅需要研習戰術，還需要鍛鍊專注力與耐力。

Xiangqi is a part of traditional Chinese culture. Those who seek to master it must learn different tactics, as well as training their concentration and patience.

下象棋讓銀髮族可以相互切磋棋藝，防止大腦老化。

By playing *xiangqi*, the elderly can learn skills from one another while preventing senility.

摄影：吴景腾

Photography: Wu Jingteng

咬牙切齿来挽脸

　　台湾民众原来并不将农历七月七日当作情人节，而是称之为"七娘妈生"。相传这天是注生娘娘生日，当夜家家户户都得准备一桌丰盛的祭品敬拜七娘妈。拜七娘妈除了牲礼水果，还得准备鲜花或纸花，还有镜子、梳子以及一盒水粉，桌下还得准备一盆清水，水盆里放置干净的毛巾。

　　水粉有淡淡的香味，粉粉的白色圆形饼状物。过去，它是妇女常用的化妆品，用来涂抹在脸颊上，可以让脸颊看来白嫩些。现在，虽然它已被形形色色的化妆品所取代，却仍有一种行业坚持用它，便是挽脸这一行。

　　挽脸，是在台湾至少已传承数百年的古老习俗，虽然在近代已逐渐淡出，没想到最近几年又悄悄复活，成为越来越受欢迎的复古美容法，真是风水轮流转啊！

　　挽脸便是美容术，没错。

　　挽脸，以两条线相绞，徐徐行过面孔的每一寸肌肤，借着收放而绞除脸上所有的细汗毛，说来便是这么简单。

　　挽脸时，挽者和被挽者面对面而坐，挽者先在被挽者脸上薄薄扑一层水粉，据说稍有止痛之效，或许也是用以柔滑肌肤。扑完粉，挽者将一条棉线对折，中间交缠后套在右手拇指和食指上，一边线头拿在左手上，

生活篇 Lifestyle

挽脸是旧时的美容术，其目的在除杂毛与去角质。摄影：何叔娟

Threading is an ancient beauty treatment that serves to remove hairs and dead skin. Photography: He Shujuan

挽脸不但可以修除脸上的杂毛，使皮肤更加白净，还可以清粉刺、去角质、修眉型，所以台湾目前还有不少女性依然迷恋挽脸。

摄影：吴景腾

Not only can threading remove facial hairs — it can also lighten the skin, clear up imperfections, remove dead skin, and shape the eyebrows. As a result, there are still a number of women in Taiwan who are devoted fans of this ancient practice.

Photography: Wu Jingteng

另一边线头用牙咬着，交缠线段紧贴被挽者脸部。随着右手一弛一张，上下左右交叉绞动，棉线跟着松紧收放，将滑过的肌肤上每一根汗毛都拔除掉。拔毛，当然疼痛难忍，第一次尝试者每每痛得咬牙切齿，甚至掉下泪水。

拔完细毛，脸上毛细孔和一些痘痘被拔除后出现的坑坑疤疤，算是小伤。挽脸师总会要求受挽者24小时内不能洗脸，以防感染。有些挽脸师则要求四小时内不洗脸，各有各的规矩。

虽然疼痛，爱美毕竟是人的本性，何况为了追求美丽，疼痛千百倍的"刑罚"可还多着呢。

挽一次面费时大约30分钟。并非只有女性才去挽脸，爱漂亮的男人定时被挽的也大有人在。男人收费略比女性高约五十块台币，据说男人的脸比较难伺候。

现代人想挽脸就去找个师傅，找家老店，顶多谨守一个忠告：挽脸不宜太频密，一个月一次已是上限，太频繁会损坏面部肌肤。而在早期社会，挽脸规矩可多呢！

过去，女孩子是在出嫁前一天才去接受挽脸的，用意当然就是大家所说的"新娘水当当"，要当个漂亮而出色的新娘子。女子经过挽脸，脸上纤毫无存，当然美白无比、焕然一新。古时中国女子一生起码要挽脸一次，那便是在出嫁之日。挽脸的习俗称为开脸，或称开面，具有带来好运的吉祥之意。许多地方的女人一生只开脸一次，之后如有离婚改嫁等不再开脸。有的地方开脸之前，主家要煮一大锅"开脸饺"分赠亲友以示吉祥，也有唱开脸歌以预祝新娘生育的。通常在完成后母方要包一份称作"修容礼"的红包给帮忙开脸的长辈，以示敬谢之意。

女性自从出嫁开过脸，取得脸部"美容权"之后，除了平日定期挽脸外，在几个特定的日子也都需要好好呵护脸庞一番。如农历春节的年俗是十二月二十四日送完神后，隔日就要挽脸，代表改头换面。端午节、中元节等重要节庆也要修面整容，据说那时的人们认为这样可以去除霉运，带来好兆头。其实说来说去谁都晓得无非就是为了一个美字。

挽脸时必须先以丝瓜水清洁脸部，再以白粉敷在脸上，挽者将一条棉线对折，中间交缠后套在右手拇指和食指上，一边线头拿在左手上，另一边线头用牙咬着，线呈交叉状，双手一拉一放，一松一紧，棉线就如剃刀一般，将脸上汗毛拔除，最重要的是还可以帮脸部按摩。
摄影：吴景腾

Before threading, the technician washes the customer's face with towel gourd water and applies a white powder. The technician then folds a thread upon itself and twists it together. Holding the ends of the thread in both hands, the technician rubs it across the customer's face in a gentle tugging motion to remove hairs and massage the muscles.
Photography: Wu Jingteng

生活篇 Lifestyle

Pain Is Beauty: The Art of Threading

Threading is an ancient custom that has been practiced in Taiwan for several hundred years. Although it had, in recent history, gradually declined in popularity, it has made a comeback in the last few years as a vintage beauty technique.

When threading, one intertwines two threads and gently passes them over every inch of the face. The slackening and tightening of the threads pulls out fine hairs from all over the face. The pain of threading may be too much for some to endure. When receiving a threading treatment for the first time, many customers clench their jaws or even let out a couple of tears. After the fine hairs are removed, there are a few swollen pores from where blackheads and pimples have been removed. However, these are hardly grave injuries. The threading artist always asks the customer to refrain from washing their face for 24 hours to prevent pores from becoming infected.

Although this treatment is painful, pain is a small price to pay for beauty. Each threading session takes around half an hour. It's not only women who receive threading treatments, either — men who care about good grooming also regularly see threading artists. Threading sessions are more expensive for men than they are for women, supposedly because men's faces are more stubborn.

One mustn't receive threading treatments too frequently — at most, one should only go once a month. Receiving these treatments too frequently can damage the muscles in the face. In the past, there were a litany of rules concerning threading. Women had to wait until the day before their wedding before receiving their first threading treatment — the reason being, of course, that they had to be pretty for their new husbands. After their faces are threaded, the young brides have a flawless, porcelain complexion. In ancient times, a woman was sure to have her face threaded at least once in her lifetime: before her wedding day.

After their face was threaded for the first time, married women would gain the "right" to receive beauty treatments. In addition to their regular threading treatments, they would also need to pamper their faces on certain special occasions, such as Spring Festival, Dragon Boat Festival and Hungry Ghost Festival. Supposedly, the people of the time believed that receiving threading treatments on these occasions could dispel bad fortune. At the end of the day, however, it was all in the name of beauty.

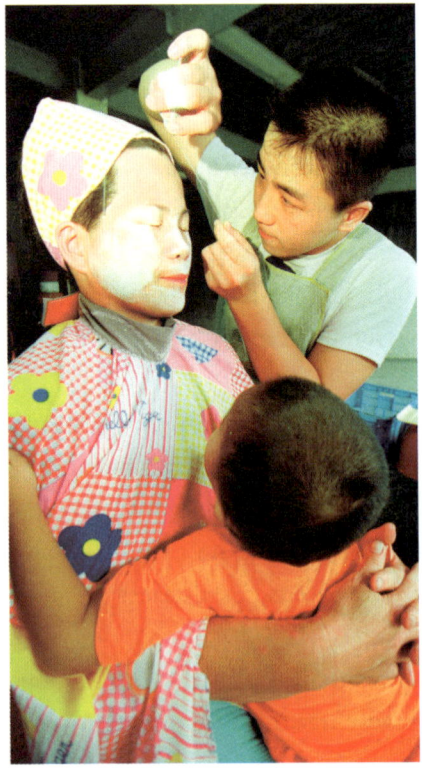

大甲镇的施圣皓，已挽过数万人的脸，而工作热情始终不减。婆婆妈妈们一面照顾孙子一面也要来挽脸，对他的手艺赞不绝口。
摄影：何叔娟

Shi Shenghao has threaded countless faces in his lifetime, but has remained just as passionate about his job as the day he began. Women have nothing but kind words to say about his skills.
Photography: He Shujuan

生活篇 Lifestyle

成年礼与高考祈福

望子成龙，望女成凤，举世皆然。人人疼爱子女，想方设法为子女祈求福运，从成年礼和考试季节的高考祈福活动中看得格外清楚，真是可怜天下父母心！

成年礼

清代台南府城五条港曾繁荣一时，当时有许多民众靠着在港边打工维生。打工者按年龄区分，满16岁才能得到全额工资。因此16岁是非常重要的一个成长阶段，每年都有许多刚满16岁的男子由父母带领前往当地信仰中心开隆宫祭拜七星娘娘，借此仪式庆祝今后可以领取成人工资。许多人都说这便是成年礼的来历。

台南人的成年礼要向七娘妈行三跪九叩之礼，然后匍匐爬过七娘妈的神桌，连续穿越三次才算完成。台湾少数民族邹族每年举办部落战祭。在仪式中，长老持杖击打当年刚满16岁的男子的臀部，并大声教诲，这是邹族人的成年礼。伊达邵的青年则在16岁接受水战训练，成年礼在模拟水战的战鼓声中进行，在日月潭上连打7天。

台北孔庙大成殿广场举行祈福仪式。
A prayer ritual unfolds in the square of Dacheng Hall (also known as the "Hall of Great Achievement") at Taipei Confucius Temple.

成年礼中晚辈亲手奉茶孝敬父母。
During a coming-of-age ceremony, children present tea to their parents in a display of filial piety.

摄影：吴景腾
Photography: Wu Jingteng

台湾各地近年来新发展出的成年礼，有的要求男子必须攀登上玉山才能视为成人，有的则让他们全副武装、背上重装备攀登海拔 3090 米的大武山。

成年礼具有历史上的时空背景，而今再度兴起则在于让孩子知道自己已经长大，今后必须自我约束、自制，对自己的行为负责，对家庭、社会、国家尽一份职责，其教育意义比过去更为宏广深远。

高考祈福

每年考季来临，台湾许多地方都会举办考生祈福活动。考季总在炎炎夏日举行，因此常有人戏称考季为"烤季"，考生因而也成了"烤生"。为考生举办祈福活动，大大降低了"烤生"心中如火般压力。

为考生祈福并没有一个统一规格，发展至今，还真是五花八门、千变万化。

祈福的举办单位包括各级地方政府，各地大庙小庙、甚至各社区和村里办公室，这正是人们常说的："有拜有保庇"，即便临时抱佛脚也是争先恐后。

许多主办单位都会为考生制作过炉加持的"2B 文昌笔"，希望这些经过神明加持的笔能为考生带来好运。还会摆设包子、粽子、青葱、萝卜、芹菜和矿泉水，包子和粽子象征"考试包中"，青葱代表"聪明"，萝卜在台湾叫作菜头，代表"好彩头"，芹菜代表"勤读、勤劳"，矿泉水指的则是"文思泉涌"，庙方准备这些供品来祈福，希望大家都能金榜题名。

孔庙会要参加者先在礼门洗手，再由礼生引领"采芹绕泮池"、过状元桥。引据《诗经·鲁颂·泮水》中，"思乐泮水，薄采其芹"的典故，意即古时中秀才的人，摘池中水芹插在帽边绕泮池，象征荣耀，而芹与勤同音，也代表勤勉向学。接着考生再穿过棂星门、仪门，前往大成殿敬拜至圣先师孔子。

Coming-of-Age Ceremonies and Prayers for College Entrance Examination

There is not a parent in the world that doesn't want their child to succeed. People dote on their children and rack their brains for ways to ensure their happiness. This is particularly clear from Taiwan's various coming-of-age ceremonies, as well as the prayer rituals that take place in the lead-up to College Entrance Examination. One cannot help but pity these parents who worry so dearly for their children!

Coming-of-age ceremonies

During the Qing Dynasty, many of the residents of Tainan worked part-time jobs in the harbor. Part-time workers could only obtain their full salary once they turned 16. As a result, 16 became an extremely important milestone in a child's development. Every year, young men who had just turned 16 were taken by their parents to Kailong Palace, where they prayed to the Seven Maids (who are said to watch over children) as a way of celebrating their right to adult wages. Many people say that this was the origin of the coming-of-age ceremonies.

During this coming-of-age ceremony, the locals of Tainan would "kneel three times and kowtow nine times" to the Seven Maids. Then, the young men

生活篇 Lifestyle

父母亲赠予成年礼生传家之宝。

Parents present their children with family heirlooms during a coming-of-age ceremony.

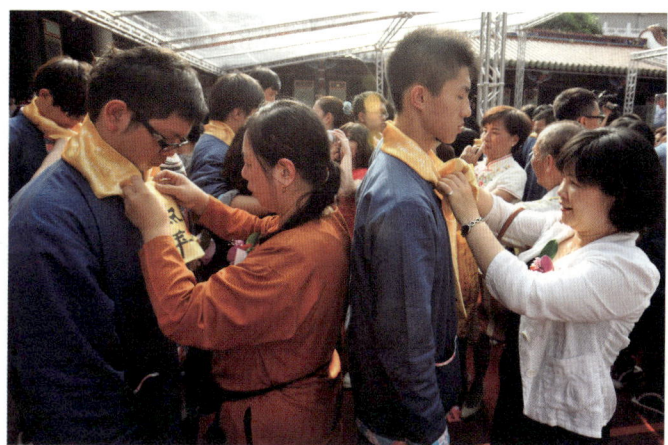

父母亲为行成年礼生系上成年领巾。

Parents tie scarves symbolizing coming-of-age around their children's necks.

摄影：吴景腾

Photography: Wu Jingteng

would crawl under the Seven Maids' altar three times before the ritual was complete. Every year, the Tsou indigenous people of Taiwan hold a tribal war ceremony known as Mayasvi. During this important coming-of-age ritual, an elder strikes with a stick the backside of young men who have just turned 16, as well as loudly sermonizing. Meanwhile, when the young Thao men of Ita Thao Village turn 16, they learn how to battle on water. Their coming-of-age is punctuated by the rumble of war drums in a mock battle on Sun-Moon Lake that lasts seven consecutive days.

Various places in Taiwan have, in recent years, come up with new coming-of-age ceremonies. Some require young men to prove their maturity by climbing Yushan ("Jade Mountain"), while others make them wear armor from head-to-toe and carry heavy equipment up to the top of Mount Dawu, situated at 3,090 m above sea level.

Coming-of-age ceremonies have profound educational significance: they let children know that they have grown up and that, from now on, they must exercise self-restraint and assume responsibility for their actions, as well as serving their family, society and country.

Prayers for College Entrance Examination

Every year, as exam season approaches, many places in Taiwan hold events where students and their parents can pray for blessings. In Taiwan, exam season — in Mandarin, *kao ji* — often overlaps with the hottest days of summer, hence some people refer to this time using a homonym of the word *kao*, or "exam", meaning "grill" or "roast". The prayer rituals organized in examinees' honor greatly reduce their sense of being "grilled" during this particularly stressful time.

The organizers of these rituals include various levels of the local government, temples of differing sizes, and even the administrative offices of residential communities and villages. The popularity of these events calls to mind the common proverb: "If one prays, one has protection". Even students who are not particularly devout feel that it cannot hurt to come pray for blessings on the eve of an exam.

Many organizers present examinees with "2B Wenchang brushes" (named after a Taoist deity of literature) that have been blessed over incense smoke by a monk in the hope that it will bring them good fortune. During exam season, temples also lay out *baozi* (stuffed buns), *zongzi* (sticky rice dumplings), green onions, radishes, celery and spring water, which, in Chinese, are homonyms of various auspicious words. For instance, *baozi* and *zongzi* are a play on words for a "guaranteed pass" in an exam; onion is a homonym for "intelligent"; the word for radish in local dialect sounds like "good omen"; and "celery" has the same pronunciation as "diligent". Finally, spring water symbolizes an overflowing source of ideas to write about.

At this time, Confucian temples also invite believers to wash their hands at the Gate of Rites, join a ceremonial official in the "picking parsnip and circling the pond" ritual, and cross the Zhuangyuan (literally "Top Scholar") Bridge. According to the *Shi Jing* (*Classic of Poetry*), successful examinees would, in ancient times, pick water parsnip from a pond, insert it in their hat, and walk around the perimeter as a symbol of glory. Next, examinees proceed to Dacheng ("Great Accomplishment") Hall to pay their respects to the Holy Ancestor, Master Confucius.

每当考季一到，父母总会陪着考生到孔庙祈求金榜题名。摄影：吴景腾

Every exam season, parents throughout Taiwan accompany their children to a Confucian temple, where they pray that their child will succeed in their exam. Photography: Wu Jingteng

生活篇 Lifestyle

童玩趣味多

扯铃

传统杂耍表演中，有所谓耍、变、练三大技艺；耍是耍坛子，变是变戏法，练就是练扯铃，可见扯铃在民俗技艺中占有重要的地位。在台湾，扯铃一度被列为体育重点发展项目，被定位为民俗体育。

70年代初台湾的民俗体育以跳绳、毽子、放风筝三个项目为主，大约10年后纳入扯铃这一项，因此开始有比赛，也因为有比赛而开始有规则规范。那时候的比赛的招数没有很多，都是以指定动作为主。多年发展下来，扯铃招数变得花样繁多，活动遍及城乡，竞赛有如一场嘉年华盛会，甚至把比赛的层级拉到国际赛。扯铃玩家得以自由发挥、展现自我，更因借着国际交流而扩大了视野。

扯铃起源于何时呢？文献记载，大概在隋唐年代就有一些街头艺人表演扯铃，在民间则是把它视为一种民俗童玩，巷弄的技艺。中国古称扯铃为"空竹"或"空钟"，据说发源自天津之"闷葫芦"，当时扯铃无声，到了清朝始能出声，康熙年间柴桑《燕京杂记》说："京师儿童，有抖扯铃之戏，截竹为二短筒，中作小干，连而不断，实其两头，窍其中间，以绳绕其小干，引两头搂抖之，声如洪钟，甚为可听。"

台湾表演团体"舞铃剧场"结合扯铃、体操、舞蹈的表演艺术,让扯铃变成一种集声光效果的炫目表演。
摄影:徐大昌
A troupe performs gymnastic tricks and dances with diabolos. Photography: Xu Dachang

孙殿起《琉璃厂小志》记载:"空竹亦名空钟,能抖出种种花样,摆摊人均擅此技,借此以广招徕。"坐观老人《清代野记》载:"京师儿童玩具,有所谓'空钟'者,即外省之'地铃'。两头以竹筒为之,中贯以柱,以绳拉之作声。唯京师之空钟其形圆而扁,加一轴,贯两车轮,其音较外省所制清越而长。"邓云乡在《鲁迅与北京风土》中说:"中间有根尖轴的小扯铃,缠上线一抽,丢在地上旋转,嗡嗡作响,叫'风葫芦'。"

扯铃在国外有两种名称,一个是 Chinese yo-yo,另一个比较专门的名称叫 Diabolo,这个词的由来,是因为它转动时,奇特的方式如同魔鬼般,所以有了这个名称。据欧洲法国的扯铃从事者 Priam Pierret 在一次国际扯铃协会筹备会上提到,扯铃可能是由马可·波罗带回欧洲,此说虽难获得确定,却也不无可能。

滚铁圈

可还记得童年时代,一根长长铁杆,推着一个轮子四处跑的得意事吗?滚铁圈,简单却充满趣味的古老童玩,是多少人难忘的儿时回忆。滚铁圈是传统乡土童玩之一,工具简单易得,只要有个铁环和一根铁勾便成。最早期常用的铁环取自废木桶的桶箍,有了单车之后的年代,拆解的老旧单车的轮框也可以当环。有了铁环,滚铁圈的游戏已完成十分之九。

弄根粗铁丝,折一个弯勾,一头镶个握柄,便是推送铁环向前转动的工具。用这工具控制铁圈的前进与方向,看似简单,初学却颇具挑战性,这种手部控制的游戏,能锻炼小朋友手部肌肉的运动能力及手眼协调,还能学习平衡的技巧。滚铁圈可以一个人玩,也可以分组一块儿比赛竞速,有些小孩还能玩出很多不同花样。例如让铁圈

一群小朋友开心地玩着自制的童玩。
摄影:于志旭

A group of children have fun playing with toys they made themselves. Photography: Yu Zhixu

飞起来再接住、让铁圈蛇行滚过种种障碍物等等。比赛除了保持轮圈不倒地,也以速度定输赢。

现代孩子有了滑板、蛇板等等新玩意,铁圈逐渐式微,说来也是可惜。

打陀螺

在台湾,陀螺被称作甘乐,打陀螺不叫打陀螺,而叫作钉甘乐。钉甘乐比单纯的打甘乐还要带劲,还要更狠一点!

从前人家没有人从店里买陀螺的,想玩就自己削。方法是截一段坚硬的木头——通常用的是芭乐树的粗枝,慢慢削成陀螺状,讲究的是形状匀称,不能有偏或斜,这往往要花上几天工夫才削得出一个完整的形状。

接下来找一根铁钉,在陀螺尖端垂直钉下去。这是成败的关键时刻,要钉得完全

新北市三峡区,休假日都会有人开心地聚在老街庙口打陀螺。摄影:吴景腾
On holidays and weekends, it is not uncommon to see people happily playing with spinning tops at the entrance to temples in alleyways. Photography: Wu Jingteng

生活篇 Lifestyle

垂直而正中圆心，不能有丝毫偏差，如果钉歪了这陀螺也毁了，就得丢了重削一个。

钉好，要有耐心地把铁钉的钉帽磨掉，再将之磨尖，一只陀螺才大功告成。有了陀螺还得有绳子，绳子也得自己打一条。方法是找来洋麻，泡水几天之后细细用石头捣掉木质部而只留皮质之纤维，再慢慢地抽取出来，分成三股将之捻合。用自己削的甘乐和自己打的麻绳来打甘乐，真乃得意事。

打甘乐除了可以自己打着开心，还可成群分组竞技，竞技可以根据旋转时间的长短来比赛，也可一人打出陀螺来后另一人再打一个出来将之击倒，于是才出现了钉甘乐这样的称呼。钉甘乐是孩童之间相互较劲的最高境界，甘乐的好坏、技巧的高下都是制胜因素，围观者鸦雀无声屏息静观，当胜败分晓立时欢声如雷，非常有趣。

台湾民俗村里一个妇人在众人围观下娴熟地打陀螺。摄影：于志旭
A skilled spinner plays with her top as a crowd watches. Photography: Yu Zhixu

The Joy of Children's Toys

Diabolo (Chinese Yo-yo)

In traditional variety shows, there are three main acts: juggling ceramic jars, making objects seemingly appear out of thin air, and performing diabolo (or Chinese yo-yo) tricks. Evidently, diabolo tricks are a privileged traditional art form. In Taiwan, the diabolo is defined as a "folk sport" and was once listed by the government as a "key physical education initiative".

In the 1970s, Taiwan's main folk sports were jump-roping, *jianzi* (an activity similar to the hackey-sack) and flying kites. A decade or so later, these sports would be joined by the diabolo. This marked the beginning of formal diabolo competitions, as well as the formation of a fixed set of rules and etiquette. At the time, there was little skill involved in diabolo performances — they mostly revolved around a limited set of pre-defined movements. However, over the years, an endless array of techniques have been developed. These days, events are held in cities and towns all throughout Taiwan, and competition venues are as lively and varied as carnivals. Diabolo competitions have even been taken to an international level.

Just when did the diabolo originate? According to textual records, street performers have been doing diabolo tricks since as early as the Sui and Tang dynasties. At the time, people viewed it as a popular children's game and a form of streetside entertainment. Although, in Western countries, this toy is

生活篇 Lifestyle

扯铃是中国传统的民俗技艺之一，花式繁多、趣味无穷。摄影：吴景腾

The diabolo is one of China's traditional folk arts. There are endless tricks one can do, and limitless fun to be had. Photography: Wu Jingteng

sometimes referred to as the "Chinese yo-yo", a more official term is "diabolo". It is said that this term was chosen because the toy's unusual spinning mechanism was said to be devil-like. Priam Pierret, a diabolo enthusiast from France, speculated at a fundraising event held by the International Diabolo Federation that diabolos may have been taken back to Europe by Marco Polo — although this theory is difficult to confirm.

Hoop rolling

Who doesn't remember the joy of running in all directions while rolling an iron hoop as a child? Hoop rolling is a simple yet endlessly entertaining children's toy that dates from ancient times and which has created unforgettable childhood memories for countless generations.

Hoop rolling is a traditional childhood pastime throughout rural Taiwan. Its materials are simple and easy to obtain: all one needs is an iron hoop and an iron rod with a kink at one end. In ancient times, people would often use the iron hoops used to bind together wooden

滚铁圈是许多中年人的儿时记忆。图为小朋友们在台湾民俗村开心地玩滚铁圈。摄影：于志旭
Hoop rolling is a common childhood memory for many middle-aged people. To this day, there are still children who enjoy rolling hoops. Photography: Yu Zhixu

buckets. Later, following the invention of the bicycle, it became common to use discarded rims. Then, one could take an iron rod, curl up one end, and mount a handle on the other in order to make the tool that pushes the ring along the ground.

Although using a rod to control the speed and direction of the iron hoop may seem simple, it can be challenging for beginners. One can roll hoops by oneself, or one can organize small races. Some children are even able to perform different tricks with the hoops. For example, they can make the hoop fly up in the air and then catch it with the rod, or they can make the hoop traverse different obstacles. A competition can be judged based on how long participants can keep the hoop from falling, or on speed.

These days, children have all sorts of gadgets, such as skateboards and snakeboards, and hoop rolling is sadly going by the wayside.

Spinning tops

In the past, anyone who wanted to play with a spinning top wouldn't buy one from a store — they would whittle one themselves. To do this, they would take a sturdy piece of wood — generally, a thick branch from a pomegranate tree. As they slowly whittle it, they must make sure that the shape remains symmetrical, without the slightest bump or slant. Whittling a functional spinning top would often take several days of work.

Next, an iron nail is hammered at a perfectly straight angle into the sharp end of the top. This is the decisive moment between success and failure: if the nail is even slightly slanted or off-center, then the last few days' work will have been for nothing.

Once the nail is in place, the head of the nail is removed and what is left is sharpened into a point. Finally, the spinning top is complete. In order to play with the spinning top, one needs a rope — also traditionally hand-made. The method is to soak the wood of the kenaf plant (similar to jute) in water for several days before using a stone to remove the fibrous bark from the wood underneath. These fibers are slowly extracted, separated into three layers, and braided together. Playing with a spinning top and rope that one has made oneself is infinitely more satisfying than buying one.

One can compete with other players to see how long one can keep one's top spinning, or one can spin one's top towards another player's in order to knock it down. Spinning tops are an ideal way for children to compare their abilities, as victory is determined not only by the quality of one's spinning top, but also one's skills. Spectators look onwards without making a sound as they anticipate the results of a duel. The moment the winner becomes known, they erupt into cheers — an amusing spectacle to behold.

传统陀螺是由木材制作，实心而无柄，打时先用绳子盘绕，抛掷出去再猛力抽回来，让它在地上转个不停。摄影：吴景腾

In order to make the top spin, one first needs to wrap a rope around its circumference. Then, one casts the top before quickly reeling it back in. Photography: Wu Jingteng

周岁抓周

台湾民众把婴儿周岁称作度晬,度晬是宝宝成长过程中一个非常重要的日子,代表孩子经历过了一年12个月春夏秋冬的考验。古来婴儿育成不易,过了度晬,平安长大就可期了。

度晬民俗中最有趣的便是抓周这个活动,通过一个活泼热闹的非正式仪式,让婴儿开心,大人也趁机探探这个小娃儿未来性格、前途的秘密。

办抓周,古礼严肃以对,现代人多半心情轻松,看着婴儿表演也开心!反正整个过程充满了如意吉祥,无论婴儿抓到的是什么,都有好解释,也都是好预兆。抓周那天,婴儿要戴上一顶有老虎图案的帽子,象征百兽之王护身而百毒不敢来侵扰。

传统抓周要准备一批具有代表性的物品来让小孩随意抓取,从所抓之物预测孩子未来从业领域,因而在仪式中要准备12种或18种东西,如:书、印章、笔墨、算盘(计算器)、乐器、相机、扑满、听诊器、尺、鸡腿、棒球、色笔、化妆盒、枪械、听筒、鼠标等等。让婴儿坐在米筛中央任意抓取。严谨的抓周古制规定要先祭拜祖先,告诉祖先宝宝满一岁的讯息,祈求宝宝健康成长。

祭拜后,在神桌前准备一个米筛,按照传统流程进行。第一个动作是脚踩红龟糕(有福气,长寿),然后吃大鸡腿(吃福,不愁吃穿)、

生活篇 Lifestyle

咬一口大苹果（平平安安）、咬一口爆米香（有人缘，得人疼），抱一下葱（聪明伶俐）、抱一下芹菜（勤奋向上）、抱一下蒜（精打细算）。之后，抱着宝宝喊一句"抓周开始"，再将宝宝高高举起，然后轻轻放在米筛中央，让宝宝自由抓取筛上物品。抓到的东西象征什么呢？

　　书：会读书，适合做学者、专家；笔墨：成为作家、画家；印章：有权势，会做大官；算盘或计算器：当商人、会计师，适合从商；钱币：会很富有；鸡腿：有福气，一生不愁吃穿；尺：成为设计师、建筑师；葱：聪明；蒜：善于计算；芹菜：勤劳；稻草：适合农事工作；刀剑：能当军官、警察；听筒：适合医护工作。

　　据说要预测得准，必须观察宝宝抓在手上玩得最久的那件东西，这反映出宝宝真正的兴趣与潜能。其实宝宝抓周算是一种庆祝宝宝诞生的小游戏，爸爸妈妈也不用太严肃去看待，把这活动当成一个亲子互动的游戏也就够了。

　　在小娃儿长到周岁之前还有许多禁忌不可违背。这些禁忌有些尚可理解，有些则匪夷所思，但大家都姑妄言之、姑且信之，能不触犯就尽量避免。这些禁忌包括：不

"抓周"，让宝宝坐在大米筛中随意选取身边之物，以此预测宝宝将来会选择的行业。摄影：吴景腾
During a *zhuazhou* ritual, the baby is placed in a large rice sieve and allowed to freely choose an object. This object supposedly represents the baby's future profession. Photography: Wu Jingteng

可让小孩啃鸡脚——以后会撕破书；大人不可亲睡觉中的小娃娃——会害得小孩子睡不好觉；日落后不能为宝宝洗澡——会犯煞（过去没有热水器，会选天气暖和的时间给宝宝洗澡）；不可用尺打小孩——以后小孩会蛮皮难带，蛮皮就是调皮的意思；不可吃茄子——以后会蛀牙；不可吃鱼卵——以后不会算数；不可吃鸡肠——以后会说话啰嗦；不能吃鱼蛋，会影响小朋友长大以后的算术能力。这些你都相信吗？年轻一代父母已经越来越不信邪，恐怕这些禁忌慢慢就没人理会了。

新生儿的收涎礼中，宝宝胸前挂上12块酥饼，由妈咪抱着，请长辈亲友取酥饼，在婴儿嘴唇做揩抹状。目的是祈求宝宝不再流口水，祝福小朋友平安长大。摄影：吴景腾

A *shouxianli* ("saliva-retaining ritual") for a newborn: 12 crispy cakes are hung on string around a baby's neck. The mother carries the baby and invites friends and family to take the cakes and wipe them on the baby's mouth. The purpose of this ritual is to stop the baby from drooling and pray that the baby will grow up peacefully. Photography: Wu Jingteng

生活篇 Lifestyle

Zhuazhou, A First Birthday Tradition

The most interesting custom for celebrating a child's first birthday is no doubt *zhuazhou*. This lively and informal ritual not only brings joy to the child — it also gives adults insights into the child's personality and future prospects.

While, in ancient times, *zhuazhou* rituals were solemn occasions, most modern families don't take them all that seriously — it's first and foremost a chance for the child to have fun. After all, the whole process is filled with good omens and auspicious signs; whatever the child ends up picking, it's sure to have positive significance for the baby's future. On the day of the first birthday, the child must wear a cap with an image of a tiger on it, as this powerful beast symbolizes protection from misfortune and illness.

Before the ritual, parents prepare an array of symbolic items for the child to choose from. The item the child picks indicates future profession. Before a traditional *zhuazhou* ritual, parents must first pay respects to their ancestors. Then, a rice sieve is laid out on an altar, and the ritual takes place according to the traditional process. The first movement the child must complete is to stomp on a red turtle pudding, which represents good fortune and longevity. Then, the child takes a bite from a chicken drumstick (meaning the child will not go without food or clothing in the future), an apple (which, due to a homonym, symbolizes peace), and popcorn (which means the baby will have connections and be loved by others), as well as holding an onion (homonym for intelligence), celery (diligence) and garlic (careful budgeting and life decisions).

Next, parents hold the baby and cheer, "*Zhuazhou kaishi*!" ("Let the picking begin!") The baby is raised up high and placed down gently in the middle of the rice sieve. Finally, it is allowed to freely choose an item placed on the sieve. What do these items symbolize?

Book: highly literate and well suited to being a scholar or specialist;

Brush and ink: will become an author or a painter;

Seal: will have authority and become an official;

Abacus or calculator: will become a businessperson or an accountant;

Money: will be wealthy;

Drumstick: will have good fortune and will not have to worry about going without food or clothing;

Ruler: will become a designer or an architect;

Onion: will be intelligent;

Garlic: will be good at calculations;

Celery: will be diligent;

Rice straw: well suited to working in agriculture;

Sword: well suited to being a military or police officer;

Stethoscope: well suited to working in healthcare.

It is said that, to ensure an accurate prediction, one must carefully observe the baby to see which item he/she plays with the longest, as this will reflect the child's true interests and potential.

父母依古俗让刚满周岁的新生儿脚踩红龟糕，祈求健康长寿。

In keeping with ancient customs, parents make their child stomp on a turtle-shaped red pudding on their first birthday, in the hope that it will bring them good health and longevity.

妈妈带着宝宝穿过挂满青葱的"聪明门"、期盼孩子聪明伶俐。

A mother carries her baby through a "Gate of Intelligence" — a doorway above which shoots of green onion have been hung.

摄影：吴景腾

Photography: Wu Jingteng

圆仔旋风

　　圆仔！圆仔！许多小朋友一进了台北木栅动物园，总会开心直嚷不停。圆仔本是对汤圆的昵称，然而此时他们口中的圆仔，可不是那道冬至时非吃不可的美味，而是一头名叫圆仔的大熊猫。5年前，木栅动物园传出轰动全台的好消息，大熊猫团团和圆圆"结婚"后产下了它们的第一个宝宝，经过公开征名，圆仔这个名字胜出，因为它是圆圆所生的孩子，更因为它长得圆滚滚极其可爱，像颗汤圆般讨人喜欢，顺理成章就称它圆仔了，就是这般的亲切和幽默。

　　圆仔的诞生，掀起了几乎比它的爹娘团团、圆圆当初移居宝岛还要轰动的一阵圆仔旋风。谈起圆仔的爹娘，可还真是大有来历。团团的妈妈华美出生在美国，长大之后被送回中国老家，是一只赫赫有名的"海归"熊猫。而圆圆则是由绰号"断掌熊猫"的雷雷所生。雷雷原是只野生大熊猫，被人发现时左手掌因受伤而严重感染，最后不得不由照护人员为它截肢，因此而有了"断掌熊猫"的称号。即使如此，它仍然能将自己所生育的五只小宝宝照顾得健健康康。雷雷有着令人钦佩的坚强母性，大陆媒体给了它"英雄母亲"的头衔。

"1600熊猫世界之旅"户外公共艺术展在台北亮相。此次展览为了强调环境保护、生态保护与熊猫保育的重要性，所有的纸雕熊猫皆采用环保材质，全人工制造。在展览结束后，所有的艺术创作都会通过义卖活动，将所得捐作生态保育基金。

The outdoor public art exhibition "1,600 Pandas World Tour" makes its debut in Taipei. This exhibition emphasized the importance of environmental protection. All of the paper figures of pandas were made from recycled materials. After the exhibition, the figures were sold in an auction, and all profits were donated to an ecological conservation fund.

面包师傅用巧克力捏塑出栩栩如生的圆仔公仔。

A baker molds a lifelike pastry of Yuan-Zai using chocolate.

摄影：吴景腾
Photography: Wu Jingteng

2008年12月23日团团与圆圆初履台湾，2011年4月16日台湾回赠一对长鬃山羊与一对台湾梅花鹿，成为两岸互赠保育类动物之首例。来自四川卧龙自然保护区的团团和圆圆被安排进住台北木栅动物园，而台湾回赠的山羊与台湾梅花鹿则获安排进住山东威海刘公岛珍稀动物园。

台湾首次迎来熊猫娇客，民众之兴奋自不在话下。次年元月26日春节起开放给公众参观，民众几乎挤爆木栅动物园的熊猫馆。2013年7月6日，这对恩爱熊猫夫妻迎来它们婚后的第一个宝宝。这是一只雌性熊猫，通过全民投票活动，圆仔之名就此被确定了。

今年圆仔已经4岁多，许多人关心它何时可以有个弟弟或妹妹。台北市立动物园表示，今春他们已经观察到圆圆出现减少采食、来回走动、奔跑、喜欢泡水及发出羊叫声等征兆，身体也出现种种进入发情期的迹象。由于雌性大熊猫的发情高峰期一年仅有一天，园方人员不敢怠慢，抓紧那个一年一度的最佳繁殖时机，立刻启动人工协助机制，希望能顺利让圆仔添个弟弟或妹妹。

动物园的数据显示，目前团团的体重为121公斤，圆圆的体重为118公斤。圆仔呢？身高体重、生活起居，天天都被完整地记录着。有一次它误吞一枚别针，那几天连它排出的粪便都被彻底翻遍！那故事发生在2015年年底，园方发现之后紧急通过诱导麻醉，将圆仔送往动物医院照X光检查，用内视镜检查肠胃，发现针头不在消化道，所幸食道未受伤。再次检查发现别针已在小肠，医疗人员只能在紧张中期盼借大便顺势排出。总算在它第3次排泄时，医疗团队在大便中发现别针，大家这才松了一口气。

圆仔的生日抓周，好像有兴趣当工程师。
According to Yuan-Zai's first birthday *zhuazhou* ritual, it seems that would she aspires to become an engineer.

圆仔生日，妈妈圆圆喂圆仔吃水果蛋糕。
On Yuan-Zai's birthday, her mother Yuan-Yuan feeds her fruitcake.

摄影：吴景腾
Photography: Wu Jingteng

Yuan-Zai Mania

From the moment one enters the Taipei Zoo, one can hear children gleefully calling out: "Yuan-Zai! Yuan-Zai!" *Yuan-zai* (literally "small round things") are what people affectionately call *tangyuan*. However, in this instance, the children are not referring to the snack — they're calling out the name of a famous panda.

Five years ago, the Taipei Zoo released news that took the whole of Taiwan by storm: after their "marriage", the giant pandas Tuan-Tuan and Yuan-Yuan had given birth to their first child. In a public survey, the name Yuan-Zai was by far the most popular suggestion, because it honors her mother, Yuan-Yuan — and, more importantly, because her adorable, round shape is reminiscent of a *tangyuan*. The name reflects local people's unique sense of humor and affectionate nature.

The birth of Yuan-Zai caused an even greater stir than when her parents, Tuan-Tuan and Yuan-Yuan, first arrived in Taiwan. Yuan-Zai's mother and father certainly come from interesting backgrounds. Tuan-Tuan's mother, Hua Mei, lived in the United States for a long time, and later returned to the Chinese mainland. Meanwhile, Yuan-Yuan was born to Lei-Lei, known as the "Pawless Panda". Lei-Lei was born in the wild; when she was discovered, her left paw had become seriously infected following an injury. Ultimately, vets had no choice but to amputate. Despite her disability, Lei-Lei was nonetheless able to raise five healthy baby pandas.

On 23 December 2008, two pandas from the Wolong National Nature Reserve in Sichuan, Tuan-Tuan and Yuan-Yuan, arrived at Taipei Zoo in Taiwan. In return,

Taiwan sent the mainland two of its local animals — the Formosan serow and the Formosan sika deer — which are held at the National Forest Park in Weihai, Shandong Province.

On Spring Festival (26 January) in 2009, the Panda Pavilion of Taipei Zoo held an open day and was packed to the rafters with visitors. On 6 July 2013, this beloved couple of pandas welcomed their first child: Yuan-Zai. Many people are keen to know when Yuan-Zai will have a little brother or sister. The zoo has stated they have noticed various signs that Yuan-Yuan is approaching her estrous cycle. As the peak of a female giant panda's estrous cycle only lasts for one day a year, the zookeepers don't dare take chances. In order not to waste this once-in-a-year opportunity to provide Yuan-Zai with a sibling, they have already begun the artificial insemination process.

Yuan-Zai's height, weight and daily life are all rigorously documented. Once, she mistakenly swallowed a safety pin. In the few days that followed, zookeepers went through her every dropping with a fine-tooth comb, but couldn't find a thing! Fearing for Yuan-Zai's life, they tranquilized her and sent her to an animal hospital for X-rays. Fortunately, her digestive tract had not been damaged. The tests revealed that the pin had already made its way into her small intestine. A team of medical specialists eventually found the pin in the third pile of droppings, and worried fans across Taiwan were able to finally heave a sigh of relief.

民众观赏以可爱逗趣的熊猫宝宝圆仔为主角的花灯。摄影：吴景腾
Members of the public admire lanterns featuring the adorable baby panda Yuan-Zai. Photography: Wu Jingteng